Scenic Design and Lighting Techniques

Scenic Design and Lighting Techniques
A Basic Guide for Theatre

Chuck Gloman
Rob Napoli

ELSEVIER

AMSTERDAM • BOSTON • HEIDELBERG • LONDON
NEW YORK • OXFORD • PARIS • SAN DIEGO
SAN FRANCISCO • SINGAPORE • SYDNEY • TOKYO

Focal Press is an imprint of Elsevier

Acquisitions Editor: Cara Anderson
Project Manager: Dawnmarie Simpson
Marketing Manager: Christine Degon Veroulis
Cover Design: Eric DeCicco

Focal Press is an imprint of Elsevier
30 Corporate Drive, Suite 400, Burlington, MA 01803, USA
Linacre House, Jordan Hill, Oxford OX2 8DP, UK

∞ Recognizing the importance of preserving what has been written, Elsevier prints its books on acid-free paper whenever possible.

Library of Congress Cataloging-in-Publication Data
Gloman, Chuck B.
  Scenic design and lighting techniques : a basic guide for theatre / Chuck Gloman, Rob Napoli.
    p. cm.
  Includes index.
  ISBN-13: 978-0-240-80806-2 (pbk. : alk. paper)
  ISBN-10: 0-240-80806-1 (pbk. : alk. paper)   1. Theaters—Stage-setting and scenery.
2. Theaters—Lighting.   I. Napoli, Rob.   II. Title.
  PN2091.S6G56 2007
  792.02′5—dc22   2006011131

British Library Cataloguing-in-Publication Data
A catalogue record for this book is available from the British Library.

ISBN 13: 978-0-240-80806-2
ISBN 10: 0-240-80806-1

For information on all Focal Press publications
visit our website at www.books.elsevier.com

06   07   08   09   10   10 9 8 7 6 5 4 3 2 1

Printed in China

Contents

Contents

About the Authors

Chuck Gloman: Chuck has been actively working in the field since 1980 when he graduated from the Pennsylvania State University with a BA in film. While persuing a Master's degree at the same school, he worked a variety of jobs in the industry, gaining valuable experience (and little money).

With MA in hand, he found a new field in its infancy called *video*. After selling his Master's thesis film, *The Butler Did It,* to HBO and Cinemax (where it remained for nine years), he worked for PBS before landing a job as an instructional designer and scriptwriter for a cutting-edge community college. Creating, shooting, and editing interactive videotapes displayed on an Apple II, he was hurled into the video industry and computer technology. After a three-year stint in Virginia working as a director shooting interactive videodiscs for the U.S. armed services and the government (traveling the country and visiting almost every base and post in the United States), he moved to Pennsylvania and became a producer, creating videodiscs for Federal Express, IBM, Turner Network, Simon & Schuster, the Singapore Ministry of Defense, the United States Department of Defense, and Ford.

In the mid-1990s he was creative services director at an NBC affiliate. There he wrote and directed over 600 television commercials. Moving back to corporate videos in the late 1990s, he handled most of Armstrong World Industries' video presentations (over 200) and shooting how-to installation videos for Lowe's. Still active in the freelance market, he moved out on his own in 2001 as a producer/director of photography, creating over 100 documentaries, 200 commercials, and dozens of corporate videos for clients such as ESPN, Fox Television, Rite Aid, Weis, PAX Network, Coca-Cola, FEMA, UGL, March of Dimes, Fuji Corporation, the History Channel, and Lockheed Martin.

His love of lighting led him into education, as adjunct faculty to Bradley Academy for the Performing Arts, where he taught production and lighting courses. Currently, he is a full-time member of the faculty at DeSales University, where he teaches TV/film courses and met his coauthor, Rob Napoli.

Chuck is also a contributing editor to *Videography* and *Government Video* magazines and has published over 300 articles for *TV Technology, Television Broadcast, Philly Tech, Mix, Sound and Video Contractor, Digital Cinema, Miata, 911 Magazine, Erosion Control, Sports TV Production, System Contractor News, Videography,* and *Government Video.* He has also published the following books: *Placing Shadows: Lighting Techniques for Video Production,* 2nd ed. (Burlington, MA: Focal Press, 2000); *No Budget Digital Filmmaking* (New York: McGraw-Hill, 2002); *303 Digital Filmmaking Solutions* (New York: McGraw-Hill, 2003);

202 Digital Photography Solutions (New York: McGraw-Hill, 2003); *Placing Shadows: Lighting Techniques for Video Production*, 3rd ed. (Burlington, MA: Focal Press, 2005).

Rob Napoli: Rob has been working in technical theatre for 20 years, but he didn't know that was he was going to do it for a living. After earning two acting degrees and touring the country with acting troupes, he was sure he was destined to be the cult favorite jumpsuited sidekick comic relief on some network buddy-cop show. While he enjoyed acting, being the son of a jack-of-all-trades and good research technician he found himself wandering backstage more often than not to find out how things worked.

Soon he was spending just as much time backstage as onstage, until he was backstage more and more. After a few years of freelance acting and tech work, he became the assistant tech director at DeSales University and worked with the Pennsylvania Shakespeare Festival as the production manager for several seasons. It was there he met Chuck Gloman and suggested that Chuck write a book on stagecraft.

Chuck, being the persuasive devil he is, suggested they write it together, and the rest is history. Rob is now designer and technical director at Penn State Berks Campus, and teaches acting and technical theatre in their theatre department. He lives in the Philadelphia area with his wife and family in a house that constantly breaks—and he repairs; however, the repairs only seem to last until the tech week of the current show.

Acknowledgments

Rob Napoli: I would like to thank my mentors Bob Mond, J. Kline, Vince Campbell, Tom Donahue, and Chuck Gloman for putting up with my questions and offering their sage advice. I would like to thank Bob Napoli for taking me to the hardware store with him and teaching me that there is no harm in walking up to a complete stranger and asking him what he was doing and how he was doing it. Also, I would like to thank all of the wonderful designers and theatre professionals I've worked with and learned from over the years, especially those I met at DeSales University and the Pennsylvania Shakespeare Festival. I'd like to thank those organizations as well as my colleagues at the HAAS Division at Penn State Berks Campus for their contributions to this book. My students over the years have taught me as much, if not more, than I ever taught them; many, now my colleagues, I continue to learn from. I'd also like to thank Cara Anderson and Focal Press for this opportunity to spread my educational madness across the world. Lastly, I'd like to thank my greatest teachers and biggest fans: my wife and family. Without their support, I'd be lost.

Chuck Gloman: I would like to thank everyone that my partner in crime, Rob Napoli, thanked (that saves me from typing their names again). This book was also a great learning experience for me. I have a background in lighting (I'm so bright my father calls me Sonny) but very little experience in scenic design. Through writing this book with Rob, he has educated me on many things I never knew, so now my experience is far greater in these areas, thanks to him. My biggest thanks in this book does goes also to Rob Napoli, whose enthusiasm, drive, talent, and the same interests in mundane things keep our friendship strong. I've written other books by myself and with other individuals, and Rob is a pleasure to work with, in that he meets deadlines, has the ability, and, when you propose a book, actually finishes it with you. Although it may sound like I'm talking about him as if he were dead and this is his eulogy—he has a gift and I'd never tell this to him—he will go far with his abilities and I am looking forward to writing again with him (then I can pay back the 20 bucks he loaned me).

In addition, I would like to thank Cara Anderson at Focal Press for her help through the process; my students at DeSales University, who let me photograph them as guinea pigs . . . I mean talent; Bob Mond, at whose party I got to know Rob better propose a book and who has been a great help with this book; Scott Paul, who let me spend the time necessary to write this book and whose guidance I appreciated; the many great people (faculty, staff, and students) at DeSales University who make teaching enjoyable, challenging, and fun; my parents, who guided me in the right direction (although the electric cattle prod was a little much); my wife, Linda, who let me do what I needed to get done when I needed to get it done (after I took the trash out); my in-laws, who stand behind me in whatever I do (hopefully not to push me); and many others who helped me get where I am today—semihealthy, overweight, undercooked, and employed. Most of all I would like to thank God for the ability he has given me to work in a field I am passionate about . . . if I could just remember what that field was.

Introduction

The most attractive thing about technical theatre is that we are constantly creating something out of nothing. When you begin, there is a dark, empty stage and an idea. Then you build it, light it, and they come. They watch the show, they leave, and you take it all down. The stage is bare, the lights are off, and the circle of life continues. How to get from empty stage to empty stage is what this book is about.

Still, even if you read this book cover to cover (which you will) and memorize every term and concept (you might), you still will need to practice the craft (not *that* kind of craft!). Practice makes perfect, and although nothing is perfect, through experience you will get better. Face it, we never stop learning. And if we ever do, we have stopped living. Technology might change the way we do things, but it is still the knowledge that creates the craft, not the tools. The tools are important and necessary, but it is the use of these tools that will take you places.

This book is divided into three sections: how to build scenery, how to design it, and how to light it. Some might want to skip around and go to the section where they think they need the most help. That's fine, but at least you will have reference to the basics that you can always turn to if you forget something. All the parts of this book are necessary to learn the basics and fundamentals of set design and lighting. It's great to specialize at something you might do best, but without a properly built set, the greatest lighting in the world won't help. In the same way, if poor lighting does not allow anyone to see the characters or set pieces, that too is useless.

What we hope is that once you have the building blocks at your disposal and the fundamentals of construction, you'll have a better understanding as to how to design and light the set. While the ideas we discuss are basic, they shouldn't be thought of as elementary. Sherlock Holmes was always telling that to Watson—maybe that was because he never quite caught on either.

As the authors of this book, each of us draws on the strengths and knowledge of the other. Neither of us alone could have created this text. Through the writing, rewriting, updating, and fact checking, each of us has actually learned something we did not know before. Since we always tell the truth (except when we lie), all of the information presented in this book was accurate at press time. All of the captions in the photographs credit the individuals or companies listed. If any have been omitted, it was an oversight and we apologize. Websites will come and go, but most of the manufacturers listed should be around for a while.

A wise man of theatre once expressed this aphorism: *K.I.S.S.: Keep it simple, stupid*. The majority of the time, you don't want a complex solution. What separates the world of theatre from that of television and movies is that 90% of what we create is in the audience's imagination. We simply give them the suggestion of a reality and they fill in the blanks. If you have ever seen a show yourself, you have contributed to the show's *tech*.

So since you already have some technical experience, we've also given you real-world tips and solutions as well as links to various resource websites. And of course we give you puns—lots of really bad puns. If you are going to be around technicians, you'd better get used to bad puns and strange humor. We're just trying to help—or is it that we're just trying?

Section 1

Building the Set

Chapter 1
The Basic Scenic Building Blocks

Let's face it. There are really only two basic scenic forms that all sets are made from: vertical and horizontal. Of the two most basic and familiar forms, we call the vertical ones *flats* and the horizontal ones *platforms*. Any variation of shape, structure, or design does not alter the fact that we have to have something vaguely horizontal for people to stand on and something sort of vertical behind them to create a believable environment to tell our stories. Even if you were to find the perfect location with the right size and shape of interior and you put your talent in front of one of those perfect walls, for our purposes it's just an overbuilt flat.

In this chapter we discuss flats, platforms, and drops and backings.

Flats

Why a Flat?
Why do they call these things flats? No one really knows for sure. A wall is one of the most familiar objects that flats are meant to represent. Walls aren't the only thing that flats can represent, but for this discussion we'll use them as an example.

Perhaps for this reason, flats are quite often rectangular or square, to imitate a wall's shape. Flats also create the illusion of a wall's solidity but use less structure, cost less, and take less time to build. To get a better understanding of how this is achieved, let's look at a flat more closely.

The main difference between a wall and a flat derives from our need to make scenery lighter and more portable than a wall. Walls are meant to be permanent. Walls are often built where they are meant to stand. They get stored in the structure they are holding upright, right where you left them last (if not, you may be in big trouble). Quite often the scenery is built somewhere other than where the scenery is used; it gets stored until it's needed, it gets loaded, transported, and then set up in its final location. To do all this we don't build flats the way a wall is built; their construction is more compact, or flat.

Hmm. . . . Could this reveal the name's origin? But before we get ahead of ourselves, let's look at the types of flats. Flats can be grouped in two different ways: by their *covering* and by their *structure*. We'll start with the type of covering.

Covering: Soft Versus Hard Flats

Flats can be covered in two ways, with a hard material and with a soft material. These types of flats are named by the type of covering, i.e., *hard-cover flats* or *soft-cover flats*. Soft-cover flats are the ones the average person is most familiar with. Hard-cover flats are more of an industry specialty.

Soft-Cover Flats

Whether we're talking about the type of flat you used in high school or the ones you see on TV sitcoms when they go backstage, this type is pretty much thought of as the quintessential flat (see Figure 1.1). Its structure is not unlike that of an artist's canvas, a cloth covering stretched over a wooden frame.

Advantages of the Soft-Cover Flat

- It is light. It may look like a wall from the front, but the fabric covering adds comparatively little weight.
- Because of its weight, it can *shift* (move into place on stage) and be braced easily, making quick scene changes and setups possible.
- It is cheap. Depending on the type of covering, these flats are relatively inexpensive to build and recover.
- Because the covering is similar to an artist's canvas, it's a medium that is easily painted, allowing the scenic artist a variety of finishes.
- Because the covering is soft, it can be removed, stored, and restretched or replaced easily, allowing the frame to be recycled.

Disadvantages of the Soft-Cover Flat

- Because of the soft covering, the flat works like a sail when air currents are disturbed nearby (e.g., someone walking behind it or slamming a door next to it).

Figure 1.1: *The quintessential flat.*

While this movement is not noticeable on a theatrical stage, it can be quite obvious in television and film.

- Any *appliqués*, which are anything you would add to the surface of the flat, such as molding or hung pictures, require additional structure behind the flat, increasing build time.
- Sometimes the flat structure creates a lump that snags the paint of a not-too-careful scenic artist, much in the way a crayon rubbing over thin paper reveals the texture of a leaf or tombstone, someone's head, or whatever you can get underneath it.
- By its nature, the surface material tends toward translucency. When backlighting the set, additional steps must be taken to prevent light transmission, such as *back painting* (literally painting the back of the flat with black paint or another color to make it opaque) and *double covering* (putting a second covering on the backside of the flat).
- While these flats may last for years, one out-of-control piece of scenery at some later time and you have a gaping hole that's not easy to fix.

Hard-Cover Flats

Hard-cover flats are the next step in adding believability to our imitation wall. The idea is the same; it is an attempt to create a lighter, more portable version of a wall. This version takes the idea of solidity to the next level (see Figure 1.2). Its frame may be

Figure 1.2: *A hard-cover flat.*

similar to that for the soft cover, but the surface material, as its name states, is hard, which opens up a variety of possibilities in creating the needed illusion of reality.

Advantages of the Hard-Cover Flat

- Its surface is hard. The surface-movement problem faced by the soft cover doesn't apply here. These flats can be walked behind, doors can slam, you may even lean against them without moving the surface.
- The surface is naturally opaque, eliminating the light leaks found with soft flats.
- The surface isn't like a painter's canvas. It's more like a wall. The texture for the most part is consistent and doesn't reveal the structure under it.
- The hard covering allows a variety of surface treatments. Whereas paint is the major treatment for a soft cover, the hard cover can easily hold wallpaper, stucco, even appliqués such as molding and hung picture frames and in most cases without additional structure.
- Depending on the surface treatment, the flat is more durable. And while the surface treatment may chip, the flat covering itself is less likely to become damaged than a soft covering.

Disadvantages of the Hard-Cover Flat

- It is heavier. In a soft-cover flat, most of the weight is in its structure. In a hard-cover flat you may have the same structure, but the hard surface has added half to twice the weight in some cases. The additional weight also makes the flat harder to shift and set up.
- It is more expensive. Depending on the type of covering, the surface materials in a hard-cover flat are more prone to price increases.
- You can't recover a hard-cover flat as easily as a soft-cover flat. It's almost easier to make a new flat, especially if you've added a textured surface treatment such as stucco.

Here is where the flat story can get a bit more complicated. As previously mentioned, there is an additional way to classify flats. This classification is according to the flat's *frame* type. Let's begin with that "quintessential flat" we spoke of earlier.

Standard Versus Hollywood Frame

The soft-cover flat we spoke of has a traditional frame type known as the *theatrical, standard frame,* or *face frame flat* (see Figure 1.3). Traditionally, it's made of ¾"-thick wood that's approximately 2½" wide on its face and whatever length is required for the flat's height and width.

As we stated before, fabric is stretched over this frame and triangular blocks of plywood or luaun called *corner blocks* are added in the corners and over any other joints for added

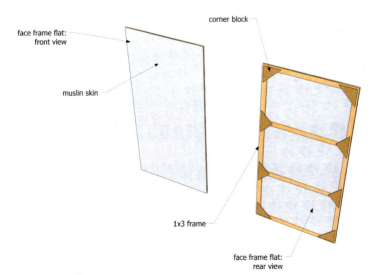

Figure 1.3: *A face frame flat.*

rigidity. In this way the overall structure is approximately 1″ thick. However, and this is where things get a little sticky, quite often this frame type is given a hard surface. Obviously doing this will increase the flat's thickness by the thickness of the hard cover. As you may have guessed, we will call this type of flat a *hard-cover standard flat*.

Advantages of the Standard Frame

- It is thin. Even with a ¼″ hard cover increasing the flat's thickness to approximately 1″, many flats can be stored back to back or face to face on edge in a relatively small space.
- Its thickness also makes it an ideal piece of scenery to fly, again allowing many pieces to be hung in a relatively small space.
- The thickness also allows it to be used in tighter spaces, even directly against a studio wall, without significantly reducing backstage passage.

Disadvantages of the Standard Frame

- It is thin. Even with a ¼″ hard cover increasing the flat's thickness to approximately 1¼″, it is nowhere near the thickness of a real wall. Additional pieces, called *reveals*, made of thin plywood or other materials must be added to create the illusion of depth.
- It is thin. By its nature the frame, when standing upright, sits on only three-quarters of an inch of thickness at its base. This requires additional support, such as *stage braces*, to keep the flat upright. The taller the flat, the more support needed.
- The thickness makes adding heavy door frames and window casements to the flats more difficult and often requires additional structure.
- The face frame structure requires additional support in the corners of the flat. As stated earlier we call these thin blocks of wood *corner blocks*. The mechanical advantage to using these relatively simple devices is great. Once added to a flat they create resistance to the twisting of the joints, the place where structural failure is most likely. The trade-off is that the process of cutting corner blocks adds another step to the flat-making process. Similarly, fastening the corner block adds yet another step.

Let's Go to Hollywood

The other type of frame is alternately known as a *studio* or *Hollywood flat* frame (see Figure 1.4). As you can guess, these flats are most widely used in the film and television industries. (Conversely, some people call standard flats *Broadway flats*. It makes sense if you realize that on Broadway, space is at a premium and quite often scenery is built somewhere else and transported on a truck to the theatre.)

Hollywood , studio or edge frame flat

front view

rear view

Figure 1.4: *A studio (Hollywood) flat frame.*

The frame is made with the widest part of the board (approximately 2½″–3½″) facing out and the thinnest part of the board facing the covering. In this way the flat resembles an open box or its scenic cousin, the platform. Most often these flats are covered with ⅛″–¼″ plywood Masonite or luaun but can be stretched with a soft cover.

Advantages of the Hollywood Frame

- It is thicker. Because of its thickness, it gains several structural advantages when setting up scenery. The depth of the frame allows clamps to be used to fasten flats together, speeding both setup and teardown. There is a popular story that the stagehands in old Hollywood could hold onto the inside frame of the flat while a scene was being shot in front of it, eliminating any need for supporting structure. While difficult to verify, the story does illustrate the advantages of the wider frame—placed side by side with strategically placed flats at right angles, these flats self-support more easily than the standard. Depending on the flat's height, it can also be weighted or sandbagged to the floor, especially useful when you can't actually fasten it to your stage floor.
- Because of the thickness, reveals aren't as necessary.
- The thickness makes adding heavy door frames and window casements to the flats less difficult and often not requiring additional structure.
- Because of its edge-to-face construction, combined with the hard cover, corner blocks aren't required.

Disadvantages of the Hollywood Frame

- It is thicker. Because of its thickness it's harder to store. Approximately three standard flats on edge take up the same amount of space as one Hollywood-style flat.
- It is more expensive, since it takes more lumber to build. Because the boards in the frame are assembled in an edge-to-face fashion, the lengths of lumber are slightly longer, and the hard covering, as we stated, increases the flat's cost.

As you can see, the differences between the advantages and disadvantages of covering and frame types aren't that great. What it basically comes down to is your choice between the styles. We may think of one type of flat as the quintessential flat, but there is no right or wrong choice between styles. How you use the flat, what kind of stage and storage space you have available, budget, and tools and skill levels available to you are all deciding factors that can help you make your choice.

Anatomy of a Flat

Now let's look at the parts of a flat. There are two basic sections to every flat: the *frame* and the *covering*. For ease of discussion we'll again use the standard theatrical flat as our example.

The frame is the skeleton of the flat (see Figure 1.5). The sturdiness of its structure determines how well it will hold whatever covering you choose. There are three main parts of the flat's frame: *rails*—the horizontal members at the top and bottom of the flat; *stiles*—the long vertical members that sit under the rails; and *toggles*—the horizontal members that sit between the stiles.

Flat Frame—Rails

Most theatre terms seem strange; however, once you understand that the majority of the terms come from other professions, some of them start to make sense. If you look at a text on making cabinets, you'll find that the terms *rails* and *stiles* apply to roughly the same corresponding pieces in your kitchen cabinet's door. Rails are the pieces found at the top and the bottom of the flat, and stiles are the vertical pieces. Each of these pieces has a specific name: The rail on the top is the *top rail*, and the one on the bottom is the *bottom rail*. Occasionally, theatrical terms do make sense.

Think about your kitchen cabinet (see Figure 1.6). If you are a keen observer or are looking at this picture, you will notice the difference between the flat and your cabinet door (*clue*: it's not that the flat *isn't* in your kitchen. I have often had flats in my kitchen). The rails on your cabinet door are inside the stiles. The rails on a flat run the entire width of the flat. What could the reason possibly be? Think again about that cabinet door (yes, I'm getting hungry too, but think about the door and not what's inside it).

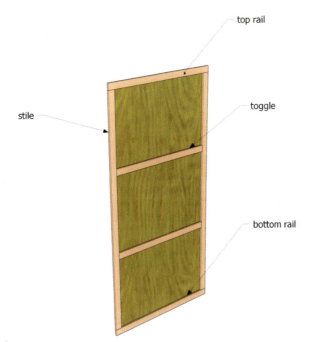

Figure 1.5: *The frame.*

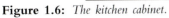

Figure 1.6: *The kitchen cabinet.*

To make the door work, it has to be hung from the side with a hinge—that's how it fulfills its function. A flat either stands on its bottom rail or is flown from its top rail—that's its basic function. The longer piece on both frames is where the stress on the structure is focused. Doors are swung on the longer piece. Flats are lifted or sat upon the longer piece. Additionally, flats are often dragged across the stage along their rails.

Since the rail runs the entire width of the flat, there is a smooth surface for the flat to slide along. If the flat was constructed like the cabinet, the long sides could catch and bump along as the flat moved or even rip off. The most important thing to remember here is that rails are on top and bottom and run the entire width of the flat.

Staying in Stiles

The long vertical pieces on the kitchen door are the stiles. On a flat, these pieces sit in between the top and bottom rails. You can think of stiles as the parts of the flat that gives it its height or think of it as its *stylish* height. How tall do these stiles need to be to give the flat its proper height?

One of the basic realities of technical theatre in general and carpentry in specific is you can't escape math. For someone like me this can seem daunting—math has never come easy. To combat my fears, I find knowing a rule or formula comforts me greatly. Just knowing that the answer is written down somewhere can be a great confidence booster. What does any of this have to do with the stiles? Although it seems to be common sense, it bears mentioning that the length of the stiles is determined by the thickness of the top and bottom rails subtracted from the total height of the flat. That's a definition; write it down or highlight it. If you are math phobic like me you may already be sweating. Look at Table 1.1, which refers to a standard flat frame.

Let's say that our flat is made with a standard 2½″-wide frame. To get the height of the stiles, we need to subtract the total of the top and bottom rails' width, or 5″, from the height of the flat (192″, or 16′). The length of the stiles would then be 187″, or 15′-7″. This simple formula holds true no matter what width you make the frame of your flat.

We talk more about standard building materials and the reasons for choosing them later in the book, but for right now we will stick with the standard 2½″ wooden frame since it is the most common. Can you see a pattern in Table 1.1? When talking about stock, whole-feet sizes using 2½″-wide framing, the height of the stiles is always 1′ shorter and the measurement always ends in 7″. Yes, you can just subtract it each time. But this is a rule, and it is comforting.

Table 1.1: *Length of Stiles = (Height of Flat) − (Width of Rails) × 2*

Height of Flat in:		Width of Rails in:		Length of Stiles in:	
Inches	Feet	Inches	×2	Inches	Feet
192″	16′-0″	2½″	5″	187″	15′-7″
168″	14′-0″	2½″	5″	163″	13′-7″
144″	12′-0″	2½″	5″	139	11′-7″
120″	10′-0″	2½″	5″	115″	9′-7″
96″	8′-0″	2½″	5″	91″	7′-7″

Table 1.2: *Length of Stiles = (Height of Flat) − (Width of Rails) × 2*

Height of Flat in:		Thickness of Rails in:		Length of Stiles in:	
Inches	Feet	Inches	×2	Inches	Feet
192″	16′-0″	¾″	1½″	190-½″	15′-10½″
168″	14′-0″	¾″	1½″	166-½″	13′-10½″
144″	12′-0″	¾″	1½″	144-½″	11′-10½″
120″	10′-0″	¾″	1½″	118-½″	9′-10½″
96″	8′-0″	¾″	1½″	94-½″	7′-10½″

That helps us with the standard frame stiles. As you know, Hollywood is *stylish* too. The formula for finding the height of stiles is still the same for a Hollywood flat, but the rule is a little different. Take another look at the picture of the Hollywood flat (Figure 1.4). You should see an obvious difference in the orientation of the framing members. For this example we are using the standard ¾″-thick rail we have shown in this illustration.

Now look at Table 1.2. This is basically the same thing, right? This time all you need to remember is that the measurement of the stiles is 1′ shorter and ends in 10½″.

Toggles Anyone?

Toggles, as we stated before, are located between the stiles. These pieces are best described as the "spreader" of the flat. If you were to use a standard flat frame and stretch it with muslin, the frame itself would pull in along its sides like an hourglass as the muslin shrinks. The toggles hold the rectangular shape of the flat against outside stresses.

There is a similar formula for determining the length of a toggle in stock whole-feet-sized flats as for the length of the stiles. This time, substitute the width of the flat for the height and the width of the stiles for the width of the rails (see Table 1.3).

Does Table 1.3 look familiar? How about Table 1.4? Again this formula can be applied to any width of flat with any frame width.

The toggle performs an additional function. The thing about walls is that when they are in our homes we always want to stick stuff on them, like pictures, moldings, or light fixtures, to make them look more interesting (see Figure 1.7). We're sure you can see the difficulty in hanging a picture frame on a soft-covered flat. One alternative is to paint the decoration directly onto the surface of the flat. This approach can work well if the style of the production is nonrealistic, but it isn't appropriate for all productions.

Table 1.3: *Length of Toggles = (Width of Flat) − (Width of Stiles) × 2*

Width of Flat in:		Width of Stiles in:		Length of Toggles in:	
Inches	Feet	Inches	×2	Inches	Feet
96″	8′-0″	2½″	5″	91″	7′-7″
72″	6′-0″	2½″	5″	67″	5′-7″
48″	4′-0″	2½″	5″	43″	3′-7″
36″	3′-0″	2½″	5″	31″	2′-7″
24″	2′-0″	2½″	5″	19″	1′-7″

Table 1.4: *Width of Toggles = (Width of Flat) − (Width of Stiles) × 2*

Width of Flat in:		Width of Stiles in:		Length of Toggles in:	
Inches	Feet	Inches	×2	Inches	Feet
96″	8′-0″	¾″	1½″	94½″	7′-10½″
72″	6′-0″	¾″	1½″	70½″	5′-10½″
48″	4′-0″	¾″	1½″	46½″	3′-10½″
36″	3′-0″	¾″	1½″	34½″	2′-10½″
24″	2′-0″	¾″	1½″	22½″	1′-10½″

Figure 1.7: *A wall with hanging "stuff."*

When actual dimensional appliqués are required, the toggle supplies the additional structure we need. Ideally, the designer has designated the locations of these appliqués so that during the flat's construction, toggles may be placed directly behind them. Toggles may be retrofitted to an existing flat if necessary. Since they live between the stiles, it's a simple matter to cut the toggle to fit and to corner-block it in. Well, at least it sounds simple. As we said before, ideally the designer knows where he or she wants the appliqué before the construction period.

Along the same vein, a toggle provides a fastening surface when hard covering a flat. Plywood and other hard-covering materials generally come in 4′ × 8′ sheets. Unless you're building a 4′ × 8′ flat there will be a seam where two sheets join. Unless backed and attached to a toggle, the seam will shift and flex as the flat is moved—potentially ruining the surface treatment.

I'm Framed—Steel-Framed Flats

Steel flats are generally made from 1″ × 1″ *16-gauge mild steel box tube* (see Figure 1.8). The term *box tube* may seem confusing. Because we generally use the term *tube*, we think of an inner tube or some such donutlike shape or even a toilet paper tube shape.

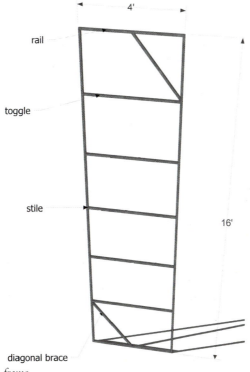

Figure 1.8: *A steel flat frame.*

As the steel manufacturers use it, the word *tube* means "hollow." You could make a flat out of solid 1″ × 1″ square steel bar, but you wouldn't want to lift it.

Steel flats are most commonly made from a square steel tube. In this respect, it is difficult to say whether a flat is a *face frame* or *edge frame* flat; that is to say, *standard* or *Hollywood*. For the sake of discussion we'll think of them as standard frames.

A steel flat has basically the same design as a wooden flat and all the same parts. Steel flats, however, need diagonal bracing to combat the natural tendency of the material to bow inward under its own weight. This is most common in taller flats (see Figure 1.8).

Another thing about steel flats: Since they are made of, well, steel, you have to use a whole set of different tools and techniques to work with them.

Advantages of Steel-Framed Flats

- Steel flats stand tall. The largest, most common length of lumber is 16′. You can order other longer board lengths, but you'll pay more for them. Steel comes in 20′–22′ lengths, depending on the type and size of the steel you're ordering.
- You may get the same rigidity as a standard flat with a smaller dimension in steel. This may be most important when you are creating a flat with a transparent or translucent section, such as a *scrim* or a front- or rear-projection screen built into it. By using steel you can have less frame and more open area (see Figure 1.9).
- You can have taller flats. Yes, it's true that you can order longer lengths of lumber. But as a wooden flat gets taller, it becomes more wobbly, unless you are building a Hollywood-style frame, which as you know is thicker. Basically, the steel frame allows you to have a taller, thinner flat.

Disadvantages of Steel-Framed Flats

- Steel is heavy. No matter what you do, between a steel flat and a wooden flat of the same dimensions, the steel flat will be heavier (unless you're just trying to prove us wrong).
- As we said, steel requires a different set of tools and techniques. It also requires technicians familiar with these tools and techniques.
- Joining steel requires welding. Welding produces ultraviolet radiation and hazardous fumes; therefore, special equipment and training are required.
- Forming and joining steel creates sparks. Sparks could ignite flammable materials, such as wood and sawdust.
- Taller flats need more space to build and store. As we said, steel can arrive in 20′ lengths. You'll need a place that can store long lengths of steel.

Figure 1.9: *A rigid steel frame from DeSales University's Production of* The Memorandum. *The open translucent area allowed by the rigid 1½″ steel tube frame allowed light transmission and created the effect of buildings that were lit from the inside.*

Platforms

The Spanish playwright Lope De Vega once said that all he needed for theatre was "three boards, two actors, and one passion." Presumably, he stood on the boards he spoke of (hence the expression *trod the boards*). Most likely these boards were suspended between two benches so that Lope could be higher than and more visible to his audience. Like Lope, directors have looked for ways to give the actor and the action of the play more emphasis—to direct and focus the audience's attention. One way is to elevate the actor. When we see a speaker at an event or a king on a throne (you see that often, don't you?), the person is generally raised above everyone else. Height gives focus. Height says importance. Height says, "This event is different—pay attention!" We even say that the theatre is *heightened* reality. Where is all of this going? If you want people raised up, you have to put something under them. In the theatre we call those things *platforms* (see Figure 1.10).

Like Lope, if you place some boards side by side; you basically have a rudimentary platform, a very *low* rudimentary platform. Over the years we have developed other ways of constructing the platforms that have allowed us to take advantage of other shapes

Figure 1.10: *Pennsylvania Shakespeare Festival's Green Show Stage.*

and designs beyond the three boards. Before we examine those, let's take a look at the parts of a platform.

Platforms have three main parts: the *skin*, the *frame*, and the *legs* (see Figure 1.11).

The Skinny on the Skin

The three boards we spoke of are an example of a platform *skin* (this is also known as the platform's *deck*). This description can be a little deceptive, since ultimately the deck is what you walk on and *skins* can be *decked* with other surfaces. Yes, this is confusing. It's another example of two theatrical terms often used interchangeably from region to region.

We say *skin* in this context because it fits the neat little literary device we are using to illustrate a point. Feel free to interchange the terms when we're not around, when you write a textbook, or if you want to confuse a group of people. (We talk about decking later in this section.) As with your body, the *skin* is on the outside of the platform, and it covers the frame, or the skeleton, of the platform. The skin has two basic purposes: It provides a surface for the scenery and actors to stand on, and it helps to spread the weight placed on it over the entire frame instead of just under the weight.

The goal of scenic building is to make it light and to construct it fast. This is also true with platforms. Platforms have the potential of becoming the heaviest units in the theatre because they need to hold people and, often, scenery above the stage floor without collapsing. It's for this reason that the standard thickness of platform skin is at least ¾″, which seems to be the combination of thickness and strength we're looking for in a flooring material.

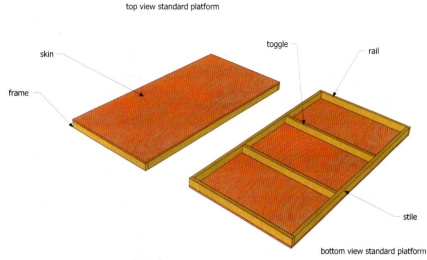

Figure 1.11: *Labeled drawing of platform parts.*

The most common and readily available material is *¾″ × 4′ × 8′ plywood sheets*. This is the same material and thickness that can be found in house floors. Because of the availability of plywood, the size and shape of the plywood sheet have defined the size and shape of *stock* platforms. Just as stores keep a *stock of merchandise* to sell right away, you need to keep a *stock answer* ready when someone says something about your mother.

Theatres keep a variety of *stock platforms* of basic sizes on hand, avoiding the time and expense of building new ones. Quite often stock platforms are built on the 4′ × 8′ *module*; that is to say, the sizes are based on multiples of, or are divisible by, 4′ and 8′ (see Figure 1.12).

Other thickness of plywood may be used; however, the thinner the skin, the more it gives when walked on and the more support you need underneath it. Whatever you hoped to save in cost or platform weight you might just add back into the unit getting the flex out of the skin (having the platform surface flex up and down is seldom desirable). We had a friend who was cutting corners on a high school set and used thinner skins without the extra framing. He told the actors that the platforms were what they used on Broadway to give the dancers that extra bounce to their step. That is, of course, not true. If, however, you have these materials on hand and you're not worried about the weight, you can make just about any thickness work for you. We have heard of examples of ⅜″ platform skins—we haven't wanted to walk on them though.

There's More Than One Way to Skin a Platform

Other materials can be used to skin.

- *¾″–1½″ wooden planks* (à la Lope De Vega) can be laid on the frame in an outdoor deck–like style (Figure 1.13).

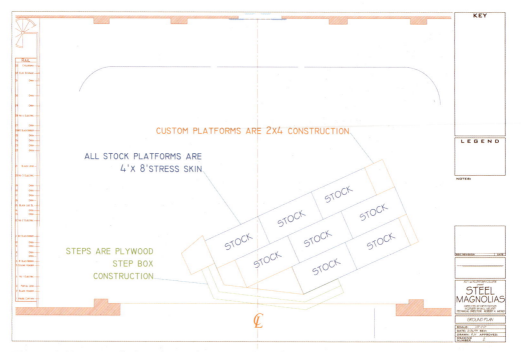

Figure 1.12: *Ground plan of a set showing stock platform usage.*

Figure 1.13: *Picture of* The Diary of Anne Frank *with poplar planked floor.*

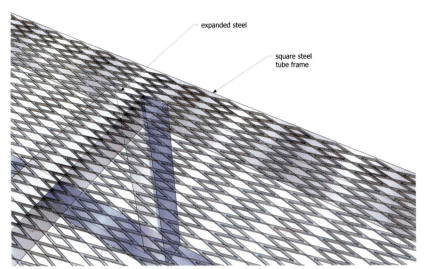

expanded steel

square steel
tube frame

Figure 1.14: *Drawing of a* West Side Story *wagon covered in expanded steel.*

- In the same way, *tongue-and-groove* planks may be laid like a traditional hardwood floor.
- As a response to increased materials cost there is a movement now toward cheaper composite/recycled wooden materials, such as *OSB* (oriented strand board) and *MDF* (medium-density fiberboard). We'll discuss the properties of these when we get to building materials.
- Steel can also serve as a platform skin (see Figure 1.14). Think of the steel-grated fire escapes you've seen. They are essentially steel platforms attached to buildings. The advantage to this style is in the look; when you start working with steel you can't worry about the weight of the platform. The grating material we spoke of is called *expanded steel*. Made from sheet metal that has been slit and stretched, expanded metal permits air and light to pass through and can be cut, formed, and welded. Sheets are lightweight yet strong due to the diamond truss pattern, which enhances the rigidity of the metal.
- Believe it or not, you can also make platform skins out of cardboard. A material called *honeycombed cardboard* or *honeycombed Kraft paper*, in a 2″ thickness, when sandwiched between a couple sheets of ⅜″ plywood, has enough strength to withstand the pressure of people walking on it.

All of these choices are of course governed by the look the designer wants, the cost of the materials, how that fits into the production budget, and the time it takes to use them.

The Frame

Let's go back to those three boards. Once Lope put them across the benches, the two actors could stand on them. Most likely the boards bowed under their weight. To prevent

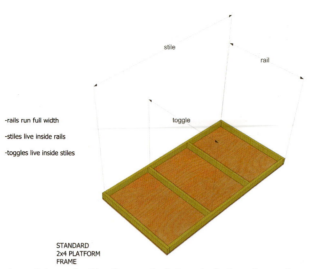

stile

rail

-rails run full width

-stiles live inside rails

toggle

-toggles live inside stiles

STANDARD
2x4 PLATFORM
FRAME

Figure 1.15: *Drawing of the underside of a standard 2 × 4 platform frame showing the frame's parts.*

this from happening, Lope's carpenter would have had to put a *frame* under the boards. The frame, as we said, is the skeleton of the platform. It rests under the skin and supports the weight of the actor, scenery, etc. To prevent the platform from bowing under this weight, several different frame styles have been devised, constructed primarily from wood and metal. All of the styles have the same basic parts in common. We start by looking at these parts and then examine how their assembly adds strength in the different styles.

Platform Frame Parts Versus Flat Frame Parts

As an example, we'll start by looking at the *standard 2 × 4 platform frame* style (Figure 1.15).

Surprisingly, these platform part names are now familiar to us: *rails*, *toggles*, and *stiles*. All the work you put into reading that section on flats has now paid off. As we said in the introduction to this chapter, flats are vaguely vertical and platforms are vaguely horizontal. So let's lay the platform on its skin and think of it for now in the same orientation as the flat as we examine the parts (Figure 1.16).

On first glance, you will notice something familiar about the platform's frame. It resembles the Hollywood flat. Both structures are made on an *edge frame construction*. As we look at the standard platform frame, we see that the parts at the top and the bottom of the platform are rails, the side pieces are the stiles, and the horizontal middle pieces are the toggles, as in the flat's structure.

The sizes of the parts can be computed with the same formula as for flat frame construction (see Table 1.4).

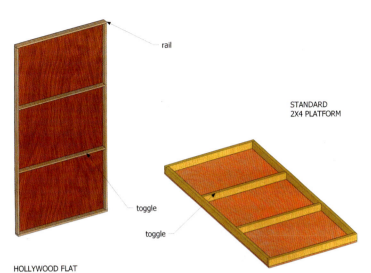

rail

STANDARD
2X4 PLATFORM

toggle

toggle

HOLLYWOOD FLAT

Figure 1.16: *Drawing comparing a Hollywood flat's structure to that of the standard 2 × 4 platform frame.*

Table 1.5: *Length of Stiles = (Length of Platform) − (Thickness of Rails) × 2*

Length of Platform in:		Thickness of Rails in:		Length of Stiles in:	
Inches	Feet	Inches	×2	Inches	Feet
96″	8′-0″	1½″	3″	93″	7′-9″
84″	7′-0″	1½″	3″	81″	6′-9″
72″	6′-0″	1½″	3″	69″	5′-9″
60″	5′-0″	1½″	3″	57″	4′-9″
48″	4′-0″	1½″	3″	45″	3′-9″

Does Table 1.5 look familiar? How about Table 1.6? Do you see the pattern in these tables? When talking about stock whole-feet-sized platforms using 1½″-thick framing, the length of the stiles is always 1′ shorter and the measurement always ends in 9″. The toggle rule is just as simple: 1′ shorter and ending in 9″.

In all fairness, the formulas work just as well with numbers that end in different foot-inch lengths. It just isn't as pretty a table, and the "1′ shorter ending in 9″" rule doesn't apply (see Table 1.7). Not as pretty, but it works for both toggles and stiles.

Frame Styles (Not Stiles)
The standard platform frame style that most people are used to is the 2 × 4 frame construction we just looked at. Let's look at its advantages and disadvantages.

Table 1.6: *Length of Toggles = (Width of Platform) − (Thickness of Stiles) × 2*

Width of Platform in:		Width of Stiles in:		Length of Toggles in:	
Inches	Feet	Inches	×2	Inches	Feet
72″	6′-0″	1½″	3″	69″	5′-9″
48″	4′-0″	1½″	3″	45″	3′-9″
36″	3′-0″	1½″	3″	33″	2′-9″
24″	2′-0″	1½″	3″	21″	1′-9″
12″	1′-0″	1½″	3″	9″	0′-9″

Table 1.7: *Length of Stiles = (Length of Platform) − (Thickness of Rails) × 2*

Length of Platform in:		Thickness of Rails in:		Length of Stiles in:	
Inches	Feet	Inches	×2	Inches	Feet
102″	8′-6″	1½″	3″	99″	8′-3″
89″	7′-5″	1½″	3″	86″	6′-2″
76″	6′-4″	1½″	3″	71″	6′-1″
69″	5′-9″	1½″	3″	66″	4′-6″
50″	4′-2″	1½″	3″	47″	3′-11″

Advantages of the Standard 2 × 4 Platform Frame

- 2 × 4 lumber is readily available.
- Its thickness makes it sturdy in use over a moderate range of platform lengths.
- At 3½″ it stores in a relatively small place.
- 2 × 4 lumber stands up to repeated abuse, drilling, and screwing.

Disadvantages of the Standard 2 × 4 Platform Frame

- A ¾″ skin and a 2 × 4 frame may be heavy.
- 2 × 4's tend to split when you drill into the ends of them.
- The 3½″ platforms may flex when walked on.
- The frame is 3½″. With a ¾″ skin, the total platform height becomes 4¼″. Designers like steps in the 6″–8″ range. If the design calls for the platforms to create a series of steplike levels, you will have to add additional structure to raise the platform to the required height.
- When transporting the platform, one common method (although not the best) is to drag it across the floor along the 8′ length. Unlike a flat, the platform is easier to drag along on its stiles instead of its rails because of its weight. This can cause the corners of the platform rails to catch and rip off.

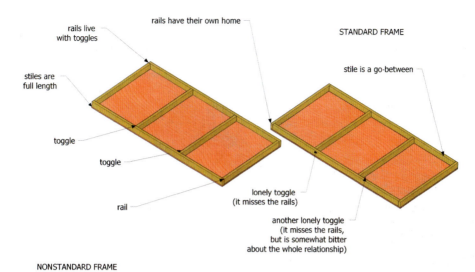

rails live
with toggles

rails have their own home

STANDARD FRAME

stiles are
full length

stile is a go-between

toggle

toggle

rail

lonely toggle
(it misses the rails)

another lonely toggle
(it misses the rails,
but is somewhat bitter
about the whole relationship)

NONSTANDARD FRAME

Figure 1.17: *Comparison drawing of the nonstandard 2 × 4 frame and the standard 2 × 4 frame.*

Nonstandard 2 × 4 Frame

One method of frame construction puts the top and bottom rails inside the stiles, like the kitchen cabinet door we spoke of earlier (Figure 1.17).

Advantages of the Nonstandard 2 × 4 Platform Frame

- This style of stile does eliminate the problem of dragging and corner ripping.
- It is also arguably easier to make, since only two sizes of lumber are being used; The toggle and top and bottom rails are the same size.

Disadvantages of the Nonstandard 2 × 4 Platform Frame

- There is the concern that it is too easy for the platform to shift when in place and to lose these end pieces without the benefit of the interlocking corners of the standard platform frame.

As you can see, there aren't a lot of advantages to this frame style. Old-timers like us just feel that "it isn't built right." In the end, our real problem with it is that it looks funny. Believe it or not, that can be a major factor in what tips the scale. A lot of what we do and build and put major amounts of time and effort into never gets seen by the audience. But we see it—as we build it. It's hard to describe, but there is a feeling that you get when you step back with your crew and look at the work you've done: The

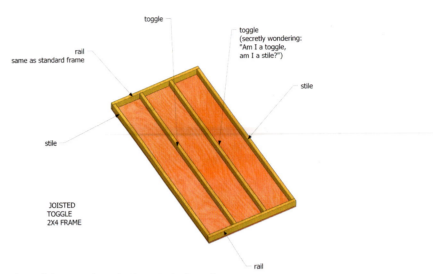

toggle

toggle
(secretly wondering:
"Am I a toggle,
am I a stile?")

rail
same as standard frame

stile

stile

JOISTED
TOGGLE
2X4 FRAME

rail

Figure 1.18: *Drawing of the joisted toggle 2 × 4 platform frame.*

well-placed toggles set in even rows, the evenly braced platform legs, the carefully cabled electric, things you've taken the time and effort to do the right way because it's the right way to do it. It's one of the things that adds a professional quality to your work, whether the audience sees it or not.

A second variation on the standard 2 × 4 platform frame is essentially the same as the standard frame, but inside the toggles run vertically instead of horizontally (Figure 1.18).

Advantages of the Joisted Toggle 2 × 4 Platform Frame

• The vertical toggles add lots of strength to the frame—they run in the same direction as the framing members of a house floor known as *joists*. When spaced along the width of the platform, they virtually eliminate flex in the skin.

Disadvantages of the Joisted Toggle 2 × 4 Platform Frame

• It's heavy. With two vertical toggles, you've added half again the weight.

The 2 × 4 standard platform frame style is also adaptable to other sizes of material. Another useful framing material is 2 × 6. While it is has many of the same advantages and disadvantages as the 2 × 4 frame, there are a few differences.

Advantages of the Standard 2 × 6 Platform Frame

- The 2 × 6 is also a readily available material.
- The added 2″ difference allows longer platform lengths without flexing.
- It stands up better to the repeated drilling and screwing and is generally more durable.
- The finished thickness of the platform and skin is 6¼″, which is in the step range most designers look for.
- It gives you more room to work with underneath.

Disadvantages of the Standard 2 × 6 Platform Frame

- It's more expensive than 2 × 4.
- It's heavy. The extra 2″ doesn't sound like much, but applied around the perimeter of the frame it can add just under twice the weight.

The 1 × 6 Platform Frame

This frame is constructed in the same manner as the 2 × 4 frame but is made of 1 × 6 pine boards (Figure 1.19). With dimensions of the 1 × 6 being ¾″ × 5½″, the platform is slightly taller and thinner than the 2 × 4 platform, whose dimensions, as you may remember, are 1½″ × 3½″ (we discuss the confusing dimensions in Chapter 2 on scenic construction materials). This frame looks even more like a Hollywood flat than the 2 × 4 frame. In fact, the tables we used for the stiles and rail lengths of the Hollywood flats work here as well.

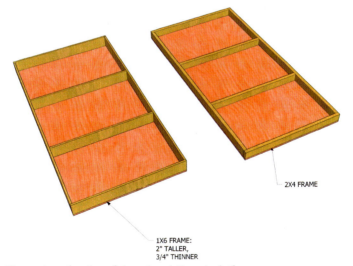

2X4 FRAME

1X6 FRAME:
2" TALLER,
3/4" THINNER

Figure 1.19: *Comparison drawing of 1 × 6 and 2 × 4 platforms.*

Advantages of the Standard 1 × 6 Platform Frame

- It is very light as compared to the 2 × 4 frame or its dimensional cousin, the 2 × 6 frame.
- Like the 2 × 6 frame, it may resist flexing better than a 2 × 4 frame.
- Its total height—frame and skin—falls into a natural step height of 6¼″. In fact, the 1 × 6 material may more easily be ripped down than 1½″ material to a width of 5¼″, giving the platform a finished height of 6″.

Disadvantages of the Standard 1 × 6 Platform Frame

- While with care these platforms can last a long time, the reality is that most people don't take a lot of care with big or heavy things. The mentality is some-thing like this: "If it's this heavy, *then it can take care of itself*—I'm outta here!" and they slam it into a corner when the TD (technical director) has his or her back turned. The frame supports the platform well and is just as thick as it needs to be for that purpose, but it doesn't take the abuse a 2 × 4 frame can.
- The 1 × material needs to be chosen carefully to avoid large knots. Knots in lumber provide weak spots that can easily crack and split. While it's true that 2 × 4 materials are prone to knots as well, structurally you don't have the same problem with them as you do with 1 × because of the additional ¾″ thickness.

All in all this is a good platform frame style. Next to the 2 × 4 frame this would be the most widely used style, since, as we said, the goal of theatrical scenery is to be strong and light and quickly constructed.

Stressed-Skin Platform Frame

One of the main functions of the platform skin is to hold the platform frame stiff and to keep it from flexing. Imagine what can happen when you add a second skin under-neath the frame. For the frame to bend, one side needs to compress and the other side needs to stretch. Since both sides of the frame are held fast, the compression and stretch-ing can't occur (Figure 1.20).

The stressed-skin platform may be constructed any number of ways. We dare say that every theatre that uses them has its own method or has heard of one or two others that you haven't. The unifying elements in the stressed-skin design are:

- There is a top skin and a bottom skin (usually the second skin is of a thinner material).
- All members must be securely joined and glued together. This is possibly the most important part of the platform formula. Well, no, it *is* the most important

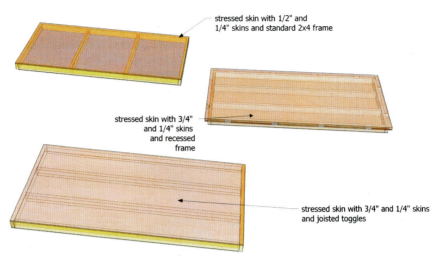

stressed skin with 1/2" and
1/4" skins and standard 2x4 frame

stressed skin with 3/4"
and 1/4" skins
and recessed
frame

stressed skin with 3/4" and 1/4" skins
and joisted toggles

x-ray view of stressed skin platforms

Figure 1.20: *Picture of several types of stressed-skin platforms.*

part. Everyone says so. Well, almost everyone. Some people weren't home and we had to leave messages. But they'll get back to us soon, and we both can guess what their answer will be.

Advantages of the Stressed-Skin Platform Frame

- The span of the platform may be greater while retaining a thin profile.
- The underside of the platform is covered, which may be helpful if it's visible to the audience.
- It takes up less room when stored.

Disadvantages of the Stressed-Skin Platform Frame

- Depending on its construction, it may be heavy. Adding a second skin, even a thinner one, may add weight.
- You can't get inside it. If you need to run wiring, plumbing, or flagpoles through the platform, it is more difficult to fish through two layers of skin.
- Legging is more difficult. Since the frame isn't exposed, bolting the legs on becomes impossible using conventional hardware.

Plywood Framed Platform

The platforms we have discussed until now have had a frame made of a dimensional lumber such as 2 × 4 or 1 × 6 and a plywood skin. There is another construction method that is a little out of the box—or rather it is the box. Constructed most often out of ¾″ plywood, the *plywood framed platform* is better visualized as a donut box

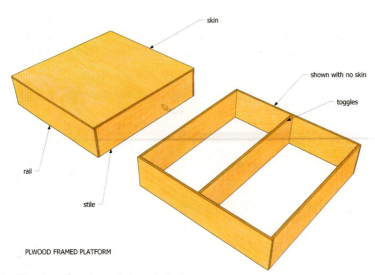

Figure 1.21: *Drawing of a plywood framed platform.*

without a bottom (Figure 1.21). The sides of the box actually create the structure where the rails and stiles would normally be, similar to a 1 × 6 platform. Unlike a 1 × 6 platform, the sides extend all the way to the stage floor, the platform beneath them, or whatever surface you are elevating away from; in effect becoming the platform's legs. Toggles, placed in the same 2′ × 4′ spacing as on more conventional styles, also run to the floor and may create additional legging for the platform.

Advantages of the Plywood Framed Platform

- The platform construction is fairly quick and simple; you're basically making a box out of plywood.
- The style of the platform lends itself very nicely to *step boxes*: platforms 6–8″ × 10–12″ wide that can act as transitional steps between levels of platforms. This eliminates the need to work with tiny pieces of dimensional lumber, which could split and crack whenever you put a fastener into them.
- Additionally, stair landings work nicely when made via this method. If the side of the platform facing the audience looks good enough, you won't have to add additional lumber or facing to keep the audience from seeing underneath the platform.

Disadvantages of the Plywood Framed Platform

- This method really doesn't work well for platforms over 4′ high.
- Plywood is heavy. A single sheet of common ¾″ plywood may weigh up to 75 pounds. To remedy this, you can cut several *lightening holes* in the material where the audience can't see them, but this adds to the platform's build time.

- Plywood is expensive. Depending on where you are, plywood is more often subjected to the market increases of the building trade than is dimensional lumber. Therefore, the more plywood in your project, the more it will cost.

Steel Platform Frame and Frame Types

The steel platform frame follows a lot of the same principles as the wooden platform frame, with one important difference. It's made of steel. Because it is made of steel, the framing members may be of a smaller dimension and still give similar support as a thicker, wooden counterpart.

As you've probably figured out by now, two of the life aspirations of any platform are to lift things up so that we can see them and to keep these things from falling down to where we can't. Remember what made the stressed-skin platform rigid? The structure is arranged in such a way that the wooden frame can't flex. Steel has less flexibility than wood, so let's look at how we can arrange a steel frame's pieces. One useful way to categorize steel frames is by the shape of the steel stock.

1 × 3 to 1 × 4 Square Steel Box Tube Frame

As we said when looked at steel flats, the term *tube* refers to the hollow nature of the steel material. 1 × 3 and 1 × 4 steel tubes are rectangular tubes whose dimensions are, as you may have guessed, 1″ × 3″ and 1″ × 4″. The frame structure used with these platform materials are practically identical to the structure used in standard platform construction (Figure 1.22).

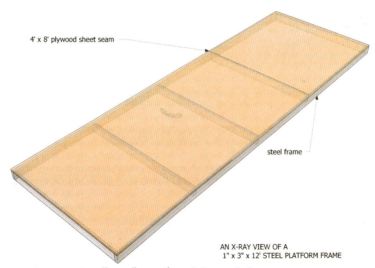

4' x 8' plywood sheet seam

steel frame

AN X-RAY VIEW OF A
1" x 3" x 12' STEEL PLATFORM FRAME

Figure 1.22: *A drawing of a 1″ × 3″ × 12′ steel frame platform.*

Figure 1.23: *Drawing of steel platforms used in DeSales University's Production of* A Christmas Carol.

Advantages of the 1 × 3 Steel Platform Frame

- The process of joining steel differs, as we said, from the process of joining wood. Wood joints, while firm, are still somewhat flexible. Whether it is weather causing the joints to expand and contract or pressure and stress from those careless stage-hands slamming the platforms around, wood joints may move, loosen, and pop. Steel, when welded, forms a rigid joint. Weather and stress won't pop the joint; in fact, welded joints are stronger than the surrounding steel.
- As we said, the steel doesn't flex. A 1 × 3 tube forms a narrow-profile frame that may easily span 6–8′ between legs (Figure 1.23).

Disadvantages of the 1 × 3 Steel Platform Frame

- Similar to the steel framed flat, whenever you use steel you need specialized tools, workspaces, and training to weld the parts together.
- Steel, as we said before, is heavy, and the 1 × 3 and 1 × 4 box tubes at 20–22′ long need a lot of room to store.
- If you have to run rope or cables through the platform, steel is much harder to drill through than wood.
- Attaching the platform skin requires specialized fasteners to go through the steel. One type of fastener most commonly used is the *self-tapping screw.* Looking remarkably like a drywall screw, these screws have a small drill point at their ends that allows them to drill into the steel and cut their own threads into it.

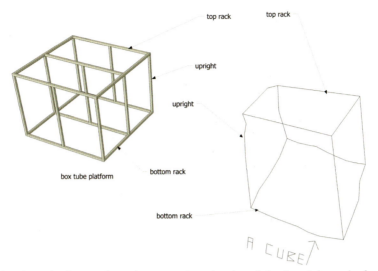

Figure 1.24: *A poorly drawn cube and a comparison drawing of the 1 × 1 box tube frame platform.*

1 × 1 Box Tube Frames

16-gauge mild steel box tube is the same material we spoke of when we talked about steel flats. This is no surprise, since it is one of the most commonly used steel shapes in scenic construction. It gives us the balance between weight, cost, and structure we look for in scenic materials. The problem with this material is that when you use it in the same manner as some of the wooden materials we spoke of, it doesn't have the rigidity we need for a platform frame. For this reason, 1 × 1 box tube platforms have a different platform structure.

Parts of the 1 × 1 Box Tube Platform

To explain the structure of this frame, let's go back to our description of the plywood framed platform. Remember the donut box? Try drawing a donut box with simple lines—it should look like those cube-shaped optical illusions we used to draw all over our notebooks in social studies class (Figure 1.24). The lines that define the sides and edges of the drawing are actually where the 1 × 1 tube would be.

Compare the two drawings in Figure 1.24. As you can see, both structures have rectangles forming the top and the bottom. These rectangles actually have names. The top rectangle is called the *top rack* and the bottom rectangle is called, as you may have guessed, *the bottom rack.* These are not unlike the more traditional frames we've seen. In fact, when viewed by itself, the top rack of a platform is almost indistinguishable from *1 × 1 box tube steel flat.* The toggle placement on the top rack is the same as on other platform frames: every 2–4′ and wherever you need one to catch the edge of your platform skin. (This is where the 2′–8″, or 32″, toggle placement construction

33

comes in handy. It's a good balance of weight, structure, and cost and still hits the eight door sheet lines of plywood skins.)

The upright members of the platform frame you see in Figure 1.24 are known as the *uprights*. If you have trouble remembering this term, try this clever mnemonic device: *"Uprights are upright."* The uprights on the donut box you drew would be the vertical lines that hold the top and bottom racks apart. These vertical members, like the sides of the plywood box frame, actually take the place of legs. Similar to the plywood box frame, the toggles also need to extend to the platform's lower rack, so uprights are used under them as well. (As you may have guessed, the bottom rack of the platform will look very similar to the top rack; wherever there is an upright attached to the top, we have to attach it to the bottom, and therefore toggle placement will be similar. Quite often it will be useful to use the top rack as a pattern for the bottom). The placement and number of the uprights are best determined by the amount of load placed on the platform, but as a rule the uprights should be spaced between 8″ and 12″ apart. The more weight, the closer the uprights.

Advantages of the 1 × 1 Box Tube Steel Platform Frame

- Just as with the other steel platform frames, the rigidity of the steel structure resists bending and can span wider distances than wood.
- It creates a strong open structure. Quite often the inside of these platforms may be used as a prop staging area, or with trapdoors in the platform they may be used to make entrances and exits.
- If placed strategically, the uprights may serve as attaching points for facing.

Advantages of the 1 × 1 Box Tube Steel Platform Frame

- There's a whole lot of parts and welding goin' on. Figure for every piece that gets cut, *at least* two welds are needed to join it to the rest of the frame.
- It is a very open structure. That may be what you are looking for in a particular design, but unlike the plywood box frame, you must face every side that faces the audience.

Drops and Backings: The Cloth, the Drops, the Backdrop, the Bedspread, and a Walk into a Spanish Courtyard

Remember what Lope said? "Three boards, two actors, and one passion." One version of this quote goes, "Three boards, two actors, *a cloth*, and one passion." We can't find it anywhere to back it up, so if he didn't say it, he should have, because that cloth is another important building block: the *drop*. Drops are alternately known as *backdrops* or

Figure 1.25: *A drop being painted.*

backings, and these names are somewhat self-defining. They can also be called *rags* or *schmattes*, but those are terms used by people who've been carrying heavy drops all day.

Think of it this way: Lope is in one of those picturesque Spanish courtyards, his *three boards* are set up on those sawhorses we spoke of, and *two actors* are "sawing the air with their arms thus," as Hamlet says, emoting the *one passion*. Suddenly, one of the many lovers Lope was reported to have had shows up behind the actors and starts to make rude gestures at Lope. The next thing you know her husband is over there, sword in hand, and he and Lope start going at it. Well, of course, no one is looking at the play at this point. Being a shrewd businessperson, Lope enlists two tall gentlemen to hold a stretched bedspread between them and behind the actors, hiding the much more interesting but extremely private events going on in back of them, and throwing the focus back on the play performance, which he was getting paid for. You can see the practical applications now, can't you? They *dropped* it in *back*—or used it as a *backdrop, backing* the play's action. Imagine what would happen if the cloth was painted with some kind of setting that relates to the play (Figure 1.25)?

So why don't we just use a flat? In the first part of this chapter we spoke of the two scenic forms, one of which was "something sort of vertical." These are both sort of vertical. What would be the advantages of using a drop over a flat? To start with, the advantages to having "the cloth" in our scenic vocabulary deal mainly with its structure.

Advantages of the Cloth Backdrop
There are, of course, many types of drops and backings, but there are a few common advantages to any cloth backdrop.

- It's made of cloth. Unless the fabric is impossibly thick, it is thinner than a flat. The drop may be rolled, folded, and stored in much less space than a flat, allowing for a greater inventory of stock scenes.
- It weighs a lot less. If you compare a painted backdrop to the same-size flat or series of flat structures, the backdrop will be much lighter.
- Depending on its size, it can be quite simple to put up or *hang*. If there is someplace to hang the drop and some way to get it up in the air, one person can feasibly do it by him-/herself.
- All of the foregoing characteristics make these units attractive scenery for touring companies.

Disadvantages of the Cloth Backdrop
The structure of the cloth backdrop also poses some disadvantages.

- It's made of cloth. As with a soft-covered flat, the drop works like a sail when air currents are disturbed nearby, in fact even more so since, in essence, it is a sail. (Common theatre lore says that the first stagehands were sailors because of their advanced sail-rigging/drop-rigging skills. Another theatre story states that these sailors gave their cues to one another with a series of whistles, which was how they communicated on ship. That explains the superstition about getting bad luck when you whistle in a theatre; the fear would be getting a drop dropped on you by a confused scenic swab. The rough-and-tumble sailor connection also explains why technicians always seem so rakishly good looking and exciting, like Johnny Depp, Erroll Flynn, Keira Knightley, or Maureen O'Hara).
- Because of its structure, the drop is a two-dimensional unit. The scenery on the drop, if meant to portray realistic images, needs to be very skillfully painted. Any appliqués, as with soft-covered flats, like molding or hung pictures, require additional structure behind the drop, increasing build time, and basically make the drop a flat.
- You have to get it up in the air, somehow, for it to *drop*. Whether it is two of Lope's stagehands, long bottom-heavy boom poles weighted down or bolted to the floor, *battens* hung above the actors' heads on ropes, pulleys, or a sophisticated counterweighted fly system, it has to be rigged safely to prevent it from falling and injuring actors or, at the very least, revealing jealous husbands backstage.

Rags to Enrich Us
Let's start by separating the types of scenic cloths we use. A *drop*, while it's most often used as a generic term for any hung cloth, is a term more correctly used to describe *soft representational scenery*; that is to say, the scenery is meant to stand in for something— a wall, a landscape, or an abstract image—that creates a mood that exemplifies or counterpoints the dramatic action. These are usually thought of as *soft show-specific scenery*,

meaning they were created for the current production and tailored to its dramatic needs.

House drapes would be the opposite of this idea (not because they are in your house; that would be opposite as well, but not what we're talking about). For our purposes, *house drapes* best describe other drapes in the theatre's stock that are *soft, neutral scenery*, neutral enough to be used in any show. Part of this grouping's job is similar to Lope's bedspread; the cloth here prevents us from seeing things we're not meant to see and focuses the audience's attention on the action.

But that isn't all house drapes can do. Sometimes a neutral cloth with nothing painted on it can be hung and lit so that we are almost able to see through it, or it can serve as a surface onto which light or images can be projected, creating a mood and atmosphere for the scene. In essence these cloths are still preventing us from seeing things we're not supposed to see, and on the surface they don't seem to look like anything; but it is their neutrality that helps them transform and focus the stage space.

House Drapes

Let's look at an average theatre (Figure 1.26). We'll begin by examining one of the most basic groups of *house drapes*, known as *maskings*.

Maskings and No–See–Me Black

The name implies its function, as you may have guessed. These cloths mask areas of the stage. That sounds simple because—well, it is. But think carefully of what it does and

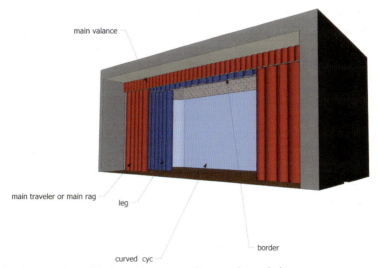

main valance

main traveler or main rag

leg

curved cyc

border

Figure 1.26: *Stage setting with the main rag, masking, and cyc cloth.*

you may realize its potential. Look at a busy street corner. If you try to focus on just one area or one activity, you are constantly distracted by the large volume of stuff around you. If you took both of your hands or a friend's hands and with the fingers made a sort of sideways "O" shape, like you were holding invisible binoculars, and held them in front of your eyes, you'd look strange; but the sides of your fingers and hands (or your friend's hands) *mask* the surrounding activities and allow you to focus on what you want to see.

But don't just think of *maskings* as hiding the wings or back walls of the theatre. That idea keeps a more rectangular image in mind—and that is somewhat limiting. *Maskings* can be hung anywhere. A better image to keep in mind is that of a stencil of a letter placed onto a piece of paper. Imagine the letter is the area you wish to focus on. The stencil creates the letter by blocking your spray paint and focuses the paint onto the paper where you want the letter to be. Once you lift the stencil from the paper all you see is the letter created from the shape of the stencil. That's how masking works: By itself it isn't obvious, but what it does is.

One of the most common types of maskings used in the theatre is the *stage black*, or *blacks* as they are commonly known. Most often these cloths are black (duh!) *velour*, a heavy fabric with a *nap*. A nap in black fabric can often be very soft, warm, and quite refreshing, but in this case we are referring to the little furry hairs of fabric that stick out of the cloth's surface. This nap breaks up the surface of the fabric and almost sucks up light like a porous sponge. Dark objects absorb light and light-colored objects reflect light. *Black* in the theatre scenic vocabulary says, "Don't look at me" or "Pay no attention to the man behind the curtain." Quite often when dealing with a space we don't want the audience to see, we get some "no-see-me black" fabric and tack it up over the spot. *Black* in our visual vocabulary is the absence of light: No light means not important. It's probably not surprising then that black maskings have been used by stage magicians for years to direct or misdirect our attention.

Fullness

Fullness describes that uncomfortable feeling you had after dinner before you took that nap in the blacks. When you awoke, you felt refreshed, but your button-fly jeans felt a little tight. In these cases, you have a pair of pants you keep handy to change into that have a pleated front with lots of extra fabric that hides your tummy. This describes fullness in masking: making pleats or folds in the masking fabric. Fullness breaks up the visual plane of the fabric and allows the curtain to absorb more light. These folds create a softer line as well as interesting highlights and shadows. Fullness is measured by these folds; if you use twice the amount of fabric as the finished width of the scenic cloth, you have created a drop with 100% fullness. Using 1½ times the amount of fabric is known as 50% fullness. If your cloth is completely flat with no pleats, you have zero fullness.

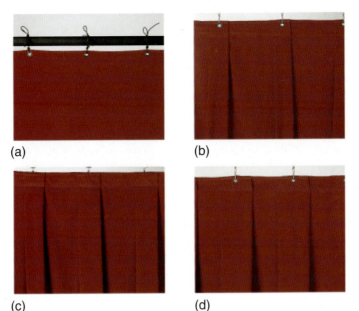

(a)   (b)

(c)   (d)

Figure 1.27: *A custom sewing guide displaying fullness treatments: (a) Flat, (b) 50% Fullness, (c) 75% Fullness, (d) 100% Fullness. (Courtesy of Rosebrand Fabrics.)*

Why do we use fullness? One reason is how it looks. Full panels create a showier, luxurious feel, and, in contrast, flat panels create a very neutral black space. One hundred years ago, and even before, the theatre was all about grandeur and opulence; the stage houses themselves were works of art. At this time fullness was the style, it was what the audience expected, and it was theatrical. When realism became the preferred style, the trend toward a more neutral flat style in masking became prominent. All in all, it depends, again, on the design team and what they think is appropriate for the show.

Another added benefit of a lot of fabric, besides light absorption, is sound absorption. Fabric and other soft surfaces suck up sound waves; hard surfaces and glossy surfaces bounce sound waves, causing echoes, and reflect other, backstage noises out toward the audience and muddle the actors' lines, music, or whatever you intended the audience to hear. Quite often you will see fabric hung on the walls of a small, black box theatre as a cheap sound-deadening treatment (Figure 1.27). *Fullness* adds ever so much more absorption to the equation.

A Leg Up on Those Teasing Terms, or a Tormenting Run to the Border
Let's try to visualize a common household window drapery treatment. Most often as you look at a window, you see a couple of drapes going up and down on both sides and one drape going horizontally across the top. Another way to classify stage drops is by where they are hung. Imagine that the window opening is the theatre's opening to

Figure 1.28: *Shot up into the flyspace showing the position of boarders with electrics and flying scenery.*

backstage, or its *proscenium*, as we call it. The horizontal curtain over the window would be known as a *boarder*. This is similar to another meaning of the word *boarder*: a house guest who pays room and board and lies on his back all day. The scenic boarder appears to be a drapery hung on its side or lying on its back. The boarder limits the audience's view into the space above the stage floor known as the *fly space*, or the *flys*. A series of boarders hung strategically above the stage can hide lighting instruments and flying scenery from view; or if you don't have any thing up there, they can help hide your open *flys* (Figure 1.28).

Let's look out your window again. Ooh, pretty! Okay, look *at* your window. Those curtains running up and down are closely analogous to *masking legs*. This term, believe it or not, can be confusing if you have several people onstage and you're hanging legs and the other carpenters are legging a platform and the prop guy is fixing a wobbly table leg and someone says, "Hey, this would be a lot easier if you'd lift that leg up!" Masking legs hide the audience's view into the wings. In combination, legs and boarders can quite nicely frame the action on stage, similar to the way your hands in the invisible binocular shape framed the street corner scene.

As we said, black masking is just one type of masking, and another way to classify stage drops is by where they are hung; if you take a boarder and a set of legs (one apiece for stage right and stage left) of any color and hang them right inside the proscenium opening, you suddenly have two different kinds of drapes. The boarder now becomes a *teaser* and the leg a *tormentor*. These are very old terms, and most people simplify it by calling them the *first leg* or *first boarder*. If you run across these terms again, here is a mnemonic to help you remember them. The boarder in your stage house is teasing you by lying around on his back, so you torment him by taking your leg and kicking him up to the flys, where he belongs. It's not a simple mnemonic but it is a vivid image.

Keeping Tabs on the Sightlines

There is another type of back stage masking known as *tab* masking; this is another way of hiding your theatre's wing space. These drapes, like legs, boarders, and all their like hung cousins, may be full or flat; but unlike them, they are hung in a completely different axis. Tabs are hung in the furthest offstage position in front of the wing space you wish to hide and are perpendicular to the legs. In this way if you have a really wide proscenium opening and the audience can see a little space between legs, you have some scenic insurance coverage, since the tabs will fill in the gaps.

This masking is also particularly useful in stopping backstage light leaks from *running* or *crossing* lights that are set up for safe backstage passage, as well as leaks caused if a backstage door to a lit hallway opens. Also, *tabs* help trap sound leaks from those leaky actors cramming their lines backstage.

Back in Black: Blackouts and Travelers (Sounds Like a Rock Ballad)

If you take a bunch of legs and hang them side to side the entire way across the stage, you have created a backing known as a *full-stage black*. Now this term may be confusing, because your full-stage black may be made of flat blacks (or blacks without fullness) making it a *flat full-stage black*; or conversely, if it has fullness it would be a *full full-stage black*. Some people avoid the entire mess and just call it a *blackout drape*.

These drapes are particularly useful if you want to hide one scene quickly or, as the name suggests, black out the stage by cutting off all the light behind it. You can manipulate them in two ways: flying and traveling. *Flying*, as we said, is the process of lifting the drapes with a series of ropes and pulleys or a counterweight system. To *travel* a curtain, you tie it to a system of little hooks with wheels on top of them called *carriers*. These carriers carry the curtain inside a track called, oddly enough, a *traveler track*. Pull lines are connected, and the whole shootin' match works just like those slide-y drapes in your parlor window (you have to read this last sentence with a cowboy accent—it's also helpful to have your character spit when you come to the period).

Everybody Wants to Get into the Act—and Out of It

Similarly, if you want to reveal the action at the top of the act or quickly exit at the end of an act, you may use another house drape, known as a *main curtain* or *act curtain*. Whenever you hear someone yell, "Curtain!" it's this curtain they're speaking of (also when they say, "It's curtains for you," in 1920's gangster films, they're referring to this curtain coming in at the end of the act. The act in this case would mean your life—you get the picture.) These curtains, like everything else in theatre, have several names: *main drape*, *grand drape*, and even *main rag*. *Main rag* is possibly the nicest term used by anyone who has ever hung one of these, because they are heavy—really heavy. Since this is the first thing your audience sees, theatres want the grand drape to look luxurious and special; it's made of thicker velour and lined with what amounts to a second heavy curtain and is rarely made without fullness. As a result, it actually stops more light and sound than a blackout curtain. Why aren't blackout curtains made like this, then? They can be, but the expense of a grand drape is such that most theatres buy one and make it last as long as they can.

Most often these curtains are travelers, however; you will add a lot of flexibility to your scenic vocabulary if you have a curtain that can fly as well as travel. Flying reveals say "Bam! Look at this!" and thrust you into the world of the play. Traveling reveals are sneakier and almost voyeuristic, since you are slowly shown and coaxed into the world of the play. Traveling curtains rarely open as fast as flying curtains. Again, it's the choice of your production team to decide what works best for your production.

There are also quite a few styles of grand drapes to choose from, and the style of the drape is mostly determined by the way it opens. The choice depends largely on the types of productions done in your theatre (Figure 1.29).

Cyc'ed You Out

Cyclorama is one of those theatre terms that have another meaning in the civilian world. MSN Encarta defines *cyclorama* as a "circular mural painted all the way around the walls

Austrian Curtain
One of the most ornate curtains, the Austrian is raised by multiple vertical riggings between which are sewn a series of swagging pleats.

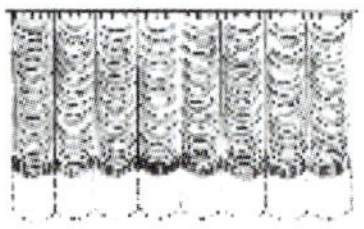

Tab Curtain
The tab curtain has two panels, sewn flat or in fullness. It is raised by diagonally lifting the two onstage lower corners towards the upper offstage sides.

Venetian Curtain
Perhaps the most versatile, the Venetian (contour) curtain consists of a pleated panel that is raised by multiple vertical riggings that are individually adjustable, making it possible to open up the view of the stage in various arrangements.

Figure 1.29: *Grand-style drapes. (Courtesy of Rosebrand Fabrics.)*

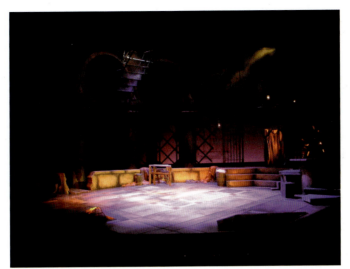

Figure 1.30: *Stage setting from the PA Shakespeare Festival's production of* Man of LaMancha *with a lit cyc.*

of a circular room." Inside the theatre, if you say *cyclorama*, or *cyc*, as most people call it, they'll send you backstage to almost the very back wall of the theatre, where you will see a large piece of fabric hanging in the air. Cycs are neutral pieces of fabric with no fullness onto which light is projected. Most commonly this house drape serves as a projection screen for lights that create realistic sunrises and skies (Figure 1.30). They can also be used for rear or front projection of images. If it is going to serve primarily to create sky effects, then the cyc can be made out of blue fabric and is known as a *sky cyc*. Most theatres opt for the neutrality of a white cyc.

While they are flat in the sense of zero fullness, cycs can be curved. *Wrap-around cycs* do just that, they wrap around the other scenery. The pipes that wrap-around cycs are tied to are slightly bent on the ends, and this curve acts similar to tab curtains; it helps seal sightlines and traps light inside the cyc.

Sinking Our Teeth into Sharkstooth Scrims

Could anything be more neutral than something that appears to be invisible? The most amazing quality of the house drape known as a *scrim* is that when lit from the front it appears solid. When it is lit from behind, or *backlit*, you can see right through it to the action behind it. This effect is particularly useful for dramatic reveals, since people or objects may almost instantly appear out of nowhere. The fabric itself is like a very fine net, somewhat stretchy, very light, and fragile. Scrim may be ordered in a variety of colors; the most common are black and white. Black scrim may work quite well as a full-stage black that can be lit to make a fast reveal; but obviously it doesn't have the sound-absorption qualities of a masking drape.

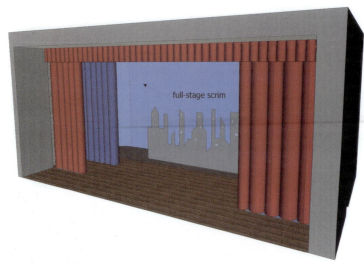

Figure 1.31: *A drawing of a full-stage black scrim revealing a scene behind it.*

Scrims may be any size, but quite often they are full-stage size (Figure 1.31). Since a seam in the fabric would ruin the transparent effect, it may be ordered in widths close to 35′. As you can imagine, fabric that size needs to be woven on a very special loom, and there aren't many that size, so a full-stage scrim may be very expensive. As a result these drapes are often packed away and carefully stored until needed.

Filled Cycs and Scrims

Actually these terms are used interchangeably to describe a scrim used as a cyc. *Filled cycs* or *scrims*, usually made of white or blue scrim, are almost ironic terms when you consider that they have little holes in them. What makes them filled is that in order to create one you actually need to take a second scrim and place it behind the first so that the holes slightly overlap, filling each other in. The result is a *cyc* with a porous texture that appears smooth to the audience. When light is projected onto this cyc it is slightly diffused and softened, creating a nice blend of colors. The disadvantage to this cyc is that projected images are also diffused and difficult to focus clearly. And with twice the fabric, it's at least twice as expensive.

The Scrimmed Cyc

A more economical version of the filled cyc is a muslin cyc with a scrim in front of it. You get light diffusion and the option to remove the scrim and project onto the cyc.

Soft Show-Specific Scenery

At this point we've framed and focused the action all around the stage. What is it we are looking at? Until the performers get there, it a good chance we are looking at *soft*

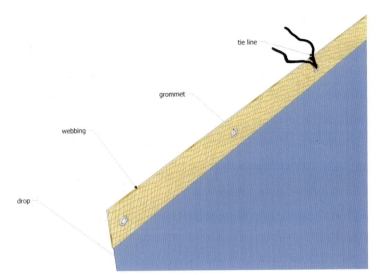

Figure 1.32: *Drop with parts labeled.*

show-specific scenery (and perhaps after they arrive as well). As we said before, show-specific scenery has been designed for the current production and by its nature is *representational* of some location or emotion pertinent to the production. These drops may be classified in two ways, by their shape and by how they are manipulated.

Full-Stage Drops or Backdrops

Painted drops are most often made of heavy muslin, although they may be made of any fabric you can paint. The shape is quite often rectangular, similar to that of a full-stage black or scrim. This is what is most often thought of as the quintessential backdrop. At this point it would be helpful to look at the anatomy of an average painted drop (Figure 1.32).

The Ties That Bind

As we said earlier, it isn't a drop till it drops from somewhere. This simple fact defines most of what the drop's structure looks like. Starting at the top of the drop we have the *tie lines*. This is another self-defining theatre term: These lines tie to the batten, hook, or stage pipe or whatever we are using to get the drop to drop. Tie line may also be substituted with cotton twill, a sort of thin, flat, woven fabric that looks a lot like the tie in your pajamas (we suppose it does—no one has been spying). Tie line seems to be in the most commonly used tie system now; tie line has so many other uses around the theatre that it always pays to have a spool around. Common colors of tie line are white and black.

Black tie line is most often used on drops, since black is our "no-see-me color"; however, one piece of white tie line may be used on a drop for a very specific purpose.

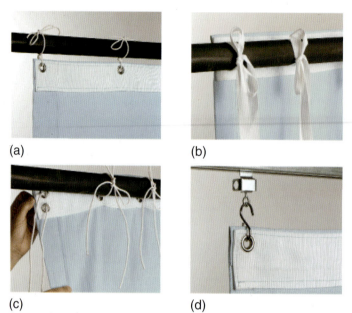

(a)   (b)

(c)   (d)

Figure 1.33: *Photographs showing (a) webbing grommets and ties, (b) sewn twill ties, (c) hidden webbing, grommets, and ties, and (d) webbing grommets and s-hooks. (Courtesy of Rosebrand Fabrics.)*

Most painted drops have the centerline marked on them, so you can easily line up this mark with the centerline of the stage. If you place a piece of white tie line above the center mark on the drop, you can quickly find the center by looking for the white in the midst of the black pieces (Figure 1.33).

The tie line has to be connected to the drop in some fashion. While in the case of cotton twill the ties are sewn on, tie line is tied on through metal-lined holes in the drop known as *grommets*. Grommets have been around forever. We're sure you've seen them, either on a tent or sail or even in the eyeholes of your favorite pair of canvas sneakers (Wallace and Gromit are also a great team).

The process of attaching the grommets involves the use of grommet-making tools and both halves of the grommet. The grommet-making set comprises a grommet hole cutter, the setting die, and an anvil or base. First, as you may imagine, a hole needs to be cut in the drop. While the muslin is heavyweight and fairly sturdy, the weight of the rest of the drop will rip open holes cut into it until it rips through to the top of the drop and the drop drops off of the ties and falls.

To strengthen the top of the drop, webbing is sewn onto the backside of the top of the drop. Traditionally webbing was woven out of jute, but now it is available in polypropylene and other synthetics. The common factor, however, is the weave. When the woven backing is sewn onto the drop, it strengthens the area and resists tears from the holes cut into it.

To create the grommet hole, the hole cutter is placed above one of the marks made approximately 12' on center in either direction from the centerline mark of the drop, and a firm but soft surface such as a 2 × 4 or scrap ¾" plywood is placed underneath. You then take a mallet and whack the top of the cutter and punch it through the webbing, creating a hole that the male half of the grommet may be placed through. The setting die base has a little indentation for the grommet and is set under the hole with the grommet on top of it, and the hole in the drop is threaded over the male end of the grommet. The washer end of the grommet is then placed over the protruding end of the male grommet. The setting die is then placed over and through the hole, and you whack it until the top of the male end mushrooms over the washer end.

The Bottom of the Drop

Hold a paper towel between your hands in front of your face and blow a small puff of air out towards it. You see how the bottom of the towel flaps around? That's what would happen every time the air currents moved around your drop if it were hung without anything holding or weighting the bottom down. There are a couple of methods to hold the bottom of the curtain down, and they all involve stiffening the bottom of the drop in some way.

The Weight Pocket

Whenever you get your drops or drapes made professionally, you always have a choice of bottom finishes, as seen in Figure 1.34. One of the easiest to deal with is to put a *weight pocket* at the bottom of the drop. The two most common types of weight pockets are known as *pipe pockets* and *pipe sleeves*. Basically the *pipe pocket* is just a long hem open on both ends that you slide sections of pipe into. A *pipe sleeve* is a long loop of fabric that is sewn onto the back of the drop so when a pipe is inserted, its bottom hangs just a little bit higher than the drop's bottom. This extra overhanging fabric can close light leaks that may be caused by an uneven floor.

Pipe-weighted drops are very easy to deal with since the pipe may be threaded together as it is inserted in sections and is rigid enough to hold the drop down but flexible enough to conform somewhat to an uneven floor. Chain may be substituted for pipe, but since it is so flexible wrinkles are hard to pull out. For this reason, you see chain most often in drops with fullness, such as main rags.

You can opt not to add a weight pocket at the bottom. This leaves you with a few other options to hold down your drop.

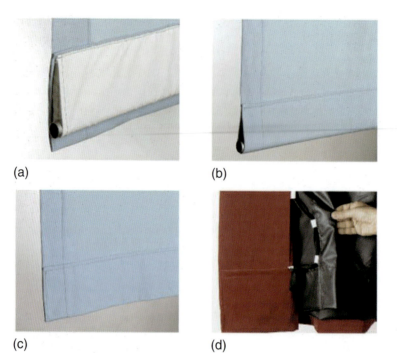

(a)

(b)

(c)

(d)

Figure 1.34: *Bottom finishes: (a) pipe pocket with skirt, (b) pipe hem, (c) 4" flat hem, (d) lined drapes. (Courtesy of Rosebrand Fabrics.)*

The Wrap

One of the quickest and dirtiest methods of holding a drop down is *wrapping*. Essentially, you just take some pipe, 2 × 4, or other weight and wrap the drop's bottom around it, creating a weight pocket.

The Wooden Batten

The wooden *batten* is similar to a wrap and is just as quick and dirty. In this instance you sandwich the bottom of the drop between two pieces of 1 × 3 or 2 × 4 and screw them together. If you paint the batten to match the floor or the bottom of the drop and the audience is far enough away or you have something masking the bottom, then this is a viable solution, as shown in Figure 1.35. Battens may also be used at the top of the drop, with holes drilled into them for the tie line. If you don't have something stiff to tie your drop to, this again is a good option. It does, however, make the drop difficult to fold.

Bottom Grommets

If you add webbing and grommets to both sides of a drop, you can easily tie your battens or pipe to the drop at the bottom when you need them and remove them for

Figure 1.35: *Quick-and-dirty battened drop.*

Figure 1.36: *A cyc that is Westcoasted for storage above the stage in the fly loft at the Labuda Theatre, DeSales University.*

storage. Many wrap-around cycs have this feature, allowing curved sections of pipe at top and bottom to hold the cyc's shape (Figure 1.36).

Stapling It to the Ground
This method is self-explanatory and is the quickest and dirtiest method.

The Sides of the Drop: Slenderizing Your Sides to Drop Weight

So you have hung and weighted your painted drop using one of the approved methods. When you step back and look at it, the sides are all crinkly, floppy, and wavy. You say, "Thank goodness, I've read up on masking," and you hang some right and left of the drop. This may have taken care of the problem, or you may have had to move it because you lost some of the image on the drop. What should you do?

A couple of things are possible. You may take some tie lines and some clamps and put some tension in the sides of the drop by clamping onto the drop and tying one end of tie line to the clamps and one end to something else that won't move. To pull this tight enough you may have to add a number of lines and loose passage around the drop, and you certainly can't fly it. You could add battens or side grommets and battens, effectively making a large soft-covered flat.

There's a handy old trick that avoids complicated spider webs of tie line, clamps, grommets, etc. When you plan your drop, leave two feet of extra fabric on either side of your image. After you paint the drop, cut the drop into a big trapezoid shape by coming down from the extra two feet of fabric at either side of the top edges with a straight cut toward the edge of the image at the bottom. Then hang and weight the drop. The sides may be seamed if you wish and the puckers pulled taut by the drop's shape (see Figure 1.37).

The Cut Drop

One of the most elegant, theatrical, and delicate pieces of soft scenery is the *cut drop;* and it is one of the biggest pains in the butt. Cut drops are similar to the painted drops

Figure 1.37: *Small trapezoidal drop from* The Gift of the Magi.

Figure 1.38: *Cut drop of Harmonia Gardens in* Hello, Dolly.

we've spoken of, but holes are cut into the drop to create an image that may be seen or even walked through.

We're sure that after your floppy-sided drop episode you are wondering, "What are you thinking? The drop is going to look like a soggy waffle fry!" Well, you're right. That's why we add a special netlike material called *scenery webbing*. Once the drop is cut, you carefully attach the scenery netting to the back of the opening. Scenery webbing, like muslin, is a natural cotton fiber, so both the drop and the netting expand and contract at a similar rate (as seen in Figure 1.38). Less expensive synthetic netting may be used, but it can pucker and bend in ways the drop doesn't.

Large open sections of the drop may be used like a doorway, but, unless you are playing an elaborate practical joke on the actors, you need to reinforce these areas with *foamcore, cardboard,* or some other light, rigid material and avoid the netting. The best solution is to incorporate the floppiness into the design.

Moving the Drop

So far we have only talked about flying or traveling drops. And as we've said so many times that you may want to slam your head into the wall, a drop needs to drop. There are a couple of other ways to drop a drop; both methods are handy for spaces that can't fly out large drops, and they involve rigging. So get out your pirate hat and "Avast ye maties! Aarrg!"

Accordion Fold (Venetian) Drop

If you've seen a venetian blind work, you understand the basis for this drop. A batten is attached to the bottom of the drop, and pull lines are run from it behind the drop through small curtain rings sewn to the back of the drop at regular intervals to keep the lines from tangling. As the pull lines are pulled, they shorten the drop, lifting the drop up and folding at the each curtain hook level as the lines slide through them.

If you don't care about wrinkles in your drop, this is an easy drop to rig and doesn't require any flyspace. As a result it may work quite nicely as a small reveal curtain under a platform or a doorway.

Roll Drop

The roll drop is one of the oldest methods of taking a drop in and out of the audience's sight and possibly the coolest. A round tube, approximately 6″ in diameter, is attached to the bottom of the drop. This is the roll part of the drop, and it sticks out of the drop on either side to allow the pull lines to wrap around the roll. The in-and-out motion is controlled as the pull lines are pulled, and they coil and uncoil around the roll. The resulting effect is a lot like a screen wipe on video: The image lowers into view from the top, unfurling as it travels to the bottom.

Soft Show-Specific Scenery We've Seen Somewhere

Many of the house drapes we spoke of have cousins in the show-specific world. Masking, while advantageous in some designs to be neutral, may also enhance the overall design by actually blending into the surrounding environment. Leaf drops and leaf boarders are two good examples. A hybrid of the cut drop and masking leg, the *leaf drop* is basically a painted drop with details and edges scalloped out to simulate leaves. Turn this drop on its side and you have a *leaf boarder* (see Figure 1.39).

Scrims may also be treated like painted drops. When the painted side is lit it appears solid, but when backlit the effect is like looking through a solid object, as shown in Figure 1.40.

Main rags may be made for the production and painted with the show's name or an image created for the show. These are referred to as the *act curtains*, or *show curtains*. The show-specific details on these curtains reveal the luxurious opulence the audience has come to expect from the grand drape.

Summary

We've talked about the basic building blocks of scenery: flats, platforms, and drops. Flats may be either hard or soft and have standard or Hollywood frames. Platforms have any number of frame styles; the most widely used are the standard and the stressed-skin. Almost all styles utilize a ¾″ plywood skin. Wood is the most common building material for both flats and platform frames, and two of the most popular cuts of wooden framing materials are 2 × 4 and 1 × 1 boards. Steel may also be used to construct frames, and 1 × 1 mild steel box tubes are among the most versatile of steel forms.

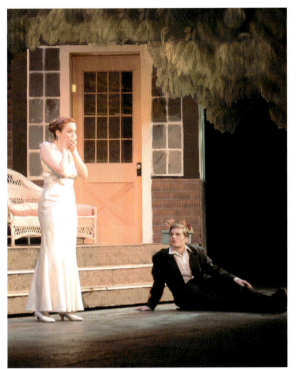

Figure 1.39: *Leaf drops and boarders mask, Act 2 of* Philadelphia Story.

Figure 1.40: *Painted scrim drop of Harmonia Gardens in* Hello, Dolly.

Drops may be classified as either house drapes or show specific. House drapes include main rags, teasers and tormentors, masking legs and boarders, tabs, cycs, and scrims. Show-specific drops include the backdrop, painted drop, cut drop, roll drop, and venetian or accordion drop. They also include versions of their normally neutral cousins, the house drapes, such as painted scrims, show and act curtains, specially treated for the current production. These drops are representational because they stand in for a place or an emotion that relates to the performance.

These, as we said, are the building blocks. The rest of this text will deal with how to construct, move, paint, design, and light these elements.

Chapter 2
What Are They Made Of?
Scenic Construction Materials

Wood

Wood Doesn't Just Grow on Trees. Wait, It Does

Wood, as we all know, is harvested from trees. And we all know the basic parts of a tree: roots, trunk, branches, and leaves. The trunk, being the thickest part, is the one that various wooden boards are harvested from. In this chapter, we discuss these types of boards. But before we do, let's think about how a tree works and how that affects a board's strength.

An oversimplification of how a tree works goes like this: The roots suck up the stuff that a tree needs to grow, such as water and minerals, the trunk sucks that stuff and sends it to the branches and leaves, and they transmit the stuff they photosynthesize back down to the roots. What's important to us is that for all this to happen, the trunk has to be made of a porous and fibrous material. Since the trunk is the main pipeline for the tree and it is supporting all the weight of the tree's canopy (leaves, branches, etc.), this material has to be strong. As the tree grows, the trunk thickens out in proportion to the size of the tree's canopy. If you sliced across the tree and looked at the cross section, you would see how this thickening piles up year after year, resulting in what is called *growth* or *annual rings* (Figure 2.1). If you were to count those rings and make a study of this kind of stuff, you could tell how old the tree was. Just remember: After you slice the tree up, it won't get any older.

Figure 2.1: *Sliced up trees or logs used in the DeSales University production of* The Foreigner. *Note the growth rings.*

Ripping Tales That Cut Against the Grain

Once you slice boards from a trunk, the rings appear to be long lines. What you're actually seeing is many rings, side by side in cross section. These long lines are known as the *grain* of the wood. To get an idea of how this works, take two colors of clay, one light and one dark. Make a little wormlike roll with some of the dark clay. Wrap that with some of the light clay until you can't see the dark. You've just made an *annual or growth ring*. Age your sapling with alternating layers of light and dark clay until you feel it's old enough or until you run out of clay. Now, with a thin blade, carefully slice the trunk down its length until you have two halves. The zebra-striped flat side of these two pieces is basically what wood grain is.

As we said, trunks are what we cut boards from (if you took another slice from behind the flat side of one of your clay trunk halves you'd have a board) and the trunk is what holds the rest of the tree up. Naturally then, it follows that if you cut the board in the direction the tree grows, you have a board with the same structural advantages as the trunk. Since by the time the board gets to us anything resembling the original tree is long gone, we need a way to see if we are using the board to its greatest structural advantage. This is where the grain comes into play. When we see those long grain lines, we know we have a piece that was ripped correctly from the tree (Figure 2.2). *Ripping* is the process of cutting wood in the direction the tree grew, or with the grain. *Cross-cuts* are cuts that go across the grain. When you cut your clay trunk the first time, you actually ripped it.

Figure 2.2: *A log that was ripped into boards at Heacock Lumber Mill. (Courtesy of Heacock Lumber Mill.)*

Water, Water Everywhere and Not a Drop to Drink

The thing about wood as a building material is that it was once a living thing. As such, to survive it needed to suck up tons of liquefied nourishment. So essentially, a tree is just a big, soggy, layered straw. When a tree has just been cut up and made into lumber, we refer to these boards as *green lumber*. Sometimes, as in the case of the wood from a poplar tree, the wood is actually green; often it isn't. *Green*, in this case basically means "new wood" (often a rookie is referred to as *green*, and in most cases the word means "new," as well). One thing common to all green or new lumber is its moisture content. As we said, there is a lot of water in a tree. When you cut the tree, the water is still there, trapped within the cells of the wood. Sometimes this trapped moisture can amount to half the weight of the green board.

Care needs to be taken when these boards dry. To gain an idea of why, take a piece of corrugated cardboard, wet or paint one side, and then set it aside to dry. Nine times out of ten the piece of cardboard will curl as it dries. This is what happens to wood if it dries unevenly. We call this curling *warping* when it happens to wood, and we don't like it. When a board warps, it curls up right along the grain line, and it's pretty much useless for any kind of construction, even hockey sticks. Therefore, the green boards need to be carefully stacked to allow air to move around them and dry them evenly. This process takes quite a bit of time and space to complete. As a result we came up with *kiln-dried lumber*, in which the boards are dried in a kiln until the moisture content is to a point where the board's moisture content is stable and warpage is less likely.

There are three different ways a board deforms because of moisture, although we seem to refer to all of them as a *warp*. *Warped* wood is actually wood that has twisted along the long grain line in a corkscrew fashion. *Cupped* wood occurs when the wood curls long the growth rings or across the grain. *Bowed* wood looks just like that: a bow; the wood has bent along its edge like a "u." All of these problems may be dealt with by gently pushing or pulling the board into shape or by cutting the offending sections out.

Facing the Wood Terms

Now that you're a somewhat experienced millwright, you should learn a little more wood jargon. That clay plank or board you made has three basic parts. They sound so simple we hesitate to mention them lest you get so completely bored you'd say, "Planks, but no planks, this is knot for me," and close this book. If you did, the book's cover would be staring you in the face right now. Imagine that your book was actually a board. What is staring you in the face right now is the *face* of the board. If you turned the book/board so you could look at its pages (sometimes called *leaves*), you'd be looking at the board's *edge*. If you rotated it once more to look at the book's top or bottom, you'd have the board's *end* right in front of you (Figure 2.3). *Face, end, edge:* it sounds simple enough, and the terms are almost interchangeable. But these three terms give us a common way to orient ourselves around the board and are the basis of terms like *edge frame construction* (Hollywood flat, platforms), *face frame construction* (standard flat), and *end grain* (which is actually from a crosscut that shows the growth rings).

Two more confusing wood terms are *hardwood* and *softwood*. They don't sound confusing, but in reality their names have nothing to do with their hardness. Hardwoods for the most part produce hard wood; but what they all have in common is that they grow a *broad* leaf. These trees are also called *deciduous* trees. Softwoods are *conifers* and grow needles instead of leaves. As anyone who has ever dropped a Christmas tree trunk or

Figure 2.3: *Picture of a book with parts labeled: face, edge, end.*

Figure 2.4: *A stack of stick lumber in a scene shop's lumber rack.*

Yule log on his or her foot will know, softwoods can be pretty hard. *Yellow pine* is one of the hardest woods out there; it's used commonly as a pallet frame for moving large stacks of goods for shipping because of that strength. *White pine, fir*, and *spruce* are commonly used for framing stage scenery, and they are softwoods.

Sticks and Sheets

We've spoken about several different kinds of lumber so far, 1 × 3, 2 × 4, ¾″ plywood, and ¼″ luaun. If you ever looked at these boards side by side, you'd notice some distinct differences between them, and these differences help us name them. The 1 × 3 and 2 × 4 are known as *dimensional lumber* or *stick lumber*. As you can see in Figure 2.4, they somewhat resemble sticks. Since the plywood and luaun resemble sheets of paper, they are often known as *sheet goods*, and they belong to a larger group of man-made materials called *engineered lumber*.

Why Is Engineered Lumber Strong?

Let's step back a minute and look at grain again. Remember, we said if you cut the board in the direction the tree grows, you gain the structural advantages of the tree. Take a Popsicle stick with its face looking up at you between both of your hands and try to bend it. You didn't have to try too hard, did you? The stick is bending along the grain lines, similar to the way it warps when wet. Now take several sticks, lay them side to side, and glue another layer on top of these—but place them perpendicular to the first layer. When they dry, you'll find the resulting sheet of lumber you made resists bending better than the original stick. The alternating grain patterns strengthen the

Figure 2.5: *Stack of plywood showing the plies.*

sheet and keep each layer from bending. The more layers, or *plies*, you add, the stronger your *plywood* gets.

When plywood is made, the log is steamed to made it softer and put on a lathe that makes it spin at a high rate of speed. Then a big knife peels the wood off in layers. The process is not unlike pulling all the sheets of a roll of paper towels (or toilet paper), and basically it just unravels the tree. These layers are cut into sheets, like the perforated sheets on the roll of paper towels lying all over your floor. And when we use them on the outside layer of the plywood they are called *veneers*. Expensive and exotic-looking woods can be applied as a veneer, with cheaper wood used on the inside layers, giving the look of the expensive wood and the strength of plywood (Figure 2.5).

Other sheet materials are made from smaller pieces of wood, from chips down to sawdust. *Hardboard* is made by blasting the wood into long fibers with steam and pressing the soggy strands into a flat, hard board that bends easily and takes paint very well. We use a lot of hardboard in the theatre because its flexibility makes it great for curved platform facings, and its hardness and paintability make it nice for floor coverings. *MDF*, or *medium-density fiberboard*, is a substance similar to hardboard, but in this case resins and glues are added to make the fibers stick together. This substance is becoming more popular as a substitute for hardboard but is quite often used in the furniture industry because of its strength and stability.

Particle board, or *chipboard*, is the forerunner of these fiberboards. It is made, as you might guess, from particles of wood that are glued and pressed together; in some cases these

Figure 2.6: *Platform covered in OSB.*

particles can be as fine as sawdust. It's the least strong of any of these materials and is most notably used in the self-assembled furniture market for light-duty bookshelves.

One of the most useful and popular fiberboards is *OSB*, or *oriented strand board*. Of the fiberboards, this is the strongest. As the name implies, strands of wood, long splinter-like things, are oriented or turned to face the same general direction and glued and thermally pressed into a layer in a sheet mold. Internal layers have strands that are randomly placed, with the oriented layers on the outside. This gives OSB a strength and structure similar to plywood's. OSB is seen quite often in house construction in the walls, floors, and roofs. Scenically, it is very useful when you have a large floor surface to cover, since quite often it is cheaper than plywood (Figure 2.6).

Old-timers feel that that "newfangled garbage board" is not as good as plywood. But in fact, industry tests and guidelines show that OSB and plywood are equivalent in strength. Because trees not normally suitable for plywood, such as aspen and poplar, or smaller, quick-growth trees may be used in this process, OSB is often cheaper than plywood. This probably adds to the myth that OSB is "that cheap stuff they use instead of plywood" (in this case *cheap* means "not good" and *plywood* means "I'm stuck in my old ways").

More Sizes and Shapes Than You Can Shake a Stick At

Stick lumber, as we said, is like a stick. It's long and thin when compared to sheet lumber, which looks like a sheet of paper. Since the size and shape of the boards lend themselves to framing purposes, stick lumber is most commonly used for framing.

Table 2.1: *Nominal and Actual Lumber Sizes*

Nominal	Actual	Nominal	Actual
1 × 2	¾″ × 1½″	2 × 10	1½″ × 9¼″
1 × 3	¾″ × 2½″	2 × 12	1½″ × 11¼″
1 × 4	¾″ × 3½″	3 × 3	2½″ × 2½″
1 × 5	¾″ × 4½″	3 × 4	2½″ × 3½″
1 × 6	¾″ × 5½″	3 × 6	2½″ × 5″
1 × 8	¾″ × 7¼″	3 × 8	2½″ × 7¼″
1 × 10	¾″ × 9¼″	3 × 10	2½″ × 9¼″
1 × 12	¾″ × 11¼″	3 × 12	2½″ × 11¼″
2 × 2	1½″ × 1½″	4 × 4	3½″ × 3½″
2 × 3	1½″ × 2½″	4 × 6	3½″ × 5½″
2 × 4	1½″ × 3½″	4 × 8	3½″ × 7¼″
2 × 6	1½″ × 5½″	4 × 10	3½″ × 9¼″
2 × 8	1½″ × 7¼″	4 × 12	3½″ × 11¼″

Unlike its engineered cousin, stick lumber is pretty much just cut from the tree, dried, and set on the shelf for you to buy, with no other structural tinkering involved. And unlike engineered lumber, it comes in a larger variety of sizes and shapes. Often stick lumber is known as *dimensional lumber* because of this variety.

Take a look at Table 2.1. You'll notice that we've included two columns for each size, the *nominal* and the *actual*. As you may have guessed, *nominal* means "name." It's what we call the board; but even though we call a board a 2 × 4, that's not its size. Once upon a time, lumber wasn't available at a store—you cut your own to whatever size you needed. There were a lot fewer people then, and a lot fewer buildings. As the numbers of each increased, a greater demand was put on the lumber industry and a need developed for lumber sizes to be standardized to simplify the lumber processes. Once kiln-dried lumber was established and boards were shrunk to stabilize their size, these *actual sizes* became the standard sizes.

How can you remember all these sizes? You don't have to. You only need to remember four things:

1. **1× (read "one by") material is ¾″ thick or has a ¾″ *edge*—**It's ¼″ smaller than its nominal size. So, for example, a 1 × 1 is ¾″ × ¾″. As you may remember, 1× is most often used for framing flats. It's the stick lumber most commonly found in the scene shop, since it is the right ratio of strength to weight of material.
2. **2× material is 1½″ thick or has a 1½″ edge—**It's ½″ smaller than its nominal size. 2× is a good framing lumber for platforms and platform legs.
3. **Face sizes between 2″ and 6″ are ½″ smaller than their nominal sizes—**in both 1× and 2× and even up to 4×. The common face sizes in this range are 2″, 3″, 4″, 5″, and 6″.

4. **Face sizes after 6″ are ¾″ smaller than their nominal sizes**—But as you can see, there are only three more sizes. After 6″ we skip the odd numbers and only focus on even sizes: 8″, 10″, and 12″.

To summarize: For dimensional lumber sizes, 1× is ¾″ on edge, 2× is 1½″ on edge, face widths between 4″ and 6″ are ½″ smaller, and face widths 8″ to 12″ are ¾″ smaller. So if you want something that would be ¾″ × 8″ in actual measurement, you would have no choice in dimensional lumber but to rip down a 1 × 10 (¾″ × 9½″) to 8″ on face.

Quite often we refer to this as a 1 × 8 *true*, which means that the face width is truly 8″. Now that we have the 1 × 8 true width ripped, you have to tell someone how long you want the board to be. The standard method of doing this for a 3′-long 1 × 8 true board would look like this: 1″ × 8″ true × 3′. You can use this method to denote the length of any board; for example, 2″ × 4″ × 8′ means a board whose actual edge is ¾″ thick, whose face is 3.5″ wide, and whose length is 8′.

When I Was a Kid We Didn't Have Running Feet, We Had Board Feet and We Didn't Like It, but We Used It!

When we started in the scenic construction business, they used a measurement known as *board feet*. It was a standard pricing formula used by lumber mills to price lumber by volume. *One board foot* is the equivalent of a board 1″ × 12″ × 12″, or 1″ thick by 12″ square. To figure out how many board feet you need, you have to figure out how many of those little boards would go into the amount of lumber you want. There are hundreds of books that have this formula in them and pretend to explain it in an easily digestible form for those of us who are math challenged. Fortunately for us, along came the chain home improvement superstore.

A lot of people have now started to "do it yourself," and the home improvement stores have boomed. As a result, the system has become more consumer friendly. Now, stick lumber is sold by the *linier foot* or *running foot*; that is to say, you simply add up the total number of feet you need and ask for that. The lumber yards have done all the pricing by stick of lumber using the board-foot formula or a magic wand or whatever. The point is if you call them up and say, "I need 1100′ of 1 × 6," they'll say, "Okay," and tell you what it will cost, and they won't make fun of you because you can't figure board feet in your head. In fact, this may be one of the last times you'll ever come across the term. But if you do, you'll just nod your head and with a knowing smile say, "Board feet— Haven't heard that one in a while," and then you'll spit. (Don't forget the cowboy accent.)

This Board Is Knot Okay, So How Do I Grade It?

Lumber grading is the industry's way of saying which boards are better than others, in other words, which boards you should pay more for. Each lumber mill or store has a subtly different way of grading the lumber. But once you get a general idea, you'll be able to decipher their code. Don't be afraid to ask how their lumber is graded; you're the customer and they are in the business to sell lumber. They want your money. It's in their interest to educate you to their methods.

Let's take another look at the growing tree to help us understand how lumber is graded. *Knots* are actually the places where tree limbs have fallen off and the tree has grown around them. Once the tree is cut, the knot appears as a darker little spot, with the grain swirling around it. Since it is harder than the surrounding wood and the grain is grown around it, it is a potential structural problem for the board. If it is large, then as the board bends, the knot, having a different grain structure, doesn't bend in the same way, or it doesn't give at all, and the board cracks, splits, and breaks. When you rip a board with a saw and run into a knot, the loose knot can pop out, sometimes with ballistic speed, and the same thing can happen again. If the knot is small and tight, it might not make a structural difference at all; however, the little dark spots may not be the look you want in your grain pattern.

A general method for grading stick lumber divides the lumber into three categories: #1, #2, and #3. The highest grade, #1, has the least knots, warps, and cups and is the most expensive. The #3 grade has big, loose knots and is used in applications such as temporary bracing, where these defects don't matter. The #2 grade is where most of us live in the scenic world. It has minimal defects, which make it cheaper than #1, but it has reasonable cosmetic appeal and strength.

Plywood has different grades as well, and those grades have to do with the type of veneer and how they look. First is the *interior-* and *exterior-grade* plywood. Exterior-grade plywood uses weather-resistant woods and glues and tends to be a little more expensive. Interior grade is the type of plywood we most often use in scenic work. Both grades have a veneer grading system. A, B, C, and D are the common grades, with A being the nicest and D having the most defects. When you see a plywood grade, you'll see two letters, for example: AB. This describes the two outside veneers. So in this case, you have one really nice-looking side and one pretty good side. Knot holes in A and B may be filled with football-shaped wood plugs or wood filler; and of course A has the fewest plugs. Both are sanded. C and D veneers have more surface defects, such as knots, splits, and deposits of stick sap resin called *pitch*. So how do you know which to use? Table 2.2 might help.

Metal

Wood, as we've stated, is harvested from trees. Carpentry is nature, it's romantic. It's almost a Zen-like feeling to bend a bowed 2 × 4 into place, and the aroma of freshly cut lumber is heavenly.

Table 2.2: *Grades of Wood and Their Uses*

Grade	Description and Use
AB	**One really good side sanded, one good side also sanded.** This is a nice plywood to work with. It's always flat and looks good. It has also become quite expensive and hard to find.
AC	**One really good side sanded, one not-so-good side not sanded.** This is suitable for a project where one face will be seen and one won't, which happens a lot in scenery. The back face will be rough and have voids where the knots were. As with almost any grade A plywood, it's become hard to find and expensive.
BC	**One pretty good side sanded, one not-so-good side not sanded.** You can use this plywood for anything you would have used AC for; for scenic purposes it's really very similar in appearance. It's less expensive than AC.
CDX	**One not-so-good side not sanded and one even worse side not sanded.** With that description, why use this at all? If, for instance, you are going to cover a platform with hardboard, it really doesn't matter what kind of veneer is on the plywood underneath it. If you're in a budget crunch, CDX has always been one option. The problem with this material is that it is very hard to work with. The X in CDX has been rumored to stand for exterior; in reality it's a designation of the weather-resistant glue used, so it amounts to the same thing. Quite often this plywood is made from yellow pine, a very hard and stringy softwood; because of this, once CDX warps you'll have a difficult time pulling it back into shape. Also, the yellow pine and exterior glue are very hard on your blades and other tools. OSB has become a common substitute for CDX because of its lower price and stable shape.

Metal is primal. We dug chunks of rock from under the ground with our newly developed opposable thumbs and smelted them in a fire until the rocks cried out their molten payload. Our mastery of metal separated us from the beasts. Flaunting our opposable thumbs at them, we cooled and shaped the metal, made tools, tamed the land, created civilization and digital cable.

You get the picture. Metal in scenic construction uses different processes than wood does. In this section you get a feel for what metal brings to the scenery party and how you can get that party started.

Metal Basics

If we break it all down, there are two types of metals: ferrous and nonferrous. *Ferrous* metals have some amount of iron in them; *nonferrous* metals don't. Now, where do these things come from? Can't you just dig them up in your backyard? Well, depending on where you live, you can—sort of. If you were to go to your backyard and dig up metal in its primal state, you'd have *ore*, in other words, one of those rocks we spoke of in the opening paragraphs. Once you melt the ore down, you have a pure metal, that is to say, the metal consists of one element, such as gold or silver or (not ore) iron.

Pure metals are great; we like them. But quite often we need to add another metal to the pure metal because otherwise it is too soft or too rare. When we do this we've created an *alloy*. Alloys are carefully formulated combinations of pure metals that retain the dominant characteristics of the original pure metal and combine to form new characteristics of their own. Steel is a common alloy of iron. Alloys are what separate us from those other cave guys—who aren't quite beasts and, well, they have opposable thumbs, but don't know how to alloy metal, so we kick their butt! (All this in an evolutionary way. Also, please note that no cave person's butts were kicked in the production of this book.)

Smelts Like Steel

Steel, as we said, is an alloy of the pure metal or element iron (chemical symbol Fe). Once the ore is heated to a molten state, a special form of coal that has been heated to remove impurities and is now called *coke* is added to the mix. The coke helps reformulate the iron to alter the brittle nature of the pure metal. This process is known as *refining*. Anyone who's seen the cartoon where the rooster smacks the dog over the head with a cast iron skillet knows that if it doesn't leave the imprint of the dog's head on the skillet (which can't really happen), it usually snaps in half (which can happen). (Please be aware that no roosters or dogs were harmed in the production of this book, real or cartoon.) The key ingredient in the coke is carbon, and the steel that is produced is known as *carbon steel*. Carbon is an ingredient of coke, but not of Coke the soft drink. But you can remember that to make steel, coke is the real thing. (However, a can of Coke is made from aluminum—keep reading.)

There are many types of carbon steel, and they vary in strength depending on the nature of the alloy. One of the most useful steels for scenic purposes is what's known as *mild steel*. Mild steel is strong but still *ductile*, or workable enough to bend, shape, cut, or weld easily. *Tool steel* is harder and less ductile, and when it is sharpened it holds an edge better than mild steel. This steel is used when you need something extremely hard, such as—you guessed it—a tool. There are other types of steel, but these two are the ones the scenic technician comes in contact with the most.

Mild steel is the steel used most often in construction. As you already know from reading about steel-framed flats and platforms, 16-gauge square steel tube is the most commonly used steel form for scenic construction. Other useful forms include flat bar, or strap iron, and angle iron and channel (which is not a perfume but a U-shaped bar of metal) (Figure 2.7). These forms get there structural strength from their shape, with flat bar being the weakest, until you gradually add more structure to the shapes in this category and arrive at square tube.

Rolled on Down the Line

Another useful shape steel comes in is the *round bar*. Usually these are made by *hot-rolling* the metal through presses while the steel is still soft and hasn't crystallized into

Figure 2.7: *Picture of common structural steel shapes.*

hardness. Similar to grain in wood, these crystal formations give steel its strength. *Cold-rolling* the bars stretches these crystals out and makes them longer and stronger. As you can imagine, hot-rolling is faster, since the metal is still warm, and produces a more pliable material; cold-rolling takes longer and produces harder bars. Hot-rolled bars are suitable for decorative scrollwork or supports in trusses, machine shafts, axles, and other applications where hardness and high strength are important.

Dislocations and Stress: It Is How Metal Functions

When any material (glass, wood, metal, etc.) is worked, rolled, cut, shaped, and so on, *stress* is added. Stress can be destructive and cause weak points (e.g., a place where a curtain would tear), or it might actually strengthen by adding energy as *dislocations* in the crystal structure. Here's an oversimplified definition of the term *dislocations*: changes in the crystal structure of the material that cause stress in a negative or positive way. What happens is a change on an atomic level: An electron is tweaked in its orbit and adds energy to the materials. It's sort of like banging your computer to get it to work correctly. Well, no, it isn't, but that does release stress. Think of it as a slack steel cable. When you add energy to the cable by pulling it taut, you can actually walk on it; in essence it has become stronger. If you keep pulling that cable, it will snap, causing a negative dislocation, and you probably dislocated something in the fall as well.

For example, when you make glass and roll it flat, you actually strengthen the surface. When metal is cold-rolled, the energy in dislocations actually builds up and the material *work hardens*, another self-describing word. When it is hot-rolled, the heat from the rollers actually helps release the previous dislocations and allows the process to continue faster.

Tempering the metal is a process where the hot metal is dipped in a liquid to rapidly cool it. This cooling freezes the tempering hot material and also weakens it. Tempering a hot metal in cold water causes a faster cooling than if you temper it in oil. The fast cool freezes dislocations in place (literally) and makes the material hard to bend. A bigger grain results from the slower cooling, which allows more *ductility*, a measure of how workable the material is. Mild steel is ideal for our use since it has that winning combination of strength and ductility.

Rolling is also used in processing sheet metal, and both hot and cold processes are used. Cold-rolled sheet metal is most often used for nonferrous metals, such as copper, bronze, and aluminum. Sheet metal, while not as structurally sound as other shapes we spoke of, is still useful, since, well, it's flat and it's metal. This allows it to be formed into shapes that are durable and relatively strong for their size and weight. *Aluminum flashing*, a thin sheet metal sold in rolls for the roofing trade, for instance, has been utilized as facing on curved platform shapes, where curving wood would take a lot more effort and time.

Aluminum: It's Not Just for Cans

When talking about aluminum we're reminded of a Broadway scenic designer who told us about *aluminum's rule of 3*. It goes something like this: When designing with aluminum, remember that aluminum is 3 times lighter, needs approximately 3 times the structure, and costs 3 times as much. While there may not be a lot of metallurgical science in that statement, it does bring up some points about aluminum.

Aluminum ore processing, when compared to iron processing, is really much more difficult. Iron production has been going on for centuries; aluminum really wasn't successfully processed until the 20th century. The main reason is that to produce pure aluminum, you need to melt down aluminum ore and shoot a whole lot of electricity through it to separate out the pure aluminum. When we say a lot of electricity, we mean gobs, chunks, and/or heaps. In fact, one of the reasons given for the centralization of the aircraft industry in the Pacific Northwest is the large hydroelectric dams that could generate the vast amounts of electricity needed for aluminum production.

There's Aluminum in Them Thar Hills!

The difficulties in the processing of *aluminum* are reflected in its price. Any people who have left the light on in a room they've exited have heard from their parents just how expensive electricity is. Translate that price to gobs, chunks, and/or heaps, and you'll get an idea what we're talking about. The website *How Stuff Works* lists this fun fact about aluminum that puts all the cost of aluminum production into perspective: "The 10-inch-high pyramid at the tip of the Washington Monument is made of aluminum rather than gold, because gold was less valuable than aluminum in 1884!" The cost of the metals is a little different now that the gold rush of the 1890s is over in California and we're no longer tripping over chunks of pure gold on our way to Sutter's Mill for some flour, but you get the idea.

Soft Cans

Like gold, aluminum is very soft and ductile, or easily formed. Unlike gold (whose atomic density is $19.3\,\mathrm{g\text{-}cm}^{-3}$ at 20°C), aluminum (whose atomic density is $2.7\,\mathrm{g\text{-}cm}^{-3}$ at 20°C) is very light. Basically, this means the Washington Monument could have been a whole lot heavier. The light weight of aluminum is what makes the aircraft and transportation industries possible. In theatre, we can take advantage of this light weight for our type of flying. Curtain tracks, flats frames, and even trusses for lighting are a few examples.

Even when alloyed, however, aluminum is still pretty soft. Anyone who has felt the soft sides of an open aluminum soda can can attest to that fact. To counteract this quality, you have to engineer the structure to prevent it from crushing when force is exerted on it. You may not need three times the structure, but you do have to carefully consider your design. The soda can, for example, is a design marvel. You'll notice that the top and bottom of the cans are slightly tapered, and the metal is a little thicker in these spots. The sides of the can are thinner. The design adds the thickness or structure where it is needed and saves material cost where the thickness isn't needed. Cans can be stacked case upon case for transport since the design of the can allows it to support weight, or maintain structural integrity, along the can's axis, which in this case (actually, in this case, in all of the cases) is top to bottom.

But once you take the can out of its specially packed case, open it, drink the beverage, and apply pressure against both ends (a common, though by no means recommended, method is to crush it against your forehead), notice how much easier it is to crush the can. The can was designed with just the right amount of aluminum to get to you in one piece, and no more (as always, please drink responsibly) (Figure 2.8).

A type of curtain track called *flex track* takes advantage of the ductile nature of aluminum. This track can be bent into gentle curves to allow curtains drawn across it to have a less traditional shape. The rigid structure of the extruded metal shape and the aluminum's alloy keep the track from completely bending out of shape. Unlike steel, this track can be cut with many of the same tools used for woodworking. In fact, aluminum's ductility will gum up the abrasive blades commonly used to cut and grind steel. Aluminum needs to be drilled at a slower speed to prevent the metal from mushrooming, trapping the drill bit, and causing it to overheat and lose its sharpness. Special coolants and cutting oils can be applied to the metal or the cutting tools to keep bits and blades from overheating and losing their temper, or, in other words, from becoming dull.

Figure 2.8: *Picture of stacked beverage cans and a crushed aluminum can.*

On the Road: How Aluminum Gets Beat

Many of the lighting instruments used in rock concerts and the truss work they hang from are aluminum (Figure 2.9). Its light weight makes it ideal for touring shows. The body of the alloyed aluminum lighting instrument was most likely cast, which is a process where the aluminum is heated to a molten state and then poured into a mold. Aluminum casts very well and transfers heat quickly, a quality that makes it suitable for CPU heat sinks, cooking pots, and Par Can, Lekos, and other lighting instruments whose lamps can get very hot.

This quality can be a pain when the roadie drops his Intelabeam lighting instrument and cracks the case. Welding aluminum is more art than skill. Aluminum doesn't change visually as it heats as steel does. Steel, when heated, turns a bright cherry red and then orangey white and then melts; aluminum looks fine one minute and then just melts into a puddle. It takes an experienced welder to successfully weld the pieces before this happens. Another drawback of aluminum includes aluminum toxicity, which, in our case, can cause people who come in contact with aluminum to break out in a rash or have other allergic reactions.

Despite all the expense, the excessive engineering, rashes, and crushed soda cans (sounds like a nerdy frat party), aluminum is extremely useful. Almost every mirror these days has an aluminum film on its back: CDs use aluminum; silvering in paint has aluminum in it; electrical transmission lines of aluminum are lighter than copper and cheaper; rubies are a gemstone variety of aluminum oxide and are used in lasers. But like any material, you need to weigh its advantages and drawbacks to see if it is the best material for your purpose.

Figure 2.9: *Loaded light truss.*

Plastic

Mr. McGuire: I want to say one word to you. Just one word.
Benjamin: Yes, sir.
Mr. McGuire: Are you listening?
Benjamin: Yes, I am.
Mr. McGuire: *Plastics.*

This quote is from the 1967 Mike Nichols movie *The Graduate*. The McGuire character was telling Benjamin that plastics were the wave of the future and he should think
about getting in on it. The rest of the movie has nothing to do with plastics, but it is
very good. *Plastic* is sort of a generic term that is used to describe several things, including soft, flexible materials, man-made materials, and credit cards. All of these are plastic,
but the substances most commonly thought of as plastic are really *polymers*. Let's break
the word down. *Poly* is a prefix that means "many." Or, if you are a parrot, you would
begin each sentence with "Polly wants. . . ." The "many" that the poly is talking about
is actually a *monomer*, a word that describes a chemical substance made of a single molecule. When you take these simple substances and link them together many times, you
get a polymer: "many" made of one thing. These substances are linked together through
the addition of other substances that sort of glue the objects together into a polymer
chain. It's the monomer and the combinations of how it is linked together that form
the different varieties of plastics.

Natural Plastic

Even though we think of plastic as man-made, there are a few naturally occurring polymers. Since one of the most common monomer bases for polymers is carbon, one of

71

the most common elements, when you think about it, natural polymers aren't that surprising. *Cellulose* is actually a kind of polymer found in trees and plant fibers, *natural rubber* is another. Animal horns and milk are two other substances that naturally contain polymers. Once these polymers were isolated, we looked for ways to turn them into usable substances. One of the earliest plastics, *parkesine*, was an attempt to create an ivory-like substance from cellulose by adding camphor as a plasticizer; it was used in dentures. *Celluloid*, another early product derived from cellulose, was used for a wide variety of things, including film stock for movies.

However, natural rubber eventually became sticky, parkesine dentures got soft when you drank hot liquids, and cellulose prints of movies faded with time. Processes like Goodyear's vulcanization, where he baked natural rubber, helped to stabilize these materials somewhat, but alternatives to natural polymers were needed.

I'll Trade You One Unentangled Polymer Chain for Some Serious Molecular Bling-Bling

That's when synthetic polymers were created. A *synthetic polymer* is man-made in fact; it doesn't have a naturally occurring molecule in it. These make up the majority of what we call plastics. *Bakelite* was the first synthetic plastic. If you've ever seen an old-fashioned telephone or radio, then you've seen Bakelite (Figure 2.10). It was hard, it insulated against electricity, and it was yet another thing that separated us from those cave people. (They had lousy phones and limited reception.) It was also one of the first *thermoset* polymers. Basically, there are two types of polymers, thermoplastics and thermosets.

Thermoplastics are made of long, flat polymer chains. The monomers are linked together end to end. Think of long chains lying side by side. When the chains are heated up, the molecules move further apart, and they become slack and flexible enough to take any shape. When they cool, the molecules move back into place, and the substance becomes hard. When you heat it again, the same thing happens and you can reshape it again.

If you think of thermoplastics as long chains side by side, think of thermosets as long chains side by side that have links linking them like chain mail. When you heat a thermoset for the first time, it will become flexible and take a shape, but after that the entangled polymer chain prevents the molecules from slipping apart the way thermoplastics do. Therefore thermosets can be used in high-temperature situations.

Making Some Plastics Can Be Sucky Work

One common thermoplastic that we use on stage is known as *vacuuform*. *Vacuuforming* is a common practice in plastic manufacturing. The process involves taking a sheet of thermoplastic, in this case vinyl, heating it until it becomes soft, and then sucking it

Figure 2.10: *Old-fashioned Bakelite phone.*

down over a mold to create your desired shape (Figure 2.11). What can you make from vacuuforming? Basically, anything that you can you can drill holes into (the holes allow air flow through the mold to enable suction) and fit on your vacuuforming table. As the name suggests, half of the table heats the plastic and half vacuums it to the mold. Care needs to be taken, however, not to create shapes with sharp undercuts, since this will entrap the vacuuform plastic on the mold and you'll have to destroy the mold to release it (Figure 2.12).

Stones and Bricks and Trees, Oh My!

One of the great advantages of using vacuuform is that it can easily mimic many textures. Heavy objects such as fieldstone, logs, and brick walls can be recreated in plastic at a great savings of time and weight. If you remember, in theatre we like things light and fast (Figure 2.13). By creating the depth and texture of the actual objects, you also save time in painting the pieces, since most of the work in stage painting is creating depth and texture.

In World War II a new plastic was utilized to deal with the increased aircraft production and specifically the glass needed for the canopies. *Polymethyl methacrylate* (it just

Figure 2.11: *Vacuuforming table at Provost Displays showing the vinyl and a mold ready for processing.*

Figure 2.12: *Various vacuuform molds showing the air holes need for suction.*

rolls off the tongue, doesn't it? Call it *PMMA* for short) is commonly known as *Plexiglas, acrylic,* or even *acrylic glass.* About half the weight of glass, acrylic sheets over 1″ thick are bullet resistant. As glass gets thicker, it develops a slight green tint, but acrylic stays optically clear. With a transparency rating of 93%, it is one of the clearest materials known. Acrylic also insulates against temperature better than glass. However, since it is a thermoplastic it can melt at temperatures between 250° and 300°F, making it less than desirable for oven cookware. We like clear acrylic sheets onstage because of its weight and impact resistance compared to glass. Actual glass on stage is scary: Actors

Figure 2.13: *DeSales University's production of* The Foreigner *showing the large fieldstone fireplace made of vacuuform panels and the vacuuform-covered beams.*

tend to get adrenaline rushes and slam things around. Murphy's Law applies to theatre, it seems, more than in real life, so we have to be prepared for anything that might happen.

UHMWPE and Other Slick Stuff

Aside from being unpronounceable, *UHMWPE* is a very useful thermoplastic in the theatrical industry. Called *UHMW* for short, it is actually an acronym for "ultra-high-molecular-weight polyethylene." This hard plastic is actually a cousin to the polyethylene that is in your plastic milk bottles, but as its name suggests it has a higher molecular weight (caused by really long polymer chains) that makes it hard and slippery. This slippery hardness makes it an ideal bushing between two substances that need to rub together, such as the bottom of a flat and the inside of a track it would ride in or a floor it might ride along. Most counterweight fly systems use lots of UHMW, especially on the T track, the track that the counterweights ride up and down. Its unique properties make it self-lubricating, it machines easily, and it is highly impact resistant. In fact, of the thermoplastics, UHMW has the highest impact resistance.

Stuck on Thermosets, or Is This Section Tacky?

Epoxy is a thermoset that gets hard through a chemical reaction after you add a hardener to it. If you go to the glue isle in the hardware store you'll see packages of glue that have either two tubes of glue in them or a clever little syringe that squirts out equal parts of two gooey liquids. Once you get a measured amount of epoxy and hardener onto a mixing surface, you mix them. Then you have a period of time to use them before the hardener makes the epoxy hard. Epoxy isn't just glue. When added to other materials, such as paint, it acts as a hardening agent that makes the new substance harder and more durable.

Epoxy is one of the key components in *fiberglass*. Basically what happens in the fiberglass process is a matlike cloth gets soaked in a fiberglass resin that has a measured amount of hardener added to it. The fiberglass mat shapes easily; the process is not unlike papier-mâché. The fiberglass can be cut into strips and shaped around an object. As the epoxy hardens, the fiberglass mat retains the shape of the object and forms a hard coating, so hard in fact that we can create fiberglass rocks hard enough for actors to sit and stand on (Figure 2.14). If enough layers of fiberglass are used, the shape can stand on its own. In the case of the rock in the picture, a Styrofoam® core was made around which the fiberglass was shaped. The advantage of fiberglass is that a sturdy structure can be made that weighs very little. By leaving the fiberglass on the foam core, fewer layers can be used and the weight of the object stays relatively low. One of the significant drawbacks of making fiberglass is the environmental hazards that surround it. Respirators are necessary because of the noxious fumes, as are epoxy-resistant gloves, since the resins harden quickly.

Figure 2.14: *Rock made with a foam base and a fiberglass shell for a production of* Carousel *at DeSales University.*

Foams or Tiny Bubbles in the Polystyrene

Foam is something we all have lots of experience with. As you know there are many kinds of foam. You can have sea foam, shaving foam, beer foam—the list goes on and on. The common ingredients in all foams are gas and something you blow the gas into, such as the sea, shaving cream, or beer.

The foam on the inside base of the rock in Figure 2.14 is a closed-cell foam known as *expanded polystyrene foam*, or, as we called it before, Styrofoam® (a registered trademark of Dow Chemical). We like this stuff because it is light, rigid, and water resistant and is one of the cheapest and most common foams available. You may also hear it referred to as *beadboard* or *white board*, since it is white in color and made out of tiny BBs of polystyrene pressed together. The polystyrene is melted and a blowing agent or gas is added to the polystyrene resin that creates little gas-filled BBs. These little BBs are put into a mold into which steam is forced, causing the gas inside the BBs to expand and stick together, taking the shape of the mold. Prior to 1990 there was a concern that chlorofluorocarbons, or CFCs, used as the blowing agent in some foam manufacturers' processes, were harmful to the ozone layer of Earth's atmosphere. Since then, manufacturers have replaced CFCs with other gases that do the same thing.

The obvious advantage to beadboard is that you can create a ridged shape that has a lot of bulk but weighs very little. One of the disadvantages is the little beads. Once they break off, when sawing or shaping the material, they go everywhere. Additionally, when painted they create a rough beaded texture that looks like painted beadboard no matter how you paint it. The most obvious way to deal with this problem is to cover the beadboard with something, much the way foamcore sheets cover the foam with paper or the way the rock in Figure 2.14 is covered in fiberglass. Cheesecloth is a common foam covering that creates a rough stone texture.

Feeling Blue About XPS, But in the Pink About Extruded Polystyrene

The polystyrene foam process was greatly improved when *extruded polystyrene foam* was developed. This foam is known as XPS for short or by its common name, *blue board* or *pink board* (guess why), depending on the manufacturer. This time the polystyrene crystal resin is mixed with a blowing agent and then heated under pressure. The resulting thick gooey mess is forced through a die, and it expands and takes shape. This process produces a more consistent and uniform closed-cell structure.

The difference in appearance, beyond color, between expanded and extruded polystyrene foam is that the little beads are even littler, and there are virtually no voids between the beads. This creates a smooth, consistent texture that paints better and doesn't require the surface covering that beadboard does. Since the naturally smooth surface takes a step out of the finishing process, XPS is replacing beadboard in a lot of scene shops.

Polyurethane Has a Cushy Job but Pads Its Resume

Everyone who has looked at a pillow or mattress has noticed those tags that say "Do Not Remove Under Penalty of Law" (Figure 2.15). If you stop laughing long enough at the thought of the pillow police coming to get you, you might notice that the pillow is made of urethane foam. Polyurethane polymer actually has thermosets and thermoplastics in its family.

Polyurethane foam is created when, as a result of the manufacturing process, carbon dioxide is released as the polymerization process cures (again: gas + substance = foam). Although you can have rigid closed-celled polyurethane foams, let's change things up a bit and talk about open-celled foam (you knew this was coming, didn't you?). Think of all those little BBs we spoke about in the closed-cell foams. Now imagine what would happen if all of those BBs popped. The result is flexible foam, since the walls of the BBs are collapsed. Also, unlike closed-cell foams, open-cell foams suck up moisture, since the majority of the material's structure is open. Common uses of this foam include cushion seats and memory-foam pillows (see Figure 2.15). In theatre when we aren't using foam rubber to upholster furniture we often carve this foam to make soft, flexible props (Figure 2.16). The cake in this picture was foam rubber covered in whipped cream. Since it was soft and flexible when the actors fell into it, they didn't get injured. Rigid or closed-cell polyurethane carves nicely and can be utilized to create molds for vacuuform shapes.

As a thermoplastic, polyurethane is tough and durable. Car tires as well as skateboard and inline-skate parts take advantage of its abrasion resistance. Another common use of polyurethane is as a finish coating for woodwork. Since in this form it is tough and

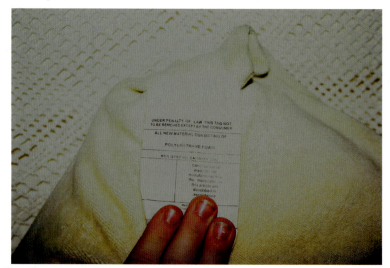

Figure 2.15: *The nasty tag in question.*

Figure 2.16: *Picture of DeSales University's production of a Christmas festival with giant foam cake prop.*

scuff resistant, we love it as a floor coating. It is highly reflective and tends to bounce light quite well, so satin finishes are more desirable for stage work than glossy ones.

Cloth

Spandex, Nylon, Acrylic, and Other Synthetic Cloths

Polyurethane is actually one of the components of spandex, that shiny, stretchy fabric that is so popular among superheroes and '80s heavy metal hair bands. In fact, one of the earliest and most sought-after polymers was *nylon*. While it is tough and durable when made into bearings and gears (many cordless screw guns have nylon gears to reduce their weight), when spun into strands and woven it makes a soft fabric intended to replace silk. Other synthetic fabrics include *rayon*, *lames*, and *polyesters*.

Synthetic fibers are desirable since whatever quality you'd like the fabric to have can be engineered into it. For example, as we said, by treating polyurethane you can create an elastic fiber (see Figure 2.17).

Remember Sharkstooth scrim, the material used in scrim curtains? As we said, it's a fine net that lets light through and can hide objects until they are lit from behind and revealed. This fine netting is also very fragile and difficult to paint. Textilene® is a synthetic substitute for Sharkstooth scrim. By coating polyester netting in polyvinylchloride, or PVC, you have created a durable material that was originally developed to cover speakers in outdoor venues. This waterproof PVC covering actually takes acrylic latex paint quite well, holds its shape when hung, holds up to actors, and can prove less

79

Figure 2.17: *Dancers using spandex.*

Figure 2.18: *Marley's ghost backlit behind a painted Textilene covered door from the DeSales University production of* A Christmas Carol.

expensive. Look back at Figure 1.41. A full-stage drop (38′) for Harmonia Gardens in *Hello, Dolly* was created out of 8′-wide sections of Textilene® placed side by side, overlapping slightly, with a stitch of monofilament line here and there. If Sharkstooth had been used in place of Textilene® scrim, the unit would have cost over 10 times more. Figure 2.18 illustrates the eerie effects you can create by suddenly back lighting a Textilene® scrim.

There are certain advantages to synthetic fibers, and yet there are designers who hate using them. Quite often there is no substitute for the light-absorbing qualities of natural fibers in stage blacks or the tight stretch that scenic muslin gives to a painted soft flat. Acrylic, polyester, nylon, and other synthetic fibers have a slight sheen that in decorative display or expo fabric add glitzy excitement to a musical. This sheen may be appropriate for some applications. But when you need absolute black or a soft, luxurious velour, you'll still get a few glimmers that make the fabrics look a little too "Vegas" for their own good. Like everything else when choosing a plastic or synthetic material, think about how its qualities best serve the production, and weigh the pluses and minuses.

Chapter 3
What Tools Do I Use?
Scene Shop Tools and Techniques

Again we ask, "What separates us from the lower beasts?" Our ability to use tools (and our ability to invent newer, cooler ones that show off our opposable thumbs to their best light). Yes, this is the chapter that will allow us to pretend that the statement "Whoever dies with the most toys wins" is true. We look at the essential tools for every scene shop (and some that aren't essential) and discuss them with loving care.

To begin with, there are really two kinds of tools: the ones you have and the ones you want. Let's start the discussion by lumping both of these types into two other basic groups: hand tools and power tools. We later discuss portable power tools and finishing tools.

Hand Tools

Hammer Time, or You've Hit the Nail Right on the Head

When the first cave person took a rock and smashed a post-dinosaur-type animal in the head, he was using a *hand tool*. In fact, he was using the most recognizable hand tool, the *hammer*. We all know what a hammer does; when it isn't smacking our thumbs it's used to pound, smack, or gently coerce something to move the way we want it to move. Be it a nail, tack, chair leg, platform, or thumbnail, your arm transfers the force to the hammer and then to the object you want to move.

Figure 3.1: *Tack hammers.*

There are a couple of parts to a hammer, and we mention them because the shape of these parts helps define the hammer. These parts are the *head*, the *handle*, and what is generally known as the *peen*. We get the idea of the handle easily enough, and the head is our striking surface, where the brunt of all the weight and force used in a hammer lies. But what's a peen? (Not much. What's a peen with you?) The peen is the part of the hammer that sits on the handle on the opposite side of the head. Sometimes this peen will be a claw shape for nail pulling, or, as in the case of a ball peen or machinist's hammer, it can have a special task-related shape. The size, shape, and combinations of various heads and peens are defined by the use of the hammer.

Here's a list of common hammer types we use in scenery construction or, as the case may be, deconstruction. Let's start small and work our way up.

- *Tack hammers* (see Figure 3.1) are little T-shaped hammers with small heads that can hit upholstery tacks and other decorative nails without an excess of force that would send them flying. Quite often they are magnetized to hold them in place and spare your thumbnails. The peen has a slot in it that acts as a nail puller. Prop departments and set dressers use these the most.
- *Finish hammers* (see Figure 3.2) are a little heavier, between 12 and 16 ounces, and have a claw-shaped peen to grab the head of an errant nail and yank it out. The curve in the claw acts like a fulcrum and gives you a mechanical advantage to remove the nail. The head is smaller than the average hammer head and has a smooth face. This lets you get in close for trim work and leaves less marring on the surface of the trim.
- *16-oz claw hammers* (see Figure 3.3) are probably the hammers most people think of when we talk of hammers. Its weight is one that just about everyone can deal with, not too heavy and not too light. And the claw peen is very utilitarian.
- *16-oz rip hammers* (see Figure 3.4) aren't that different from claw hammers. Their peen has a claw shape, but it has less of a curve to it. These hammers are

Figure 3.2: *Finish hammer.*

Figure 3.3: *16-oz claw hammer.*

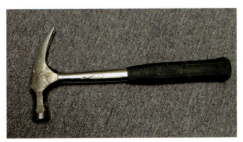

Figure 3.4: *16-oz rip hammer.*

Figure 3.5: *Framing hammer.*

especially nice if you are going to do a lot of prying as well as pounding. The flatter shape can easily get in between surfaces like a pry bar and wedge them apart.

- *Framing hammers* (see Figure 3.5) can have rip or claw peens. Their handles are a bit longer (sometimes as long as your forearm), and they weigh around 20–24 oz. The advantage to the longer handle and extra weight is the mechanical advantage they give when pounding large framing nails into softwoods such as spruce and fir used in the building trades. The heads are slightly chamfered to prevent chipping and can also be waffled to prevent glancing blows to the nails. The waffling in scenic work can be disadvantageous to the finish work on the set, so quite often scenic carpenters prefer smooth-faced hammers. The head can also have a slot with a magnet in it to hold the nail. The nail head is placed against the magnet in the slot, and the first hammer blow makes the nail stick in the wood without exposing your hand to the mechanical advantages of extra weight and longer handle. (Not to mention the waffle head. Did we say it resembles a meat tenderizer?)

- *Dead-blow hammers* (see Figure 3.6) are soft-covered, hollow hammers filled with metal shot. These hammers generally have two heads. The shot is loosely packed inside, adding weight to the hammer as well as directing the force of the hammer and preventing it from bouncing when it strikes a surface. This is the "dead blow" in the name. These hammers are great for careful disassembly of furniture and props, where a well-directed tap can help a lot. They are also the first in the class of what we wood butchers call *scenic micrometers*, or "big heavy hammers that can make scenic elements fit where they are supposed to go."

- *3-lb sledgehammer* (see Figure 3.7) is another scenic micrometer. It can have a double head or a wedge-shaped head for machinist work. At this weight it generally has a short handle, making it handy to use in tight spots, such as under platforms.

- *10-lb sledge.* (see Figure 3.7) This would be the granddaddy of the scenic micrometers. If you're moving scenery with one of these, you're in big trouble. Try and figure out why the parts don't fit first. With its heavy weight and long handle, the 10-lb sledge is best suited to demolition work at set-striking time or for making sure the radio station you hate is never played again.

Figure 3.6: *Dead-blow hammer.*

Figure 3.7: *Sledgehammers.*

Which Hammer Do I Need?

Some of us can never have enough hammers. It's such an elemental tool, and it feels good in your hand. The ironic thing is we are using hammers less and less since the advent of the cordless screw gun. That doesn't mean that you don't need one. Sometimes you need to give something a good whack or a gentle "directed-force persuasion." It's also a handy lever for lifting things up to get under them, such as heavy platforms, or punching holes in flat skins to cut out windows (see the later sections on routers and jigsaws). That said, there are a couple of things to think about when you are choosing your hammer.

- *How heavy of a hammer can you hold?* Yes, the more you wield a heavy hammer, the easier it will be to hold its weight as you build up muscles. And big hammers are cool. But, as we said, hammers are being used less and less in scenic construction. Do you want to carry a heavy hammer around all the time? Go to a hardware store and try the various weights, feel their balance, and see how the handle fits in your hand. Get the hammer that is overall the most comfortable.

- *How big are you?* Really, it's a consideration. Long handles give you a mechanical advantage and are great fun to swing, but they can be a pain (literally) for someone with short arms. Carefully try it out. How close do you come to smacking yourself? Additionally, if you have short legs and wear your hammer on your tool belt, every time you kneel the handle will hit the floor and push its way out of its hanger. Tools are like sports equipment—you need to fit them to your body. Try your tools out, see how they feel, and choose what's best for you.
- *What are you doing the most of?* Yes, most tool belts come with two hammer hangers. Again, do you want to carry around that much extra weight? If you find you are doing a lot of whacking and demolition work, a rip hammer or framing hammer might be best for you. If you are doing a lot of trim and finish work, carry a trim hammer.

After you add up the considerations, pick the best fit. When it comes down to it, most people choose between the 16-oz claw and a framing hammer. But let's face it—there is nothing more personal to a carpenter than his or her tools, so choose carefully. Your hammer could save your life one day. Well probably not, but you get the idea.

And Now a Subject with Teeth: Handsaws

Again, handsaws are being used less and less since the advent of cordless power saws. But when you need one, you need one. There is no real substitute. Power saws have their limitations. When you are cutting square corners and can't get the saw to cut neatly into the corner, a couple of strokes with the "original cordless saw" will do the trick. Which kind should you have around? Let's first look at the parts of a saw and the different types.

Parts of a Saw (Figure 3.8)

- *The handle.* We must often think of the handle of the saw as a D-shaped grip that sits behind the blade. That is starting to change with the introduction of the Japanese saw technology, which is growing in popularity. These saws have a

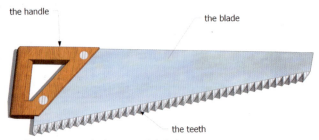

Figure 3.8: *Picture of a ripsaw with the parts labeled.*

Figure 3.9: *Picture of a Japanese saw.*

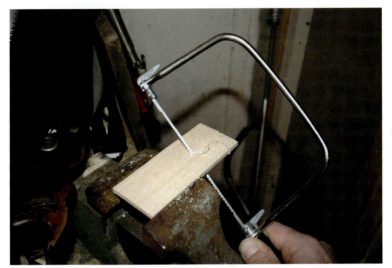

Figure 3.10: *Close-up of a handsaw, its saw kerf, and sawdust.*

broomstick-like handle, and the saw looks much more like a knife handle than the D handle (see Figure 3.9).

- *The blade.* This makes up the majority of the saw. It is usually thin, strong, but flexible tool steel and can vary in shape from wedge shape to keystone shape to thin bands of steel. The most important thing about the blade is that it connects the teeth to the handle.

- *The teeth.* These do the cutting. When we say that a saw blade is sharp, it's the teeth we refer to. There are two main wood-saw teeth types, rip and crosscut.

More About Teeth: Tooth Set, Rip and Crosscut Teeth, and Saw Kerf—or Things You'll Never Hear from Your Orthodontist

Remember how a tree is created: The fibers grow into long strands that form into rings. The best way to cut across (or *crosscut*, as we spoke about in the Wood section of Chapter 2) the tree, is to use teeth shaped like little shark's teeth. These grab onto the fibers and cut them. The *set* of the teeth describes how they are set in relation to the blade. If you turn a handsaw up so the teeth are facing you, you'll see that the teeth are set in a zigzag fashion. This helps grab the wood, remove sawdust from the cut, and keep the blade from binding in the wood. The space left in the wood after the teeth cut it is called the *kerf*. The wood that was in the kerf is now called *sawdust* (Figure 3.10).

It seems silly to bring up kerfs and sawdust, but it's important to realize that if your saw blade cuts an ⅛″ kerf into a board, you never get that wood back. Therefore, if you crosscut a sheet of 4′ × 8′ plywood in half across the 4′ width, you will get two sheets that are 3′-11¹⁵⁄₁₆″. You'll never get two 4′ pieces out of an 8′ board. So you have to plan your materials accordingly.

Rip teeth have a different, chisel-like design. Since they cut *with the grain*, or along the length of the long fibers, they more or less plane or chisel the wood out, removing the fibers that are in the way. Also, rip teeth have a coarser set than crosscut teeth; that is, there are fewer teeth per inch in general. This takes a bigger bite into the wood and shaves it away in larger pieces. If you look at the sawdust after a rip cut you'll see it isn't as fine as crosscut dust. Typically a common crosscut handsaw has something like 9 TPI, or teeth per inch, and a rip set of 4 TPI.

Types of Wood Saws

- *Bow saw (see Figure 3.11)*. This may be the earliest type of saw. It consists of a thin, narrow blade that is held under tension to keep it stiff in a bow-shaped frame (that's a bow and arrow type of bow, not a gift box type of bow). These days bow saws are used mostly to cut tree limbs and have a very coarse set. It is important to mention them since the hacksaw and the coping saws are similar in design.
- *Rip saws (see Figure 3.12)*. These saws are used to rip along the grain of the wood. You hardly see anyone make that long of a cut with a handsaw these days.
- *Crosscut saw (see Figure 3.13)*. As we said, this saw is used to make crosscuts, which is the cut most people make with a handsaw.
- *Back saw (see Figure 3.14)*. The back saw is a crosscutting saw used mainly in combination with a miter box. A *miter cut* is a cut that goes across the edge of

Figure 3.11: *Bow saw: Its blade can be replaced with a hacksaw blade to cut metal.*

Figure 3.12: *Rip saw: "Grandma, what sharp, pointy teeth you have!"*

Figure 3.13: *Crosscut saw.*

Figure 3.14: *Backsaw in a miter box.*

Figure 3.15: *Crosscut saw (top) and toolbox saw.*

Figure 3.16: *The coping saw: a favorite of Dr. Phil's.*

a board on an angle, usually to make a tight corner with trim molding. The box itself is U shaped, with slits cut at 90° and 45°. The backsaw has a piece of metal over the back of the blade that keeps it stiff as it travels inside the slots of the miter box. The slots act as a guide and keep the cut straight.

- *Toolbox saw (see Figure 3.15).* The first thing that defines a toolbox saw is its size. It's small enough to fit inside a toolbox. These saws can be either rip or cross-cut or (are you ready?) both. There is an aggressive tooth set that combines both properties. It's replacing the other two because of the convenience offered, and it cuts plastic equally well.
- *Coping saw (see Figure 3.16).* The saws we mentioned earlier are mostly straight cutting saws. If you need a curved cut, this saw will help you cope with that problem. The saw has a D-shaped bow attached to a handle by a screw. As you tighten the handle, you put tension on the thin blade suspended in the bow. Since the blade is so thin, you can turn it into tight scrolling curves without its binding.

Fun with a Coping Saw

You can even cut patterns on the inside of a board with a coping saw. Drill a hole and place one side of the coping saw blade into the hole. Reattach the top of the blade and then tighten the bow frame. You can now make an interior cut as deep as the space between the blade and the bow frame.

The term *coping* actually describes a method of cutting molding used in finish carpentry. When two pieces of molding join in a corner, a joint results. If the molding isn't complicated with lots of in and out shapes, you can make a simple miter cut (see the discussion of the backsaw), however; if the corner angle is sharp and the molding is extra fancy, tight corners are hard to make. What you can do is take your coping saw and cut, at a bit of an angle (20° or so), the profile of the molding from the back of one of the pieces. This piece will then lay over the other and look like a tight joint. It takes some practice, and that's why finish carpenters make so much money.

Other Handsaws

We mentioned hacksaws and their similarity to bow saws. Hacksaws have a fine-toothed narrow blade that, like the blade of the coping and bow saws, is kept under tension. And as with the coping and bow saws, the blades are removable and reversible. But what makes the hacksaw different is that it is meant to cut metal (as anyone who's seen a prison movie can attest to. *Note*: Baking hacksaw blades into pies is not recommended).

One of the disadvantages of the hacksaw is that the bow prevents it from being used in close quarters. Jab saws were invented to remedy this situation (Figure 3.17). A jab, as you know, is a quick, sharp movement, usually done in the backseat of your parent's car on a long trip, with some sibling as the intended target. In this case the jab is you inserting the jab saw into a confined space or a cavity. Basically, what a jab saw consists of is a hacksaw blade and a short handle that supports most of the saw but leaves the front end free to slip in between what you want to cut and what's in your way (it also fits nicely into a pie, but see the earlier note).

Figure 3.17: *(from top left to bottom right) Jab saw, drywall saw, hacksaw, and keyhole saw.*

Similar to the jab saw are the keyhole saw and the drywall saw. A *keyhole saw* is basically the same thing as a jab saw, and as the name implies it is made to cut small holes. Where it differs is that the blade is narrow at the end and widens toward the handle. The handle can look like a pistol grip or a traditional D handle. The idea behind it is that the narrow end of the saw can be inserted into a hole and the saw cut can be an inside cut, similar to the cut you can make with a coping saw, without the size of the bow frame getting in the way.

Another similarity to the coping saw is that curved cuts can be made by using just the narrow end of the saw. Since the narrow end of the keyhole saw is nowhere near the size of the coping saw, the intricate, jigsaw puzzle–like curves you can cut with the coping saw aren't really possible with this saw. The *drywall saw* operates on the same principle. It has a straight handle and a blade that goes from narrow to wide. With this saw you can make inside cuts to drywall-covered walls easily (after you make sure of where the wiring is, of course).

A further adaptation to the bow/hack/coping family is the *rod saw blade* (Figure 3.18). This blade is a stiff steel cable impregnated with carbide chips. It looks like a metal pretzel covered in chunky black salt. The chunks act like a very aggressive toothed blade. Since the chunks go all the way around the blade, you can easily change direction without turning the saw. You only need to push or pull the saw in the direction you want it to go.

This brings up an interesting point. Most of the saws we spoke of cut on the *push stroke*, which is to say that the teeth are set to cut when they are pushed through the wood. Yes, you do move a saw back and forth to cut, hence the terms *seesaw* and *sawing a log* (which can mean cutting the log or sleeping. Never operate tools while asleep or drowsy). The *back stroke* on a pull saw clears the sawdust and returns the blade to the starting position, to be pushed through the wood again. So when you use a push saw, you really only need to apply effort to the push stroke and not the back stroke. This will save you effort and embarrassment as the old-timers stand and snicker at the rookie who works too hard.

Figure 3.18: *Hacksaw with a rod saw blade in its frame and the regular blade.*

As you may have guessed, the pull saw works the same way in reverse. The Japanese saws we mentioned earlier work as pull saws. Some people find these easier to use, and some people can't use them at all. It's just like the hammer. Borrow one and see which works for you.

Which Handsaws Should I Have?

We can start by asking a similar question to one we asked about the hammer: What are you doing the most of? Obviously if you are cutting a lot of steel, you'll need a saw with a metal cutting blade. Do you often find yourself squeezed under platforms trying to cut free a frozen bolt? Or are you just cutting wood and the occasional piece of PVC pipe?

For the most part, the current toolbox saws with aggressive-set teeth are going to answer all of your wood and plastic crosscutting needs as well as handle the occasional rip cuts you may make. Hacksaws are nice to have, and there are a few models out there that can break down and make a jab saw if you are the resident platform spelunker.

The coping saw is also nice to have, but for the most part most shops' coping saws are found in a corner with loose handles and broken blades. Compared to the power versions of this saw, it's just too slow for most people, and that can be said for the hacksaw.

When it comes to push or pull saw choices, as we said, borrow one and try it. There are nice advantages to the Japanese-style saws. They are aggressive toothed with a fine cut and are flexible enough to saw flush to a surface and make a flush cut. Yet these very qualities sometimes confound the push saw vet. All in all, before you start filling your shopping cart, see how often you need a handsaw and go from there.

Pliers, Knives, and Their Mutant Cousin, the Multitool

There is no doubt about it: Pliers are just as useful as the opposable thumb. The most common pliers people think of are *slip-joint pliers* (Figure 3.19). These have a broad nose with serrated jaws that grip staples and small nails well when you need to pull them out. A second set of larger serrated jaws on the inside allow you to grip bolt heads and nuts. The biggest gimmick to this tool, as you may have guessed, is the slip joint. The pivot point where the pliers come together isn't fastened tight; in fact the joint has a wide figure 8–shaped slot that allows the jaws to open wider, much like a snake does when it wants to swallow a deer. In this way you can adapt the tool to the job. Additionally, it has a rudimentary wire cutter set right above the slip joint.

Pliers basically allow us to grip things we couldn't grip with our bare hands. Whether it's a jammed nut, a staple that needs to be pulled out, or a piece of hot metal, pliers are just an extension of our fingers and thumbs. The job we need them for determines

Figure 3.19: *Slip-joint pliers in action.*

Figure 3.20: *A fencing tool that's seen a lot of fences.*

the size and shape of these new über-digits. You can get by very well with slip-joint pliers and for a long time. But, as with any multipurpose tool, the slip-joint pliers do some things well and do others okay, and some are just a quick solution when you don't have the right tool. Let's look at some of the things these pliers do for us in theatres.

Pulling or Prying

Possibly one of the coolest tools around for pulling staples and small nails is the *fencing tool* (Figure 3.20). It is another multipurpose tool, but it was designed with a single purpose in mind. When barbed wire was developed, these pliers were created to be a one-piece toolkit. A cowboy could reach into his saddlebag, pull these out, and remove staples with the long, curved pointed end. Compare this end to that of the claw hammer and you will understand the design choice; it's basically half a claw. The sharp point gets under the crown (the U-shaped top) of the staple, and the curve gives you a mechanical advantage when you rock it out. This feature alone makes the tool worthwhile.

Figure 3.21: *(clockwise from top) Vise grips, needle-nose pliers, and water pump pliers.*

To carry the comparison further, the other side of the pliers has a serrated hammer face. Basically, these are only effective for driving the wider, flat-crowned fencing staples. We hardly ever use these. Even at that, they are hard to use as hammers since the legs of the pliers are harder to grip than a hammer handle. The top of the fencing tool's head are wide-nosed pliers jaws. With the mechanical advantage of the claw peen, these jaws are effective pulling tools.

Under the jaws are the wire cutters. These were designed to cut hardened barbed wire, so they work pretty well.

Gripping

There are many types of *gripping pliers* (see Figure 3.21). The types we use most are listed here.

- *Vise grips, or locking pliers:* These pliers don't help you come to terms with those regrettable habits you'd like to quit; they actually refer to the clamping tool that firmly holds objects, also known as a *vise*. They have a bolt that tightens and loosens the jaw opening and a spring and locking lever that holds the jaws in place. These are especially nice for grabbing frozen bolts or screws.
- *Needle-nose pliers:* As the name suggests, the nose on these pliers is thin like a needle. While they are great for getting into small spaces and picking up and holding small objects, they are also great for shaping wire for craft work, and they have handy wire cutters as well.
- *Water pump pliers:* These are better known by the brand name Channel Locks® and are like slip joints on steroids. When you have plumbing to do on stage, these are handy to have around. Their adjustable jaws and serrated grip make grabbing pipe and the fittings used in plumbing easier.

Table 3.1: *Common Types of Pliers*

Name	Material	Features
Wire strippers	Electrical wire of different gauges	• Strips insulation and cuts wire. • Many have crimpers in the nose for crimping electrical connectors to wires. • May also have small bolt cutters in them to cut the various small bolts and screws used in electrical work.
Diagonal cutters, parrot-nose cutters, or "dykes"	Electrical wire and thin-gauge wire and staples	These will cut flush to the surface.
Bolt cutters	Bolts and chain	These are also known as "the universal key" when you can't open a padlock.
C7's	Aircraft and other steel cable	These have a coiled spring between the legs that add a mechanical advantage to make cutting stranded steel cable easier.
Rope cutters	Synthetic or natural hemp rope	These look a lot like a combination of bolt cutters and scissors.
Swaging tools	Swage sleeves (look like metal licorice bites)	• These make secure aircraft cable terminations for rigging by crimping swage sleeves over the cable. • They look a lot like bolt cutters with the crimpers from the wire strippers on their nose. • They come accompanied by a GO–NO GO gauge that tells you if you've crimped enough.

Cutting and Stripping

We can cut a few different things with pliers. Table 3.1 lists the most common types of pliers and what they cut.

Which Pliers Do I Need?

Pliers can be as specialized as surgical tools. In fact, some pliers *are* surgical tools. So how do we answer the topic question? By asking the same question we've been asking: What are you doing? If you are an electrician you'll want pliers that cut and strip. If you're a carpenter you'll want something that pries and grips. Carpenters can't go wrong with fencing tools in their toolbox as well as a pair of locking pliers. Electricians, or "sparkies," would do well with wire strippers and diagonal cutters. Both groups would profit from needle-nose pliers. But reserve final judgment until you get to the end of this section.

Knives: An Edgy Subject

There may be more kinds of knives than hammers and pliers combined, and the choice between them is pretty personal. But when it comes down to it, there are only a couple

Figure 3.22a: *Mat (utility) knife.*

Figure 3.22b: *Snap-off knife.*

of types we use in theatre, and the rest are variations on those themes. We'll start with the most commonly used knife in scenic work, the mat knife.

Mat Knife, or Utility Knife

The mat (utility) knife (Figure 3.22a) is sometimes known as a *box cutter*. It has a replaceable blade with two sides so that you can reverse it when one side becomes dull. We like this knife because it is razor sharp and can cut a variety of materials, including fabric on soft-cover flats, plastic package wrapping, wallpaper, tie line, and carpet; the list goes on and on. The replaceable blades make it possible to have a sharp edge quickly. The razor-sharp edge, however, is thinner and more prone to breaking than a conventional knife blade. The blades can be fixed or retractable, and there are blade styles available for a variety of materials.

Snap-Off Knives

Snap-off knives (Figure 3.22b) are the little cousins of the mat knife. They have a smaller and longer blade than a mat knife, and this blade is scored at regular intervals. By removing the special slotted tool at the bottom of the knife and placing the dull end of the knife blade into it, you can snap off the dull edge and get a sharp one with a new point. This cool feature has a drawback: Sometimes the blade will snap by itself. Therefore you can't cut tough materials with it.

Precision Blade Knife

The precision blade knife (Figure 3.22c) is the little brother of the mat knife. Most commonly known under the trade name Xacto knife®, this is a sharp, replaceable blade knife that comes in a variety of blade styles for cutting thin materials such as stencil paper into intricate patterns.

99

Figure 3.22c: *Precision blade knife.*

Figure 3.22d: *Serrated-edge knife.*

Folding Lock-Blade Knife

The folding lock-blade knife is also known as a *pocketknife* or a *jackknife*. The folding nature of the knife makes it convenient and easy to carry. Unlike standard pocket knives, these are rugged and have a locking mechanism to prevent accidentally closing it on your hand while you're making a difficult cut. Many now have belt clips, making them even more convenient, and even have one-handed-opening features. There are many blade options. Next we present a few of the most popular and useful options.

Serrated-Edge Knife

The serrated-edge knife (Figure 3.22d) is characterized by the little waves on its edge, called *serrations*, that allow you to cut more easily through tough materials such as rope and plastic hose. Police officers and paramedics carry serrated-edge knives to quickly cut through seatbelt webbing.

Folding Mat Knife

The folding mat knife (Figure 3.22e) combines the mat knife and the folding lock blade. The knife grip style actually gives you a bit more leverage than do standard mat knives.

Marlin Spike Knife

As you may have guessed from the name, the marlin spike knife (Figure 3.22f) was designed for use at sea. The marlin spike is used to push in between rope fibers in order

Figure 3.22e: *Folding mat knife.*

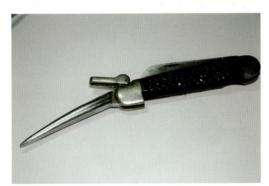

Figure 3.22f: *Marlin spike knife.*

to splice lengths together. This is an ideal knife for rigging since it is designed to cut rope.

Half-Serrated Blade
This is an option on many knives in which the front half of the blade is conventional and the back half is serrated.

Which Knife Should I Get?
According to a few Edgar Rice Burroughs novels that were scanned for research on this book, Tarzan did quite nicely with a piece of sharpened flint (the precursor to the serrated edge). Since most of us can't pull off the loincloth look, there's not much point to using that knife. A mat knife will serve most of your scenic needs and is a good place to start. After that, the cardinal rule of tool choice reigns: What are you doing the most of? If you are cutting a variety of materials, think about a combination blade, such as a half-serrated blade.

Say Hello to My Little Friend, the Multitool
Technically, any tool that serves more than one purpose is a multipurpose tool. Pliers, such as the slip-joint and the fencing tool, have done this for years. Pocketknives have

Figure 3.23: *Knife-shaped and pliers-shaped multitools.*

also had multiple blades, each suited to a need; the Swiss army knife is an excellent example of this. It seems natural that these two tools should be combined into one tool that we now know as the *multitool*. These may be the sexiest and most seductive of the hand tools. They give you the power of instant tool access, and they feel good in your hand.

Multitools come in a variety of shapes and blade types. Which you choose is again based on the cardinal rule of tool choice. The two basic shapes of multitools can best be described as pliers shaped or knife shaped (Figure 3.23). The design is governed by the primary tool usage. That is to say, if you use pliers more, go with that shape. But if you use knife blades more, go with the knife shape. The main reason behind this decision is that in the pliers shape the pliers are easier to get to and in the knife shape the blades are easier to get to.

Aside from the shape, there are two more considerations that are linked: How big is your hand? And which accessories do you want? The accessory blades in a multitool can be varied, but there are constants: straight-blade screwdriver heads, Phillips-head screwdriver blades, smaller versions of both blade types, files, saws, and even the eternally cool little pair of scissors. The more accessories, the wider the tool and the harder it is to hold (and as you may guess, the more expensive it is). Try it out. Ask people how they like theirs.

And please remember, these tools are for convenience. Seven times out of 10 you'd be better off getting the single-purpose tool that does the same job. That eternally cool little pair of scissors in your multitool won't do a good job of cutting out the fabric for a ball gown. But we've seen people try.

Figure 3.24: *PSU Berks stagecraft class trying to see who can get the longest standout.*

Tape Measure: The Measuring Tool You *Must*—Repeat, *Must*—Have

We mean it. You absolutely, positively need a tape measure. There just isn't a handier, more compact way of measuring the materials and the stage layouts that we need in this business. So get one. But before you do, here are some things to think about.

If you have a small space, you don't really need to go out and get a 35′ tape measure. 12′–16′ tapes can do the job. But if your proscenium opening is wider than 20′ and your stage is deeper than 20′, you probably do. If you're going to be measuring lots of vertical objects, such as flats, you'll need a tape that has a wider *standout*. The standout is the length of tape you can pull out vertically without its bending (which is called *breaking*). This is useful for measuring things taller than you. The standard standout is about 9′ feet, but wide tapes go higher. Quite often at break time you'll see the carpenters out back behind the shop trying to see who can get the longest standout (Figure 3.24).

The numbers on the "tape" can be quite important, as you may have guessed. The precision on a tape measure can go down to ¹⁄₆₄″. We rarely need to go beyond ¹⁄₁₆″ and that brings us to another important "tape" consideration. How good are you at reading those fractions? If you have trouble, try a fractional-read tape (Figure 3.25). These tapes have the fractions, such as ⅛″, ⅝″, and ¾″, written right on them in the appropriate places. If you are going to be going back and forth between metric and imperial measurement (which means not metric but the standard units used in the United States), get a metric/imperial read tape. Otherwise, don't buy one. They can be confusing.

Figure 3.25: *Fractional-read tape blade and metric/imperial tape.*

FAQs About Tape Measures

- *Why is the silver thingy on the end of my tape loose?* I just bought it! Should I smack it with a hammer? No. While that may be fun, the tape is supposed to be that way. We'll answer that question by explaining the two types of measurements: inside and outside. And to make this easier, we'll tell you that the silver thingy's name is the *slip hook* or *floating zero*.
  - *Inside measurements* are when you take your tape measure and push one end up against something (such as the base of a wall) and take your measurement.
  - *Outside measurements* are when you take the tape and measure something from outside to outside, such as one of those vertical flats we just spoke of. This measurement is characterized by hooking the slip hook over something. So why does it move? There is play in the floating zero so that when you push it, it adjusts to the inside measurement, and vice versa.
- *Why are some numbers in red?* Look carefully (see Figure 3.25). These numbers appear every 16″. This is a quick reference to the standard distance between the *studs,* or vertical 2 × 4's in a house's wall frame. This works for us too. A nice standard construction placement for our rails and toggles is 32″, or 2′-8″. That would be *every other* red mark.
- *What are all those little lines? There are way too many. They're just showing off.* These lines are what we use to measure. Let's break it down. Basically, in imperial measurement you have ⅟₁₆″, ⅛″, ¼″, and ½″ (they can get smaller but we don't need that kind of precision). When you are looking at a map, you can remember your route easier if you remember landmarks along the way; let's find some on the tape measure (Figure 3.25).
  - If you count every line between 0 and 1″ you'll find there are 16. Two of those represent ⅛″, and if you look carefully you'll notice that the second one is longer than the first. Four make up ¼″, and that fourth line is longer than the other two. The ½″ mark is longer still. Remember, as the denominator gets smaller, the lines get longer.

- If you need to find ⅜″, just count over three groups of two little lines. You'll find yourself in the area of ⅛″ longer than ¼″. As you become more familiar with the tape measure you'll find you remember shortcuts, such as ⅛″ longer than a quarter inch, or 1⁄16″ longer than half an inch. Just like driving through a neighborhood, you get these shortcuts down cold. Don't be afraid to count the little lines. Most people would rather you take more time and be exact than waste materials. (We won't use the old adage "Measure twice, cut once" because it's old and a little trite. But it's true. We just won't say it.)
- *Why is there this slot in the end of—what did you call it—the slip hook?* This horizontal slot in the slip hook is actually there to allow you to take outside measurements from a point, for instance, a point in the middle of a floor, where you don't have anything to hook onto. Simply drive a nail or a screw into the point and the slot on the slip hook grabs the nail head and allows you to pull as far away from the point as you like. This slot-and-nail system also lets you use your tape measure as a compass. Hook the tape as before, and place your pencil or marker at the side of the measurement on the tape that matches the radius of the circle you'd like to trace. Slowly, holding the marker next to the tape as you move, pivot around the screw, keeping it tight to the nail head as you circle your center point, until you come back to where you started.

It's Hip to Be a Square

Another extremely important tool you need for your toolbox is a *square*. Ironically, squares aren't really square. Most are L shaped, and a few are actually triangular. First let's define what being square means. When we say something is square we aren't referring to its shape; we are referring to how close it is to 90°. We like flats to the square where they're supposed to be square. The same thing goes with platforms. This makes covering platforms and flat frames, joining flats to other flats, and legging platforms easier when there is a square corner. They also look better.

The most important kind of square every scene shop needs is a *framing square*, or *carpenter square*, as it is sometimes called. This is a giant L-shaped square. It has many uses. Being as large as it is, 16″ on the short leg of the L and 24″ on the long leg, makes it possible to square large scenic pieces and do floor layouts.

How do you check something for square? The basic idea is to lay the square on the object and see if it matches the L shape. There are two ways of doing this. You can place the square directly on what you want to check for square, such as paint lines on the floor, lining up the outside edges of the square to the paint lines. The other way is to hook the square over the edge of the object—let's say a flat. Hold the square as tight as you can to the edges of the flat. If you see any light between the square and the edges of the flat, then the flat isn't perfectly square.

Figure 3.26: *(from top to bottom) Speed square, combination square, and carpenter's square.*

As you look at the framing square (Figure 3.26) you'll notice measurements all around it. These allow you to do inside and outside measurements. As you may notice, the measurements on the outside and the measurements on the inside of the L start in different places and don't really line up side to side exactly. The long leg of most framing squares is 2″ wide. The short leg is 1½″ wide. That's one reason. The second reason is a lot like the flooding zero on the tape measure: By starting the numbers on the inside edge of the L you can do inside measurements, and vice versa.

Speed squares are used in the construction trade to quickly cut angles for roof beams, which is why they are sometimes called *roofing squares*. For us, the squares are handy because they fit into our toolbox and squeeze quite nicely into quarters of flats and platforms. There's a little slot in the corner of every framing square; this is the *pivot point*. When lining it up to the degree lines on the hypotenuse of the blade of the triangle, you can measure and mark angles to cut. This is a handy feature. Most stage carpenters don't use this feature, however. There's another tool that we will be mentioning soon that works better for this.

Another thing that makes the speed square nice for your use is the raised edges that allow you to hook the square on the edge of a flat or platform. This gives you a firm grip and ensures that you have good contact with the board. While this lets you draw a nice square line, it also lets you use the speed square as a saw guide. By holding the square firm to the board, you create a square fence you can run your circular saw against, giving you a square cut.

Some Other Useful Marking Tools and Layout Tools

We mentioned *layout* when we spoke of the framing square. We weren't referring to tanning. Laying something out is basically drawing it (the angle or the shape you want) in full scale on whatever you want to cut, paint, or build your set. This needs to be

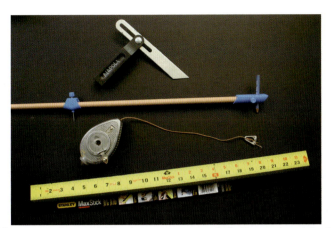

Figure 3.27: *(from top to bottom) T bevel, beam compass, chalk line, and straightedge.*

done precisely, especially in the case of a scenic artist transferring a designer's rendering to a flat or drop for paint treatments.

The angle-marking tool we mentioned earlier is known as a *T bevel* or *angle bevel*. Some people call it "that angle thingy you use to measure the corners that aren't really square and stuff." Try going into a store and getting one of those (Figure 3.27). There are three parts to a T bevel: the handle, the blade, and the knob to tighten the blade to the angle you want to set. The way you use the T bevel is to loosen the blade and pivot it to whatever angle you need to trace, let's say an irregularly shaped corner of a platform skin. Tighten the knob to hold the angle till you trace it to the board you want to cut. When you are done, loosen the knob again and store the blade in the slot of the handle. This tool would bake nicely into a pie, but, really, what is the point? Other versions of this tool contain protractors and can be quite large by comparison.

Another useful layout tool is the *straightedge*. This is just a big, straight ruler made of steel, or a yardstick, or a board. The longer it is, the longer line you can draw. But that isn't the only way to draw a straight line.

A *chalk line* can draw a straight line between two points without a straightedge. This tool, shaped like a diamond, has a little crank on the side. At the top of the chalk line is a little hook or clip similar to the one on the tape measure. It has the same kind of slot in it for a nail or screw head. Place this end on the first point and stretch it to your next point. You'll notice as you pull on the chalk line that some string covered in chalk dust is following you. Don't be alarmed. This is good. This is where the chalk line gets its name. Once you reach your second point, snapping the taut line will transfer the chalk dust to the ground. Since chalk, for the most part, is removable, this makes a good temporary straight line. There are several colors of chalk dust to choose from, with white being the most temporary and red the most permanent.

When you used your tape measure as a compass, you actually created a rudimentary *beam compass*. There are actually little gismos you can buy that do the same thing. We call them *trammel points*. They look like that old school compass that was in your pencil box (your mother probably took it away from you because it was too sharp), but split in half and with clamps on each piece. These clamps attach the point side and the marking side to the beam, board, or piece of steel or straightedge. The pivot end goes on your center point, and the whole thing works like the tape measure compass.

Other Items in the Toolbox

So far we have the hammer, a toolbox saw, a pair of slip-joint pliers, a fencing tool, needle-nose pliers, a mat knife, a multitool, a speed square, a tape measure, and a chalk box. You'll also need to carry a pencil. It's really important. Just like the tape measure, you can't work without one. A small notepad for writing measurements is also a good idea.

Screwdrivers

Additionally, you'll need to have a Phillips-head screwdriver (from the top it looks like a little × point) and a straight-blade screwdriver (self-defining). Yes, cordless screw guns are easily available and very cool to use. But they aren't good for everything. Sometimes only a hand-turned screwdriver will work, such as when you assemble a doorknob set or remove the packing screw from a battery case. A powered screwdriver could strip the screw head (which means destroying the head, so you can't turn it, also called *caming*) or snap the head off because of the motor's powerful speed and torque or because its bulk could not reach into a tight space.

Personal Protective Equipment (PPE)

Next is your *personal protective equipment* (*PPE*). This includes safety glasses, dust masks, and earplugs. Some shops provide these. If you're serious about this work, you should have your own (Figure 3.28).

Safety Glasses

Safety glasses come in different styles. Some work like goggles and slip on with a strap, most work like regular glasses, and some are made to fit over your own glasses. Whichever you choose, pick a pair whose style and fit are comfortable enough for you to keep them on.

It's not a good idea to wear tinted outdoor safety glasses indoors for shop work. As cool as you may look, it won't be so cool when your reduced vision causes you to cut off your finger. There are new lenses out there with a UV coating and slight tint that

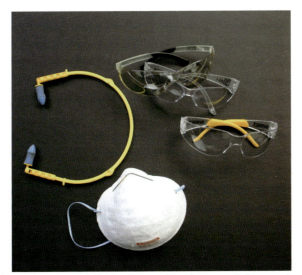

Figure 3.28: *(clockwise from upper left) Earplugs, safety glasses, and dust mask.*

are called *IO glasses*, or *in/out glasses*. These don't impair indoor vision, and they cut glare outside. They are a better choice.

Dust Masks

Dust masks, or nuisance masks, are a good idea. Breathing particulates into your lungs for a long period of time is a bad idea. Use one when sanding most woods, cutting Masonite or Homosote or other boards that produce a fine dust. Remember, these masks protect you from dust or other fine particles, not fumes or vapors. *Respirators* (masks designed to filter specific fumes) and adequate ventilation should be provided for you when working with hazardous substances. Consult your TD, the product warning label, and the MSDS (material safety data sheet) for the product before using it. If you don't have all the safety equipment you need, don't use it.

Earplugs

The most effective earplugs are the expanding foam plugs. A lot of shops provide these, and they are disposable. You scrunch these things up between your fingers and insert them directly into your ear cavity. This foam has a memory, so once you scrunch it, it wants to return to its original state. This forms a tight seal that reduces noise. Other types are banded together and inserted into your ears or worn like earmuffs over the ears. These plugs don't block out all noise; they just reduce it to safe levels.

Earplugs are rated according to their NRR (Noise Reduction Rating, governed by OSHA, the Occupational Safety and Health Administration). These guidelines state that prolonged exposure to noise over 85 decibels (dB) requires hearing protection. Just to give you an idea, a baby's cry is about that loud. Table saws are louder. You'll want an NRR of 26 dB or higher for the work we do.

Wrenches

Under these in your toolbox you'll need an 8″ adjustable wrench. It's a good size for the work we do, and by turning the adjustment dial you can expand and contract the jaws to fit the size bolt or nut head you want to turn. If you want individual wrenches, that's up to you. The sizes we use most are $5/16$″ ($1/4$″ bolt heads and nuts), $7/16$″, ($1/2$″ bolt heads and nuts), and the most common, $9/16$″ ($3/8$″ bolt heads and nuts). You can also get these sizes in a socket set. *Sockets* are tubes of metal that fit over the nut or bolt head, with facets or points on the inside to catch and grip the edges of the fastener. You can insert these on a *ratchet handle*, a geared crank that mechanically increases the amount of force you apply by turning the socket faster, or with an adapter on a cordless screw gun, or a pneumatic wrench like car repair shops use. The last two won't fit in you toolbox, however.

Power Tools

Just say the name: *power tools*. It's a tool, but it's powerful. What could be better? Let's start with the king of the power tool beasts: the table saw. It's one of the scariest tools for beginners to use. But once you comprehend its terms and the safety procedures that go along with it, the other tools will be a snap to understand.

Circular Saw Family

There is a story about the origin of the table saw: A Shaker woman in 1813 was watching men using a two-man pull saw to saw logs and thought there must be a better way. So she took a pie pan and cut little teeth into it. Then she attached the pan to a spinning wheel, and the power saw was born. One of the important things you can take from the story is that we need to work smarter, not harder; and another is that the blade in the spinning wheel saw is round or circular. (The third thing is that you shouldn't eat directly from a Shaker woman's pie pan because the edges could be sharp.) Therefore, the table saw belongs to the family of circular saws. Let's examine this blade (Figure 3.29).

The first thing you'll see is the hole in the center of the blade. Besides making the blade look like a vicious donut, this hole is where the saw blade gets attached to the *arbor*, or the part of the saw that turns the blade. This arbor can be turned directly by the motor, making it a *direct-drive* saw, or can be turned by a belt, making the saw *belt driven*. The next things we'll examine are the teeth. They look remarkably like the teeth on a handsaw, a ripsaw to be exact. Each of these teeth has a set to it, like the handsaw teeth.

Figure 3.29: *Circular saw blade.*

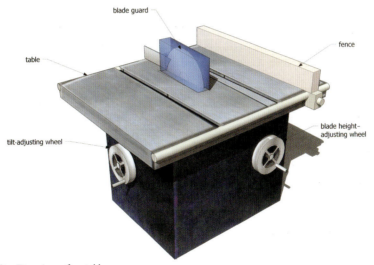

Figure 3.30: *Drawing of a table saw.*

The blade is supported on both sides of the arbor by a thick washer called a *blade flange*. These keep the blade stiff and prevent it from warping side to side. One goes on first and the other sandwiches the blade between them. Then the arbor nut goes on to hold this all in place. Sounds easy, right? Well, it is if you know that the majority of arbors and their nuts are reverse threaded, which means to put it on you need to turn it like you're taking it off. This prevents the spinning action of the blade and arbor from loosening the blade.

Saw Terms Wheel Need a Hand Adjusting To

Now that we know a little about the blade let's look at the rest of the saw (Figure 3.30). Another important part of the table saw is the *table*. It looks like a table. The blade sticks through the surface of the table and nestles snuggly under the *blade guard*.

The blade itself doesn't really need to be guarded. There's not much that can happen to a blade that would hurt it. The guard covers the blade to prevent your accidental contact with it. The blade can be raised or lowered by turning the *blade-raising hand-wheel*, located under the face of the table. Another handwheel, located near the blade-raising handwheel, controls the tilt of the blade. We call it the *tilt-adjusting handwheel*.

Give Me Kerf, Lots of Kerf, Under Sawdust Skies Above . . . Don't Fence Me in, or Ripping Tales You Can Sink Your Teeth into

Back on the tabletop, to the right of the blade on most saws, is the saw's *fence*. You can remember the name by means of this simple mnemonic. Imagine there are little horses, cows, or sheep running across the saw table until they are stopped by the fence. Okay, so it's not really a great mnemonic, but it is a vivid image, and you can't forget it if you try. The fence rises up out of the table just like a real fence rises up out of the ground. The difference between them (besides size, shape, material, and, well, they really don't look a lot alike) is that the saw fence is meant to move.

By sliding the saw fence, you can adjust the distance between the blade and the fence and thereby the width of the cut. For instance, imagine we are cutting a 1 × 6 (which is 5½″ wide, remember?) into two 1 × 3's. The board is pushed with its face flat down on the table saw's table, and one edge rides along the fence, using it as a guide. You have adjusted the distance between the blade and the fence to be 2½″ (the size of a 1 × 3, but you knew that). As you push the board, the saw blade spins toward you, ripping a ⅛″ kerf into the board, leaving you with two pieces, one that is 2½″ wide and one that is 2⅞″.

"Hold it buckaroo," you say. "That doesn't add up." Yipee-ki-yea! You noticed! Remember the kerf? Again, you never get that wood back. Run this 2⅞″ board through the table saw again without changing the fence's setting and you get a 1 × 3 and a thin ¼″ strip of wood and, of course, sawdust.

Safety Devices and Accessories on the Table Saw

Blade Guard

Another important piece of the table saw is the blade guard (Figure 3.31). If your saw doesn't have one, you need to add one to it. It's vital to your personal safety. A TD we know went to a small family-owned fence shop to scout out some fencing supplies for a show. While he waited to speak to someone, he noticed that their radial arm saw had obviously been in service for many years and it didn't have a blade guard. When he saw the shop's foreman come through the door, he thought he'd ask him about it, but changed his mind when the foreman took off his gloves to shake the TD's hand. You guessed it: He had only three fingers on his right hand.

Figure 3.31: *Blade guard.*

The blade guard, as our story illustrates, guards you from the blade. It sits above the blade like a cage. Usually it is made of a tough, clear acrylic that is shatter resistant but soft enough that if it should by chance make contact with the blade, it wouldn't hurt the blade or send broken teeth flying like little carbide missiles.

Splitter

The next safety device on the table saw is the splitter. It sits behind the blade, and quite often it is built into the blade guard. It consists of a stiff but thin piece of metal that rides in the kerf and splits the two edges of the kerf from pinching together. To understand why this is so important, it helps to know what *kickback* is. Kickback is what happens when a board edge moves away from the fence and comes in contact with the backside of the blade where the teeth are coming up out of the table. This can lift the board off the table and throw the board back at you. Sitting behind the blade, the splitter prevents the edges from making contact with the blade.

A Pawl-ing Safety Device

Near or connected to the splitter are the *antikickback pawls*, or *pawls* (Figure 3.32). These are two spring-loaded devices with little barbs on the bottom. They are curved on the bottom so that the edge of the board pushes them up as it passes. Since on kickback the board raises up a bit as the blade's teeth catch it; the spring-loaded barbs on the pawls dig into the wood and trap it against the table. Some old-timers don't like these safety devices. They say, "I can count on one hand the times it's saved me." We say, "How many fingers are on that hand?"

Support Your Local Dead Man

Once the board has passed the saw blade, there are three possibilities for what happens to it: It falls to the ground, a helper supports the end of it and keeps it from falling,

Figure 3.32: *Close-up of the saw's safety devices: guard, splitter, and pawls.*

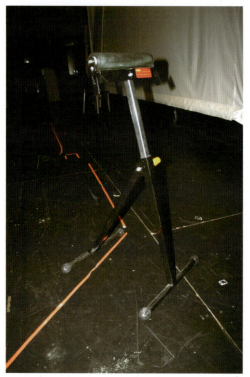

Figure 3.33: *Folding dead man.*

or it rides against the top of the *outfeed table*. This table is really just an extension of the saw table, but positioned behind it. And it is particularly helpful with long lengths of lumber. But as we said, that is not the only possibility. The helper who supports the lumber is actually acting as a *dead man*. This has no reflection on his acting ability; he's taking the part of another outfeed device, similar to the outfeed table, known as a *dead man*. This device is basically a roller on a stand (Figure 3.33). This is an option if you don't have room for a permanent outfeed table.

Figure 3.34: *Operator adjusting the blade height with the assistance of her not-so-dead man (notice the unplugged saw plug).*

Safe Ripping Procedures, or How to Be a Dead Man and Still Be Useful in the Shop

It's not as easy as you think to play dead. Let's look at the process involved with ripping a sheet of ¾″ × 4′ × 8′ plywood into 6″ strips and see how it's done.

1. First, the person who will be operating the saw (let's call her the *operator*) puts on her safety glasses and ear protection and checks to make sure that her partner (the *dead man*) is wearing his. Then they secure any loose clothing, hair, or jewelry that could catch in the saw's machinery or on the board itself.

2. Next the operator unplugs the saw. This seems counterproductive, but it isn't. Anytime you are doing any kind of adjustment on a power tool, you need to disconnect it from the power source to prevent accidental starting of the tool (Figure 3.34).

3. Third, she lifts up the blade guard and adjusts the blade height with the blade height–adjusting handwheel. The height of the blade should be adjusted to approximately ¼″ higher than the thickness of the wood. In this case, that would be 1″ from the top of the table. Once it's adjusted, she'll lock it down with the adjustment lock. On most saws this is just a knob on the handwheel that you will tighten down.

➤ **TIP** A quick way of doing this is to have a piece of scrap the same thickness as the board you are going to cut. Lay it beside the saw blade (again checking that the power is disconnected) and raise it up flush to the top tooth of the blade. If you then take a piece of ¼″ material and lay it on top of the board and raise it flush to this height, you'll get the height you need above the board without measuring. You've just created a *jig*, a device used to make repetitive tasks faster and more accurate. You'll be hearing more about these soon.

4. At this time she wants to check the fence and the blade angle to see if they are square to the table. If the fence isn't square, the board can slide into the back of the spinning blade and, as we now know, cause kickback. Checking the blade angle the first time you use the saw is a good idea as well. Quite often someone who used the saw before you (and forgot the universal table saw etiquette of returning the blade to 90° when done) can make a bevel cut that puts a shallow angle, such as a 1° tilt, to the blade that she won't notice with her naked eye. She inspects the safety devices—the blade guard, splitter, and pawls—at this time to make sure they are working. Sometimes people break a tool and either forget to tell someone or just walk away from it so that they don't get blamed. This is a bad idea. Every TD and shop foreman wants to know when a tool isn't functioning, especially safety equipment, to save time and prevent injuries. They may not be thrilled to discover it's broken, but if someone gets hurt they'll be even less thrilled. So it's best to check everything. You never know what you may be walking into.

   ➤ **TIP** A quick way to check a fence for square is to slide it up to a *miter gauge slot*. These are shallow slots in the table that the miter gauge slides into. The miter gauge looks like a protractor on a metal stick. The stick rides in that slot. You use it to make crosscuts and miter cuts on the table saw. For that reason it needs to be square to the table, and you can slide the fence right up to it and use it the same way you check for square with a framing square.

   • You would normally check the blade's "squareness" with a speed square or some other small square. Nowadays, most push shoes have a 90° setup jig built into them, along with other common angles and blade heights. More about push shoes in a minute (Figure 3.35).

5. Next the operator sets the fence. There are two ways to do this.
   • One way is to look at the set of the teeth on the blade. She'll find one that has its set pointed toward the fence. This tooth is what will cut the inside edge of the saw kerf toward the fence. With her tape measure she takes an inside measurement from that tooth to the fence, in which the slip hook is on the fence and the numbers are above the point of the tooth. Then she adjusts the fence until she gets the measurement she needs (Figure 3.36).
   • The second way is simpler but not always as accurate. Many saws have a tape measure built into them that sits on the rail the fence rides on. A

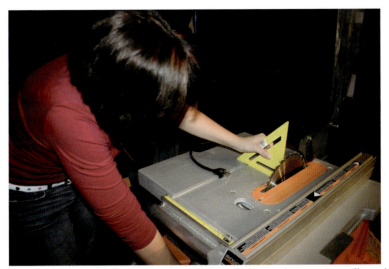

Figure 3.35: *Operator checking the square of the blade with the speed square (we still see the unplugged plug).*

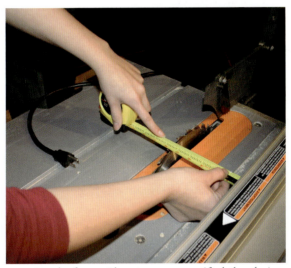

Figure 3.36: *Operator setting the fence with a tape measure (find the plug).*

cursor is offset to read the measurement to the fence from the blade's tooth, just like the operator did in the last paragraph. It's not as accurate because until you make a cut you don't know if the tape is correctly calibrated or adjusted. The first method is a good way to check the fence tape's accuracy (Figure 3.37).

6. There is a *fence lock* on all fences to prevent accidental shifting of the fence; that would cause kickback, and we hate that. At this point she uses that lock, which clamps the fence to the table and fence rail.

Figure 3.37: *Close-up of the saw rail showing the saw's built-in tape and fence rail lock.*

7. Now, with everything adjusted, she lowers the blade guard, makes sure the table is clear of anything that might be pushed into the blade or catch on the board, and plugs in the saw. Notice we didn't say turns it on.

8. Here's where we talk about the *push shoe.* (You can make your own from plywood or hardwood, but we discuss the commercial type). It looks like a shoe. It has a toe with a little rubber gripper on it that holds the board down and points toward the blade. Also, as with any good shoe, it has a heel that catches the back edge of the board. Above both of these is a handle with which you push the shoe and the board you are ripping. By using this shoe when ripping strips thinner than 8″ you can still push the wood through the space between the fence and the blade and guard with your hand up and away from the blade. The operator takes the shoe and places it where she can easily reach it when it comes time to use it.

9. Next she wakes up the dead man and tells him to wipe the drool off his face. Then she walks to the back edge of the sheet of plywood, and the dead man lifts the leading edge onto the edge of the saw's table (Figure 3.38).

10. He stays on the side opposite the fence and *supports the edge of the plywood from that side.* That's all he's supposed to do. In spite of any temptation he may feel, he should *never* push the board. That's the operator's job. If it was his job, he'd be the "not-so-dead pushy" guy or the "I'm looking for all the glory, so I'm going to push the board too, causing massive kickback when I jam my side into the back of the blade" man. But he's not either of these because they are wrong and unsafe and no one wants a name that's a really long and wordy sentence.

11. Now they can turn on the saw—that is, after they check to make sure the board is not up against the blade when the motor starts. This is unsafe and is

Figure 3.38: *Dead man and operator in their start positions (he is there to support her).*

bad for the motor and blade. It may also cause a series of two-headed cats to be born in the local vicinity, but we have no way to verify that. Just don't do it. Most times the dead man is closer to the start button.

12. The blade is spinning and the operator is smiling because her dead man is letting her do all the pushing. She's standing a bit to the left of the blade in case the piece of wood she's cutting jams and kicks back. This keeps her out of the path of any possible ejections.

13. She begins to push. The leading edge of the board slides under the blade guard, and the antikickback pawls rock up a bit in their ready position as the leading edge passes them on its way to the splitter.

14. The board doesn't kick back though, because as she is feeding the lumber she is watching the blade and the fence (similar to the way you watch the road ahead of you and glance at your rearview mirror while you drive). She is looking to make sure the edge siding against the fence stays against the fence. She's feeding it nice and easy, letting the saw do the work. The dead man is slowly moving his hands with the board as he supports it.

15. Now the trailing edge is just about at the edge of the saw's table. She slows down or stops feeding for a second, secure in the knowledge that her partner

Figure 3.39: *Operator pushing the trailing edge with the push shoe.*

would never think of pushing, and she pulls out the push shoe by its handle from wherever she kept it, hooks the heel on the trailing edge, and continues to push the board all the way through, past the blade (Figure 3.39).

16. She now turns off the saw, waits until the blade stops spinning, and clears the cut piece from the path of the blade. Her partner has just slid the plywood back into the starting position. She takes out her tape measure and checks the board to see if it is the correct measurement.

17. Since it is, they can start the cutting again without any further adjustments. It makes them feel good that they both know the proper safety procedures and can work well together and trust each other. And they'll sleep well tonight, knowing that no two-headed cats were born on their watch because of some careless action of theirs at the table saw.

Miter Gauges and Crosscuts

We spoke of miter gauges and crosscutting on the table saw briefly. Here's how it works (Figure 3.40). You set the angle of the cut by loosening the adjustment knob, turning the protractor, and tightening the adjustment knob to lock it when you set it to where you want it. The gauge has its own fence, which faces the blade when it's in its slot. You mark your measurement on the piece of wood so that when you place an edge up tight to the fence you can see the mark as you look over the miter fence.

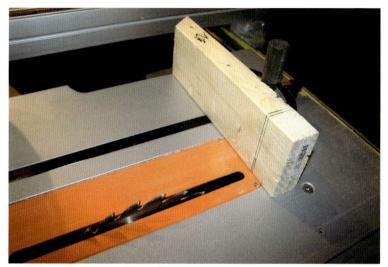

Figure 3.40: *Miter gauge with auxiliary fence and saw cut.*

> ➤ **TIP** There are screw holes on the face of this fence that let you attach an auxiliary wooden fence to the miter gauge. This can give you greater surface area to clamp your workpiece to or add a stop block to. Run the miter gauge with the new fence on it past the blade and make a cut into the gauge. This gives you your line-up mark to the saw's kerf. Place your board's measurement mark to line up with the kerf edge you just cut. Make sure that the kerf is on the same side as the miter gauge.

The rest of the process is similar to ripping. You stand clear of the blade's ejection path, just like before. Your right hand holds the adjustment knob, and your left hand holds the workpiece against the fence, staying at least 6″ away from the blade and guard. (The fence is removed in this process to prevent the scrap from binding between it and the blade, which would eject it).

Another cut that the miter gauge allows you to make is known as a *dado*. A dado is made when the blade is lowered so that it only partially cuts through the board. This comes in handy when creating wood joints, such as a half lap joint. The board is held against the miter gauge fence as with a miter cut, and repeated passes are made, each time sliding the board over so that you are widening the kerf you already cut by another blade's width.

Yes, these repeated cuts are time consuming. That's why they invented the dado blade (Figure 3.41). The advantage to the dado blade is that it makes a wider cut, either by stacking blades together (a *stacked dado*) or by cocking the blades at a bit of an angle to each other on the arbor. The last type is known as a *wobble dado*, which describes what it looks like when it spins.

(a)

(b)

(c)

Figure 3.41: *Dado blades: (a) the blade in the saw; (b) dial-style dado; (c) detail showing the bottom blade and the chipper blades used to widen a cut (top blade not shown).*

Figure 3.42: *Operator turning on a 14" delta radial arm saw.*

I Miter Saw That Crosscut (This Title Must Be Read Aloud with a Pirate Accent)

Since we have miters fresh in our minds, let's talk about the crosscutting branch of the circular saw family, which we call *miter saws*. This branch is a bit different from the table saw in that, to cut, you move the saw instead of the wood. The patriarch of this family is the *radial arm saw*. Let's look at how it works.

The radial arm saw has five major parts (Figure 3.42). The first two we are familiar with, the table and the fence. The table on a radial arm saw is relatively shallow when compared to a table saw (but then again it doesn't need to be wider. If it did, we'd call it something like a "radial table saw" and we don't want to). The fence, unlike the table saw's fence, doesn't move at all and, perhaps because of this, is better suited to preventing those little horses and sheep we spoke of from running all over the table. You'll see why the fence doesn't need to move in a minute.

Hanging above the table like an outstretched metal arm is the radial arm saw's . . . well, you've probably figured it out, but we'll say it anyhow, arm. This piece is what allows the saw to cut miters. If you remember the miter gauge for the table saw, there was a fence and a protractor-like part that you could set at an angle. The arm can be set to an angle as well.

123

If John Was the Walrus, Why Am I the Horse?

The fifth part of the saw is the *carriage*. This is the actual saw part of the radial arm saw. The carriage is basically everything on the table saw, except the height adjustment, in a small package. Right now you're thinking "Why do they call it a carriage? That has nothing to do with cutting. Does it have anything to do with the little horses and sheep we keep hearing about?" Well actually, it describes the way it moves.

The carriage is suspended from underneath the arm by the *yoke*. This is more horse imagery: A yoke is a U-shaped harness made to fit over a horse's neck. The yoke is then connected to whatever the horse is pulling, a carriage, for instance. The yoke has little wheels that ride in the arm's track, and by taking the carriage's handle and pulling it towards you, you actually become the horse in this metaphor and move the saw across the table. (Another example of why we call it a crosscutting saw).

A Multi-Power Tool

The yoke's U shape allows the saw to do a lot of interesting things that made the radial arm saw pretty cool when it first came out. The carriage can be tilted inside the yoke, which tilts the blade, similar to the way the table saw blade can be tilted. The blade can be rotated at 90° to the arm and locked in place. In this position you can actually use your crosscutting saw to rip. You can do this by locking the carriage in the 90° orientation, adjusting the arm to the distance from the fence you want your cut to be, and locking the carriage there. Then you push your board through the saw, using the fence as a guide, just like with the table saw. As with any multipurpose tool, it's harder to rip like this than with a table saw, which is designed to rip. Table saws, by comparison, are harder to crosscut with than crosscutting saws.

As we said, you can also rotate the saw in the yoke so that it creates an angled cut, similar to the blade tilt on the table saw. When you combine this adjustment with the arm's miter adjustment, you've created a *compound miter adjustment*. This allows you to cut a *compound angle*, which is a cut that has two angles, an angle to the face and an angle to the edge.

There are attachments you can add to the radial arm saw that take further advantage of the yoke and its pivot. But for what we do, they really aren't much help, and fewer and fewer people are using this saw for anything but crosscutting. The major disadvantage to these attachments, such as a planer, router, and molding head, is the time lost converting the saw back and forth.

Miter Be Getting Cranky? I Dado, What About You?

One last adjustment to the radial arm saw we haven't spoken of yet is the blade height. Most saws have a crank at the front of the table facing you; some saws place it above the arm. Wherever it is, by cranking it you can raise and lower the blade, similar to the table saw. But the entire arm goes up and down, carrying the carriage and the blade with it.

Kerfing and Dados

By adjusting the height, we can make dado cuts easily. In fact, we often make a series of dados, loosely spaced, called *kerfing*. Kerfing is designed to allow you to bend wood. The kerfs in these cuts, as you know, are slots in the board where there is no longer any wood. After you make the cut (set to a depth with the height adjustment crank about half the thickness of the board) and begin to bend the wood, the edges of the kerf want to bend in to touch each other. If you've ever scored cardboard with a sharp knife and bent it, you've done practically the same thing. This process works exceptionally well on the radial arm saw.

You can put a dado head on a radial arm saw. Since it's too wide to fit inside most saws' blade guards, you have to leave them off. As our three-fingered friend illustrates, a guardless radial arm saw is a spooky proposition. So think carefully before leaving off a guard.

Safely Cutting on the Radial Arm Saw

The key to being safe on the radial arm saw is to know where your hands are. This sounds like common sense. It is. But when we get busy, we get distracted and the simple things are forgotten. It's best, then, to make safety procedures a common practice.

One of the universal safety procedures around power tools is to use your PPE (personal protective equipment). In addition to protecting your hearing and your eyes, you need to secure your sleeves, hair, jewelry, or anything else that may dangle and get caught in the path of the saw. This brings us back to where your hands should be. Let's start with marking your board.

It's All About Kerf

There are two parts to a board you're cutting: the part you want and the part you don't. We call the part you want the *workpiece*. You can also call it the *good piece* (not because of some moral criteria it fulfills, but because we have to call it something, and you didn't like the term *workpiece*. It's always about you, isn't it?). The other piece is the *scrap piece*. Why is this important? It's all about kerf. And what do we know about kerf? You never get it back. So we want the kerf to come out of the scrap. This is one of the most common mistakes beginners make. You know you've made this mistake if all your good pieces are short by ⅛″, or the thickness of the blade.

Figure 3.43: *Picture of a board showing the bird's beak, measurement, and scrap markings.*

Making Your Mark

The way to avoid this mistake is to carefully mark the board so that you know which side of the kerf is the good side and which is the scrap side. Start with your tape measure by taking an outside measurement along the edge of the board that will face the fence. Then place a mark on that edge at the measurement you need. The mark that is the easiest to see is the *bird's beak*, or a little arrow with a very short tail (Figure 3.43).

The Cutting Edge

Now our board is divided into two different sides: the one we want and the one we don't. How do we tell them apart? The best thing to do is immediately to mark the scrap side before you even bring it near the saw. You can do this by marking it with the word *scrap* or just a big "X". Why is this important? You would be surprised how often you can be distracted between marking the board and cutting it.

Take the board over to the radial arm saw and lay it up against the fence. Before you place the board against the fence to cut it, check the board for staples, screws, nails, or loose knots that could be caught by the blade and kicked back at you.

Next, look along the fence and sweep away any sawdust that might be piled against it. Even a little bit of sawdust between your board and the fence can take your cut out of square, since the board won't be square against the fence, which is square to the blade. Slide the board over to toward the fence until the bird's beak on your board is even with the blade. (The bird's beak we are referring to is the mark on your board; we're not implying anything about your appearance—after all, we can't see you.)

Without turning the saw on, pull the carriage up to the bird's beak. Adjust the board so that one edge of the blade is against the center of the bird's beak and the other is

126

inside the edge you marked scrap. By doing this you will cut the kerf out of the scrap and your board will be the right size.

Cutting the Board, Not Your Hands

Your board is lined up. What's next? Here is where we decide where your hands are going to go. We know that one hand is going to be on the handle of the carriage pulling the spinning blade through the wood. That hand is clear of the blade's path. We need to make sure the other one is as well. The other hand needs to hold the board tightly against the fence to prevent kickback and to keep the board from sliding out of proper alignment with your bird's beak (the mark, not your appearance). To avoid injury, this hand should be well clear of the blade, at least 10″–12″.

Cutting from the Armpit

Next, make sure the carriage is all the way back under the arm as far as it can go—let's call this place the *armpit*—and it won't come in contact with the board before the blade starts to spin. Before you turn on the saw, check your hand position on the board again. When you are sure you are safely in the clear, switch on the saw. Reach into the armpit and grab the carriage handle. Slowly pull the carriage toward you. Once you are through the board, return the carriage back to the armpit and shut off the saw. That's when you can release the hand holding the board to the fence. If you move it too soon, you risk hitting the blade with the board, which at best will nick it and at worst kick it back at you.

Miter Be Another Saw That Crosscuts?

The little brother of the radial arm saw is the *power miter box saw* or, as some call it, the *chop saw*. It cuts miters just like the radial arm saw, but it doesn't have a radial arm. Instead this saw looks more like those paper cutters your teachers wouldn't let you touch in grade school (Figure 3.44). It works pretty much the same way: You grab the handle, squeeze the trigger, and lower the blade into the wood. After that, all the same safety measures apply: Hold the board tight to the fence and keep your hand clear of the blade.

Actually, when you think about it, that chopping action is the same action you use to cut paper, and it's where this saw gets the name *chop saw*. The chopping action actually helps you set the blade depth. There is usually a depth-stop adjustment screw that stops the blade from lowering past whatever depth you set it to. Imagine that paper cutter. Imagine that when your teacher wasn't looking you jammed a pencil under the blade and tried to cut a stack of paper thicker than the pencil. Only a few sheets would get cut until the blade was stopped by the pencil. The pencil is acting like a depth stop. If you pulled a stunt like this, it explains why your teachers wouldn't let you near the paper cutter.

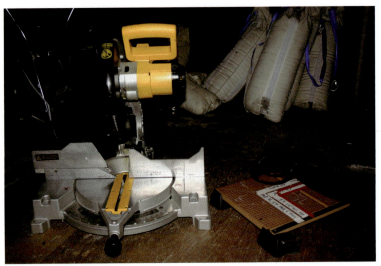

Figure 3.44: *DeWalt chop saw and paper cutter.*

Adjusting the Angles

The angle of the miter box saw is adjusted by rotating the saw's table and blade arm. It looks a bit like the table saw's miter gauge. The difference is the adjustment knob sticks straight out of the table. By loosening this knob and rotating the table you turn the blade arm at an angle to the fence. You can also cut a compound angle with the blade tilt adjustment. This is usually behind the blade arm and tilts the entire assembly to an angle to the table.

Electric Slide

The big brother in the crosscutting saw family is the *sliding compound miter saw.* Aside from having a really cool name that makes you sound like you really know something when you use it ("Joe, go get me that sliding compound miter saw on the double! We have a compound miter emergency! Move it man!"), the sliding compound miter saw is a combination of the radial arm saw and the power miter box saw, in a portable package (Figure 3.45).

It looks like a chop saw and can cut like one, and its tilt adjustment, blade depth, and miter adjustments are pretty much the same. However, the sliding function of the saw lets you slide the carriage out to cut wider boards than a chop saw might. It's slightly bigger than a miter box saw and smaller than a radial arm saw. And it's a lot less expensive than a radial arm saw. Many people don't see the reason for buying a radial arm saw since the sliding compound miter saw or slider has the features you commonly use and you don't have to pay for the features you don't, like routing and planing. The versatility, size, and cost effectiveness are why it has replaced the radial arm in many shops.

Figure 3.45: *"Slider" on the job site during DeSales University's production of* The Foreigner.

Scrolling Saws

A *scroll cut* is a cut in a board that takes a loopy or curving path. As you might guess, none of the saws we've mentioned is good at this. In fact, when using these saws, that is the very kind of cut you would want to avoid. So how do we make those kinds of cuts? There are two main saws we can use to make curved cuts.

Bandsaw

The bandsaw could technically be considered a circular saw. Its blade travels in a circular motion. But really we don't think of it that way. Unlike the Shaker woman's pie pan, the bandsaw blade doesn't look like a vicious doughnut. The saw gets its name from the shape of its blade (Figure 3.46). The blade is literally a band with teeth that travels in a circular motion stretched between two giant wheels that keep it spinning. The teeth on the blade travel down toward your workpiece, and this actually helps hold the workpiece to the table.

It's All in the Band

So why can you make curved cuts with the bandsaw? Because the blade is thinner than a circular saw blade, it can turn while it's cutting and not kick back. In fact, the smaller

Figure 3.46: *Delta bandsaw.*

the width of the blade, the tighter the curve you can make. A good working blade width is anywhere between ⅜″ wide and ½″ wide. This width allows you to make moderately tight curves and still be wide enough to make straight cuts with ease. One application of that wider blade is known as *resawing*, or the process of cutting thicker material into thinner material. For example, some saw mills use bandsaws to process logs into boards. Thinner blades allow you to do intricate scrollwork.

Big Loop Versus Vicious Donut

Unlike the table saw or the radial arm saw, there is no blade-depth adjustment on the bandsaw. Since its blade travels around in a continuous loop, the material is cut straight through. You can make beveled cuts with a bandsaw, but here again the bandsaw differs from its circular saw cousins. While in the case of the crosscutting and table saws you tilt the blade to make a beveled cut, the bandsaw asks you to kindly tilt its table.

You can add a fence to a bandsaw, if it didn't already come with one. These are most useful in resawing, where you are trying to get a consistent thickness of material. The biggest difficulty in resawing is what is known as *blade drift*. This describes what happens when you're cutting the material on the bandsaw and the blade drifts off the path you wanted to take. To counter this tendency, you need to be able to make minute adjustments as you're running the material through the blade. A conventional fence such as on the table saw makes this difficult since you can't maneuver the material to adjust for drift. A *resaw guide* added to the fence helps keep you on the straight and narrow (or thick, depending on what you are cutting). The resaw guide is generally domed in the middle, which allows you to adjust your workpiece slightly from side to side to keep it on the straight path.

The kerf on the bandsaw is usually very fine; in some cases the width of a pencil line. Quite often, with the thinner, finer-toothed blades, people just run the saw down the pencil line without worrying about the saw kerf.

The continuous loop of the bandsaw blade allows you to cut through thicker materials than you could with a table saw, which is generally 10″ in diameter, or even some of the larger crosscutting saw blades, which can be up to 14″ in diameter. The drawback of the continuous loop blade is that to the left side of the blade you are limited to the width of the bandsaw blade's loop.

Playing with the Band

This saw has many useful applications for theatre crafts. It's especially nice for cutting many kinds of foam, since circular saw blades are very thick and by comparison have coarser teeth that like to chew up foam. Of course the thinness of the blade makes the bandsaw an excellent tool for cutting the intricate curves we like to use in decorative pieces and props. You can also make long, angled cuts, especially those greater than 45°, which are difficult on crosscutting saws. Also, equipped with the proper blade, you can cut a variety of materials with the bandsaws, including metal.

Safe Cutting with the Bandsaw, or Avoiding Band-Aids

Probably the most important thing to remember when using the bandsaw, besides wearing your PPE, is that the blade guard should be in place. This saw is incredibly easy to use. It's quiet, it doesn't have angry-looking teeth, and kickback is almost non-existent. In fact, many people in your shop will try to use this saw for everything. This can be a problem, since this really isn't the best or fastest saw in your shop for making straight ripping cuts. "Familiarity breeds contempt," as the saying goes; people tend to get careless around the tool they find easy to use. The blade guard adjustment is one of the easiest things for them to forget.

Remember that with the table saw, we didn't want more than ¼″ of the blade to stick through the material we were cutting. Generally, no more than 1″ of the bandsaw's blade should be exposed above your workpiece when you're cutting. The blade guard adjustment is very easy to make. Behind the saw is an adjustment knob that you loosen, and then you slide the blade guard down to the height you need it and tighten up again.

Not only does this protect your fingers, it helps you make a more accurate cut. The blade guard is incorporated into the blade guides for the top part of the bandsaw. These guides hold the blade from flexing above and below the table. The more blade exposed above your workpiece, the more dangerous it is and the more likely the blade is to flex, which can cause drift or even snap it in two.

Relief Efforts

Another way a bandsaw blade can snap is to make too tight of a turn with too wide of a blade. The way to get around this is by making relief cuts. *Relief cuts* are kerf-widening cuts made to allow your blade to turn within these wider kerfs without binding. You can think of them as "k" turns for your bandsaw.

Let's take, as an example, the cutting of a simple key-shaped prop (Figure 3.47). Begin roughing out the shape by cutting a wide swath around your pencil outline (Figure 3.48). Then make straight cuts directly into each corner on the key shape. The next step is to come back in with another cut, just wide of the first cut, that pulls up to your pencil line the way you would pull into a parallel parking space. Drive the blade right into the first cut (Figure 3.49). This should release a piece of scrap (Figure 3.50). Slide the scrap out of your way. Rotate your workpiece around the blade so that you can drive into the opposite corner (Figure 3.51). If necessary, make another relief cut to clean out the opposite corner.

Another way to cut a relief cut is simply to back the blade up into its own kerf and then forward again, nibbling a wider kerf, and so on, until you get enough room to turn

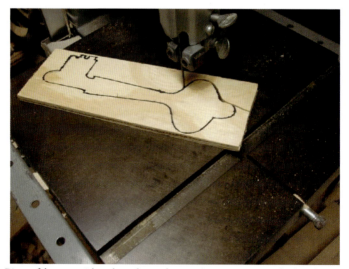

Figure 3.47: *Piece of luaun, with a key shape drawn on it, resting on the bandsaw table. (Courtesy of Bob and Theresa Napoli.)*

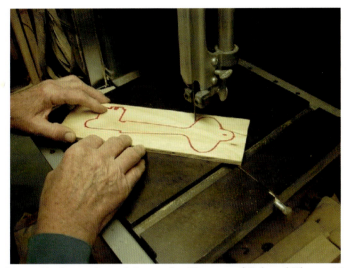

Figure 3.48: *Piece with the rough cut being made. (Courtesy of Bob and Theresa Napoli.)*

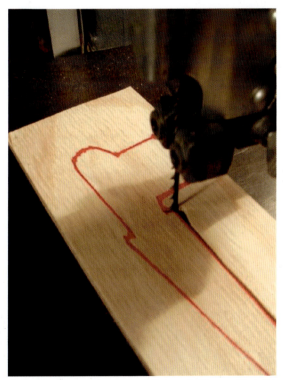

Figure 3.49: *Driving into the corner. (Courtesy of Bob and Theresa Napoli.)*

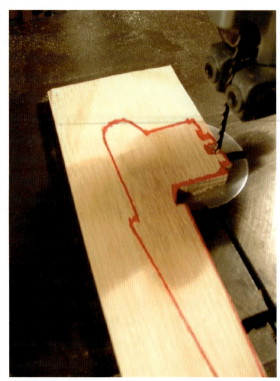

Figure 3.50: *Close-up of the cut around the key's teeth, with the scrap relieved from the cut. (Courtesy of Bob and Theresa Napoli.)*

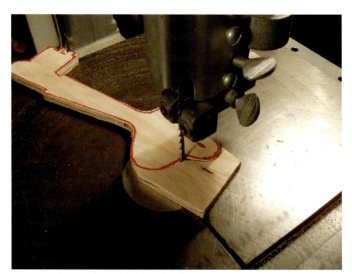

Figure 3.51: *Key rotated around the blade to finish the cut. (Courtesy of Bob and Theresa Napoli.)*

Figure 3.52: *Scroll saw. (Courtesy of Bob and Theresa Napoli.)*

your blade. This really is best done with thinner blades since you only have to nibble a bit. Wider blades require more nibbles. And who wants to fill up on all that fiber?

Scroll Saws

Scroll saws aren't even remotely circular. They actually would best be described as a motorized coping saw. They have the same upside-down D look about them (this look, upon reflection, is really a Q). Their tables tilt the same way the bandsaw's table tilts to give you bevel cuts, and they have the same limitations as the blade that the bandsaw has because of their *neck*. This is the part of the saw that travels up and down (the round part of the upside-down D (or Q). This motion moves the blade the way your arm moves a coping saw (Figure 3.52).

One disadvantage of the scroll saw as compared to the bandsaw is that it won't cut thicker materials. Most scroll saws are only good up to about ¾"- to 1"-thick materials. The advantage to the scroll saw is that the blade works just like the coping saw blade. When you need to make an inside cut, let's say the inside of an upside-down D or Q, you drill a hole in the round part of the upside-down D or Q, unfasten one side of the blade, feed that through the hole, refasten the blade, and make your cut. Because of the bandsaw's continuous loop, you can't make inside cuts.

Scroll Versus Band

Most moderate to large shops have bandsaws. The most common is the 14″ size; the 14″ describes the distance from the inside of the bandsaw's neck across the table to the

135

blade, although larger shops may go larger. The scroll saw is nice for prop work as an auxiliary saw to bring some relief to the bandsaw traffic, but when given a choice, most techies will take the bandsaw for its beefy versatility.

Drill Press

Probably the second thing the earliest carpenters wanted to do after they figured out how to cut a board was to stick a hole into it. The first thing was to complain about how hard it was to cut the board, since no one had bothered to invent the power miter box saw yet, or perhaps to complain that electricians have it easy since no one had bothered to invent electricity yet. So how can you do it? With a drill.

The earliest drills were hard sticks that they rubbed between their hands to get them spinning into the wood. Eventually, the stick was replaced with metal, made pointier, and sharpened a bit; and then they called it a *bit* because it was Friday and almost quitting time. The hands were replaced with a variety of motion-enhancing devices, including a bow and string, cranks, and gears hooked up to cranks (Figure 3.53) and eventually a motor. While this was easier, one problem remained: how to get a perfectly straight hole. All the turning and cranking and motor torque was hard to steady with the human hand, leaving you with wobbly holes.

Pressed for a Better Drilling Solution

The *drill press* was the answer to this problem (Figure 3.54). The name pretty much describes the drill's action. A motor turns a belt that spins the drill bit, and the bit is lowered or pressed into the material. The lever that lowers the bit is a three-handled crank called the *feed handle* that gives the operator a mechanical advantage, making it much easier to operate the drill press than if you had to do the same thing with a

Figure 3.53: *"Eggbeater" drill. (Courtesy of Bob and Theresa Napoli.)*

Figure 3.54: *Drill press. (Courtesy of Bob and Theresa Napoli.)*

handheld drill. When it comes to repetitive drilling or drilling through hard materials, there is no substitute (aside from getting someone else to do it).

The drill press has a few basic parts: the column, the table, and the chuck. We'll start from the bit and work our way around. The bit is chucked into the *chuck*. This is a viselike structure with three jaws that hold the bit tight. Why is it called a chuck? We're not sure, but the research we did come up with indicated that the Fred was a name that just didn't catch on. Whatever the reason, the bit is locked into the chuck by means of the *chuck key*. The chuck key is a geared key that fits into a hole above the chuck; that hole is geared as well. The chuck key turns these chuck gears, which tighten the jaws, which hold the bit, which drills the wood that lives in the house that Jack built, or your theatre's shop.

Of course if you are going to press that bit into something, you have to have something to press against. That something is the *drill press table*. This table can tilt, similar to the bandsaw and scroll saw tables. It's held under the bits by an arm that connects it to the *column*. The column is just that, a column that separates and supports the base of the drill press from the rest of the drill press. The column is geared, and the table's arm is also geared, and there's a crank that raises and lowers the table along these gears in relation to the bit. The table can also rotate in relation to the column, which allows you to drill very large pieces that you couldn't fit between the table and the drill press's base.

The chuck is attached to the drill press's *spindle*, or *quill*. This is the part that the motor actually spins and the part that the feed arm lowers into the workpiece. All of this goes up into the *head*, which is where the motor and the pulleys live, sort of like the brains of the drill press. By adjusting the drive belts' positions between the spindle pulleys, the idler pulley, and the drive pulley, you can get the drill press to turn at different speeds, much like shifting gears on your bike.

Drill Press Safety: The Table Does Have a Vise

There are slots in the table that allow a drill press vise to be bolted down to it. This vise holds the workpiece while it's being drilled. Imagine what would happen if your bit jammed into your workpiece and you lifted up the crank handle: You'd have the equivalent of a small upside-down helicopter aimed at your midsection. We don't like this idea, so what we do to avoid it is to bolt a vise down to the table and tightly clamp our workpiece into it.

Drum up New Business

The drill press can also be used to sand by chucking a sanding drum into the drill press. The *sanding drum* is basically a rubber cylinder with a sandpaper sleeve slipped over it and a little spindle that you chuck into the press. You sand by lowering the sanding drum with the feed arm, locking it in place, and sliding your workpiece along the table, feeding it lightly into the sanding drum. Many times people make an auxiliary table with a recessed hole in it that keeps the sanding drum from making direct contact with the table and gives the workpiece a bit more surface to feed on (Figure 3.55).

So we've examined the larger power tools. In the next section, we'll be looking at handheld power tools. You'll find that the parts and safety practices you've learned with the large power tools also apply to the handheld power tools.

Portable Power Tools

Now that we've seen the grown-up models, let's look at their smaller counterparts. While large floor-model power tools are great, sometimes the only tool for the job is one you can hold in your hands. Let's start as we did in the last section, with the table saw, and work our way down in size.

The table saw most people think of when they speak of a table saw is actually classified as a cabinet saw. It's called a *cabinet saw*, not because you can make cabinets with it, which you can, but because it is built around a closed cabinet. The closed cabinet encloses the saw's motor and its housing and also makes dust collection easier. These saws are usually made with heavy cast-iron parts, heavy cast-iron tables, and heavy-duty motors. These things make them heavy. Their heavy-duty motors run on 220-volt current instead of 120-volt, which is the standard household current. They also run up a lot of currency, making them only affordable to larger shops and universities.

Figure 3.55: *Drill press table with a drum sanding jig. (Courtesy of Bob and Theresa Napoli.)*

Benchtop saws are by comparison lightweight and light duty (Figure 3.56). They have smaller light-duty motors that run on 120-volt current. These are mostly used by hobbyists and weekend warriors, because they don't require special current and you can carry them without help. As the name implies, these saws have no legs or cabinets, because they are meant sit on the benchtop (you need to bolt or clamp them down; they are so light you could easily push them over with your workpiece). Also, they are really inexpensive. Just remember, in the tool world, if the price seems too good to be true, it probably is. There is always a trade-off in quality, durability, or performance.

So what do contractors use when they travel to the job site? The benchtop saw isn't an option because its light-duty structure and motor won't hold up. Contractors need something heavier duty than the benchtop saw but more portable than a cabinet saw. This is how the *contractor's saw* was born (Figure 3.57). They have heavier motors than the benchtop saw, and the parts are thicker and designed to take some abuse. The price is also a lot lower than for the large cabinet saws, but you are getting a smaller saw. The fence capacity on contractor's saws is somewhere between 24″ and 30″; this means that from the blade to the fence in its fully extended position you can make a 24–30″ cut.

139

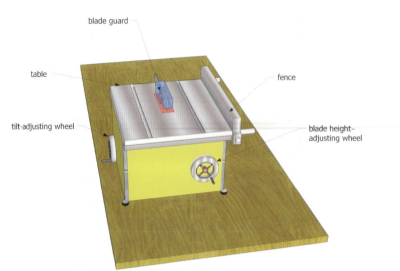

Figure 3.56: *Drawing of a benchtop saw on a bench.*

Figure 3.57: *Rigid contractor's saw with folding wheeled stand.*

Contractor's saws will work for most any ripping application and will even crosscut with a miter gauge like a cabinet saw. Many models have some clever engineering to make up for their smaller size. Tables often telescope to expand fence capacity. Many of these saws are equipped with wheeled folding stands for easier mobility, and their fences, miter gauges, and even blade guards are removable and easily stored for transport (Figure 3.58). All in all, these saws are a good choice for a second portable table

Figure 3.58: *Rigid contractor's saw folded and ready for transport.*

saw for onstage work, but they have enough muscle to function as the primary saw in smaller shops.

Circular Saw

The term *circular saw* is in some circles used to describe the *handheld circular saw*, or *circ saw*, for short. In fact, enter "circular saw" into a search engine and see what you get. This saw is also known as a *Skil saw*, which is actually a brand name of a popular saw manufacturer. This saw is just a little handheld table saw; it has a table or shoe, blade height adjustment, and a blade tilt, just like its parent saws. One major difference between this saw and the table saw is that, like many handheld tools, you move the tool through the wood instead of moving the wood through the tool. Let's look at the basic parts and then discuss the various sizes (Figure 3.59).

This Saw's Got Sole

The *table* or *shoe* or *sole plate* (or *base*, which is the least colorful name we found) is what rides against the workpiece as you make your cut. This piece would be the table on a table saw, and, as you can guess from that description, the blade sticks through the

Figure 3.59: *Circular saw with a blade guide attached to it.*

sole plate and cuts down through the workpiece. There is an alignment notch on the sole plate, which is basically the size of the kerf. Depending on which side you are cutting from, you line that notch up to your pattern line so that the kerf cuts through the scrap.

The blade height adjustment would actually be best described as a blade depth adjustment. A lever releases a clamp so that the rest of the saw drops down and lowers the blade through the blade slot in the base. The blade tilt adjustment is also released by a lever, and it tilts the rest of the saw at an angle to the base so that the blade slants inside of the blade slot.

A Smaller Vicious Donut or a Tinier Shaker Pie Pan

Since you brought up the blade (it was you, wasn't it?), the circ saw blade is smaller than ones we've been talking about. The average size is 7¼″ for corded circ saws, compared to 10″ on the table saw. By using a smaller blade, you can get the same saw speed from a smaller motor, and this keeps the weight of the saw down. (Some models go even further in weight reduction by using magnesium alloys, which are stronger than aluminum and lighter than steel. They also lighten your wallet.)

Snuggling into Circ Safety and Other Current Safety Concerns

Inside the blade slot and snuggled around the blade like two spooning puppies is the blade guard. Unlike the table saw, the circ saw blade guard is made of aluminum and is spring loaded to retract when it comes in contact with the wood. The more you push into the piece, the further it retracts until it is in its final position, riding on the surface of the workpiece, protecting you from the rear of the blade. Unlike the table saw, the blade is completely exposed under the workpiece. For this reason you should always keep the blade depth just a ¼″ lower than the workpiece's thickness, to minimize safety hazards.

All of those other safety practices still apply: Loose clothing, hair, and jewelry should be secured and PPE used. You need to be aware of where all the parts of your body are in relation to the saw blade, and make sure they are out of its path and a safe distance away. Also, whenever making any adjustment to the saw, you need to unplug it.

Speaking of the plug: One concern you don't have with the table saw is that of the saw cord getting in the path of the blade and getting cut by the saw. This, as you would expect, is a shocking development and should be avoided. While the saw is insulated, the other end of the cord will still be live and you could get shocked by that. Checking your blade path with handheld power saws doesn't just include checking for staples, nails, crews, and loose knots; it also includes removing the saw cord from the blade's path. A lot of carpenters flip it over their shoulders; others use after-market devices such as hooks or Velcro tabs that let you attach the cord to your belt.

Whatever you do, make sure the cord remains free from obstructions. If the cord catches on something as you are traveling through the workpiece, the saw will stop like a dog caught on the end of a leash. This can loosen the cord in the saw's body and cause it to short out or make the saw twist in its kerf and kick back. You also look silly.

Everybody has seen the cartoon where the carpenter saws through the board he is kneeling on. Well it is a concern. When you make a cut, you need to make sure your saw isn't resting on the side that's going to fall. No one wants 7¼″ of spinning terror falling toward his legs. You also need to make sure that the supports under the saw, for instance, sawhorses, aren't on the wrong side of the cut. If the support is on the outside of your cut, the kerf will pinch the blade as you cut and cause kickback. Place your sawhorse inside the cut and clear of the saw's path so that the cut piece can fall free. And, of course, stand to the side of the piece so that it doesn't fall on your feet.

Fences and Guides

One thing this saw doesn't have is a fence. Often times you will see people cutting freehand with a circ saw. They simply follow the pattern line (possibly a chalk line marking) with the alignment notch. It isn't simple, though; it takes a lot of practice and causes a lot of kickback. There are a variety of guides (see Figure 3.59) you can use with the circ saw, including a speed square, as we said in the Hand Tools section of this chapter, that will act as a fence and give you a more accurate cut. Some beginners feel the saw guides are a copout and good carpenters don't need them. Good carpenters do good work. They'll use whatever it takes to safely produce good work, with the

Figure 3.60: *Worm-drive saw.*

least waste. The time setting up a good cut is never wasted if it prevents you from having to do it all over again.

Worm-Drive Saw: Direct Drive and How the Worm Turns

Worm drive, what the heck is that? Is it an address for invertebrates? Is it a sci fi system of propulsion? Full of questions aren't you? Most circ saw arbors or spindles are driven directly from the motor, with no pulleys or belts in between. This is called *direct drive*.

A *worm-drive saw* (Figure 3.60) utilizes a gear to turn the blade, and as you know from your cars and your bikes, gears multiply the turning force, or torque, from your legs or a motor. The upshot of this is that you get a beefier saw that has a little larger motor and more torque for cutting thicker, tougher materials. Since the saw is bigger than a regular circ, it's heavier. Many models are made out of magnesium, but the back-heavy balance definitely takes some getting used to. The larger size of this saw means a larger sole plate or base. Once you get over the weight, you may find this added surface area makes this saw easier, not harder, to control. And, of course, it cuts like a hot knife through butter.

Trim Saw: To Cord or Not to Cord

Sometimes you don't need a beefy saw. When cutting thin materials there is just no need to lug a heavy saw around. So you reach for a *trim saw* (Figure 3.61). These are smaller, lighter saws (under 10 lb, compared to a 7¼″ worm drive at 17 lb) with blades that can be anywhere from 4½″ to 5⅜″ in diameter. Usually these saws can only cut up to ¾″ in thickness effectively.

(a)

(b)

Figure 3.61: *(a) Corded and (b) cordless trim saws.*

Many trim saws are cordless now and utilize a battery pack to power their motors. Again, another reason for downsizing the blades is the smaller amount of power needed to turn the blade, making the battery last longer. The main thing to realize with trim saws, or any saw, is that you have to make sure the saw's limitations aren't exceeded by the task you've given it. When you try to force any power tool, you run the risk of creating an unsafe situation.

Jigsaws and Other Up-and-Down Types

The portable version of the scroll saw is the jigsaw (Figure 3.62). Its blade travels up and down like a scroll saw, but it's only connected to the saw's body at the top. This

(a)

(b)

Figure 3.62: *(a) Jigsaw being used; (b) close-up of a jigsaw.*

lets you easily make inside cuts without removing the blade from the saw. Like the circ saw, to cut with the jigsaw you move the saw through the workpiece, and like the circ saw, you can tilt the blade to the saw's sole plate or base. Unlike the circ saw and similar to the bandsaw and scroll saw, this saw has no blade depth adjustment. It cuts straight through the thickness of the workpiece.

For scenic work, this saw is a great tool. Since you can take the saw to the workpiece, you can scroll out larger patterns in bigger boards than the shallow necks of the scroll and bandsaw would let you.

Figure 3.63: *Reciprocating saw.*

Reciprocating Saws: The Velociraptor of Power Tools

Imagine you had a cybernetic arm and put a handsaw in that arm's hand. You could do some serious cutting, couldn't you? That's basically what a reciprocating saw does (Figure 3.63). The reciprocating saw is often known by various brand names, such as Sawzall and Tiger Saw; it is basically a motorized handsaw. But if you change the wood-cutting blade to a metal-cutting blade, you suddenly have a motorized hacksaw. Both kinds of blades are very aggressive in their cutting style. These are not finishing tools. While the blade's up-and-down action is similar to a jigsaw and you can make curved cuts, the width of the blade prevents you from making tight scrolling cuts. This saw is best for set demolition or strike work or in a tight space where a circ saw couldn't fit. It can also be used to cut difficult angles in wood or steel.

Handheld Power Drills: A Boring Subject

There are a few types of handheld power drills that we use in theatre: the ⅜″ or ½″ chuck VSR drill, a hammer drill, and, of course, the sexiest power tool, the cordless drill, or screw gun.

What the Chuck?

What does ⅜″ or ½″ chuck mean? As you probably remember, the chuck is the part of the drill into which the bit fits, so it makes sense that the measurement ⅜″ or ½″ describes the widest diameter to which you can open the jaws of the chuck. As with circ saws, the bigger the bit, the more power it needs to drill. Therefore, a ½″ drill has, by necessity, a little more oomph than a ⅜″. For the most part; ⅜″ chucks are a good choice if the majority of the holes you will be drilling are under ½″. For that occasional ½″ or larger hole you may need to drill, you can buy a *reduced-shank bit*, which is made with a skinnier shaft to fit into the ⅜″ chuck. The ½″-chuck drills are nice for their lager size and extra power. Flat shovel-shaped bits with a point on

Figure 3.64: *Various bits, including hole saws.*

the end can make wide holes in wood. Theses are called *spade* or *speed bits*. Also, even larger holes can be drilled with a *hole saw*, which is a combination of a drill and a saw (Figure 3.64).

Since we're talking about chucks, we should look at the *keyless chuck* (Figure 3.65). These chucks have no key. That's a big surprise, right? Instead of taking a geared key and turning it to open the jaws of the chuck as we did with the drill press, we can hand-tighten the keyless chuck. Some keyless chucks have two sections that you tighten against each other, and some have a spindle lock that holds the chuck from rotating while you tighten the jaws. This makes for some quick bit changes, as when going from a drill bit to a screw bit. Whether you have a keyless or keyed chuck, it's important to unplug the drill before you do any kind of bit change.

Variable-Speed Reversing (VSR)

VSR stands for *variable-speed reversing*. By varying the pressure you apply on the drill's trigger you can vary the speed the drill turns at. This is particularly useful for starting drill bits in hard materials. The reversing part is great for removing screws but also very helpful when you are drilling. If you occasionally reverse the drill and pull it out of your workpiece, the chips and shavings the bit cuts come with it, trapped in the bit's *flutes* (the curvy, sharp gullies on the bit that do the actual cutting). Once free from the hole they fall off of the bit, and you can insert the bit again without its binding against the chips packed in the hole.

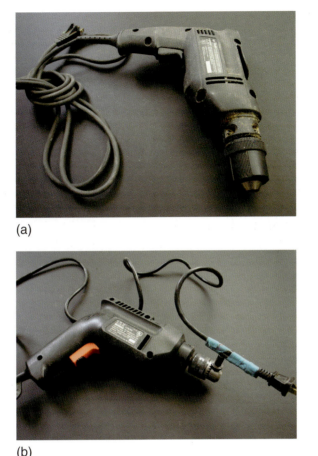

(a)

(b)

Figure 3.65: *Two drills: (a) keyless chuck; (b) keyed-chuck hammer drill.*

It's Hammer Time Again

There's an expression among carpenters that's meant to be funny: "Everything's a hammer," meaning that when you can't find your hammer, you can use whatever is at hand as a hammer. Obviously this is not a good idea, especially if the only thing at hand is a live grenade. In the case of the hammer drill, even though it has the word *hammer* in it, it's not meant to smack something.

So far all we've been talking about are drills meant for metal, wood, or even plastic. There is another type of drill bit called the *masonry bit*. Instead of coming to a point in the same way other drill bits do, the masonry bit looks like it has a little house roof on the end of it. It's made, as you might guess, to drill masonry: cement blocks, brick, or poured cement walls or floors. You can do a decent job of drilling masonry with the bigger motor in a ½″ drill, but if you're going to be doing a lot of drilling in this kind of material, you need something with a little more power that gets the job done faster. The hammer drill's spindle not only turns in a circle, but it actually moves back

Figure 3.66: *14-volt cordless drill with a ½″ spindle-lock keyless chuck.*

and forth while it's turning. This is the hammer action, and it makes quick work of holes in masonry.

Obviously, if you going to be putting any kind of holes into the walls of your theatre, you first need to check the locations of the electrical service and plumbing within the walls. And before you go fastening anything to the walls or any other part of your theatre structure, you should consult your facilities manager to make sure the structure can take the weight of whatever you're hanging on it.

Cordless Drill (Screw Gun): I'm Too Sexy for My Cord

The cordless drill, or screw gun, does have a little bit of attitude. Since it doesn't have a cord and runs from rechargeable batteries it thinks it can go anywhere. Cordless screw guns most often have keyless chucks. This doesn't help their attitude very much either. "Whee! No cord, no key!" And the next thing you know, they've gone completely Pinocchio on you. But they are really cool and sexy, and that attraction stems from their power and convenience (Figure 3.66).

Choosing Your Drill

When you are picking out a cordless drill, there are a few things to keep in mind. Cordless drills are just another version of VSR drills, with no cord, and they are available in ⅜″ and ½″ chucks as well. You can start your tool search by picking out your chuck size. What next? Just like you did with the other hand tools; the first things you need to think about are what you're going to be doing with this drill and how heavy of a drill you want to be lugging around.

150

If you are just doing trim and set decoration work like hanging draperies or pictures, you probably only needed a 7- to 9-V Martha Stewart–sized drill. If you are going to be driving a lot of long screws into thick materials for long periods of time, you'll need as much power as you can carry. The available voltages range anywhere from 7 V to 24 V, and the drills increase in size, weight, and power as the voltage rating increases. Most carpenters find the 12- to 18-V range the most comfortable to work with. Smack dab in the middle of this range is 14.4 V, which has a nice ratio of power to weight.

Accessories are another consideration when you're buying your cordless drill. Cordless technology has taken off to the point where you can actually have just about any corded tool in a cordless version. Many manufacturers are packaging cordless toolkits that include several different kinds of cordless tools along with your cordless drill: cordless circ saws, hammer drills, cordless reciprocating saws, and cordless jigsaws. As you can imagine, these tools are extremely convenient, but the smaller the voltage, the smaller the motor, the smaller the blades, and the smaller the stock they're able to work with. So once again you need to ask yourself what you're going to be using these tools for. Look at your overall work picture and then decide what power/weight ratio you can deal with. Also, ask yourself whether you really need all those cordless tools. You may. Your theatre may not have a lot of available power outlets. Your shop might be so small you need to work on larger pieces outside, away from available power. But if this isn't the case, perhaps you don't need those cordless tools. In the long run, cordless tools are all about convenience. And remember, with power tools there's always a trade-off between convenience and performance. You're not going to be able to cut the same types of materials with a 5½″ cordless trim saw blade as you can with a 7½″ worm-drive saw. But we've seen people try who just sank a lot of money into one.

Also keep in mind that these things are cordless. They need rechargeable batteries. Battery technology is changing almost daily; however, there are two major concerns when you're looking at batteries: capacity and recharge time. Having a bag of cordless tools isn't very helpful if your batteries don't last long and take a long time to recharge. If you're going to be doing heavy-duty work for long hours, you want a battery that recharges quickly. There are cordless toolkits out there that include three-hour-charging batteries. You don't want one of these. You need a battery and charger that work in a half-hour to an hour.

Believe it or not, cordless screw guns have gears and a clutch. Maybe that's why we say we drive screws. By turning the clutch adjustment, found just behind the chuck, you can set the depth of the screw you're driving. Once the clutch feels the selected resistance, it disengages from the motor and prevents the screw from driving any deeper. If you turn your clutch adjustment up the entire way, you'll notice a tiny little drill bit drawn on the dial. This is the clutch's drill selection; the clutch won't engage when you have this selected. The gear-selection switch, usually found behind the clutch adjustment, controls the drill's speed, much like the belts and pulleys did on the drill press.

Cordless drills have between two and three gears. First gear has the most torque; third and second gears have more speed. Remember, when drilling through metal you want to go slower, and you need to go faster through softer materials. Screwdriving is best done in the lowest gear, which gives you the most torque and avoids snapping the screw heads off. So think about what you're doing and how that affects the kind of speed you need from your drill.

Finishing Tools

Pneumatic Tools Versus Your Cat

Pneumatic tools are air powered. That means that behind the pneumatic tool, somewhere at the end of the air hose connected to it, is an air compressor. The compressor sucks up air and forces it into its tank, where the air is compressed. Once gas is compressed, by its very nature it wants to escape, the same way your cat wants to escape when you stick it in a pillowcase. Not exactly the same way; once the cat gets out it won't do anything useful for a while. By plugging an air hose into the compressor, you've given the compressed air an opening to search for a way out. The air keeps traveling through the hose into the air tool, spinning turbines or pushing pistons until it can escape. In the process it has powered your tool and proven itself more useful than your cat. Here are some common air tools.

- *Impact wrench or pneumatic wrench:* This is the tool garages use to remove and tighten lug nuts on tires. We sometimes use these wrenches to tighten nuts on bolts or lag pipe flanges down to the floor. Because they spin so fast, care needs to be taken to prevent snapping the fastener or stripping it out.
- *Drills and die grinders:* Without a heavy motor attached to it, a pneumatic drill can be more compact and lighter than its corded or cordless counterparts. Die grinders are a lot like dentist drills; they can be used with a variety of attachments that can drill, grind, or polish. These are very useful in prop work.
- *Pneumatic staplers:* There are four main types of pneumatic staplers we use in scenic work, and they're classified by the size of their crown or the head of the staple. These staples are inserted into the staple gun in a long clip and fed under the stapler's drive head by a spring.
  - ➤ **SAFETY TIP** Most of these staple guns, as well as the air nailers, have a safety on their nose (which is where the fastener comes out) that allows the gun to fire only when the safety has been depressed. By holding the trigger down and bumping the nose against the workpiece, you can shoot a fastener as fast as you can bump the nose. This is also great fun (until you try to take the piece apart and realize that you had too much fun). But remember that if you bump the nose against your foot while holding the trigger, the air tool doesn't know it's your foot and will blithely do its job.

- *Narrow-crown stapler:* As the name implies, these staplers use a very narrow-crown staple. This size is very useful for trim work because the staple leaves a very small hole in the workpiece. It's also nice for attaching corner blocks to flat frames while the glue dries.
- *Medium-crown stapler:* This stapler has a wider crown and works well for putting plywood boxes together.
- *Wide-crown stapler:* The wide crown on the staple makes it particularly useful temporarily joining flat pieces together before you lock them into place with corner blocks or flat skins.
- *Fabric stapler:* This stapler shoots a staple that more closely resembles the desk or office stapler staple. Upholsterers use these guns to stretch fabric and padding over furniture. So do we. And we use them for practically everything else. They are incredibly handy tools for both the scenic and prop shops, and quite often both want them at the same time. The fine-gauge wire staple it shoots has a wide head. This makes it really nice for stapling set decorations such as curtains, paper, or greenery such as garland or vines. It's also indispensable when it comes to stretching soft-cover flats or putting up soft maskings under platforms. There are hand staple guns that do the exactly same thing, and there are even electric staple guns that will work faster than the hand staple guns, but none of them works as smoothly as the pneumatic fabric stapler.

  ➤ **SAFETY TIP**   One drawback to the pneumatic fabric stapler is that unlike other pneumatic fasteners, it has no safety. Every time you pull the trigger it shoots a staple, whether against your workpiece or your leg. So extra care must be taken when using it, and no matter how silly it sounds you need to wear your eye protection while using it or any other pneumatic tool. After the air does its useful job inside the tool pushing a piston or spinning a turbine, it escapes from the tool's air exhaust. While it spins around the tool's moving parts it carries a little bit of pneumatic tool oil with it, so it can coat and lubricate them. This oil is constantly in the pneumatic system, supplied by a filter regulator lubricator that also sucks out water vapor and regulates the air pressure. This tool oil isn't good for your eyes when the tool's exhaust blows it into them. Also, just about everything we do can cause sawdust or metal dust or some small piece of material that can get picked up by the exhaust and blown into your eyes.
- *Air nailers:* Essentially, air nailers are power hammers. As with the pneumatic stapler, the air nailer holds a clip of nails that a pneumatic piston drives into the workpiece. There are three types of air nailers to consider.
  - *Framing nailers:* These shoot larger, heavier-gauge nails that are good for attaching 2 × 4's together, such as in platform frames. The nails are held together in a long clip joined by a coating of glue and a strip of paper on either side. This glue also adds holding power when it goes into the 2 × 4. Anyone who's ever tried to take an air-nailed platform frame apart can attest to this.

- *Finish nailers:* Thinner-gauge, smaller-headed nails come out of this gun. Finish carpenters use these for moldings and other trim. Stage carpenters use them for finish work as well and also for decorative prop work.
- *(FAQ) Why doesn't my finish nailer drive the nail all the way into the wood? Is it broken? Why did I buy this thing? I'm always getting ripped off!* Calm down! You should never work when you're angry. Some of these nailers are set to stop the nail just above the surface of the wood. Just like finish carpenters (not Finnish, although certainly Finnish finish carpenters could do this), stop hammering the finish nail just above the wood to avoid putting a union label in the workpiece. You flush the nail head by using a *nail set,* a punchlike tool with a wide end for being struck and a smaller end that fits on the finish nail's head. Just take a hammer, put the set on the nail head, and tap it down.
- *Brad nailers, or wire nailers:* The thin, wirelike nails that come out of this gun are nice for attaching thin materials, such as a ⅛″ or ¼″ luaun. There isn't much of a head to these nails, so they don't have very much holding power on their own. That's why you need to make sure you glue your materials carefully.

Router

While a router is a very efficient computer networking device that forwards packets of information around the Internet, it does very little to help us finish a scenic piece. The router we're talking about (Figure 3.67) is a much more useful scenic device. Basically it's a motor that turns a bit designed to trim away wood. There are a many different types of bits but only two main types: edge bits and nonedge bits.

Edge bits are meant to cut the edge of the board. Quite often they have bearings on them that ride against the surface of the edge and prevent the cutting flutes of the bit from taking too large a bite and kicking back. Bearings are also found on *flush trim bits,* which allow you to flush one surface to another, such as the luaun skin of a hardcover flat and the flat frame. Other edge bits include *round-over, cove, roman ogee,* and *rabbeting bits* (Figure 3.68).

Nonedge bits cut slots, or *flutes,* into the face of materials. These bits are best used with some kind of straightedge guide or template, but they can be used freehand. The trick with these bits is in starting the bit in the surface of the wood. You can always drill a small hole the size of the bit and start the router inside that, or, if you have a plunge router base, you can slowly lower the router or plunge it into the wood. Some common nonedge bits are *V-groove, round-nose,* and *dovetail* (see Figure 3.68).

Using a Router Safely, or Taking the Safest Route

You absolutely want to wear eye and ear protection when you use a router. They are loud and kick up a tremendous amount of dust. It wouldn't be a bad idea to wear a dust mask as well. Here are some other safety guidelines.

Figure 3.67: *Router with fixed and plunge bases.*

Figure 3.68: *Router bits.*

- The bit rotates clockwise; the safest way to move the router is from left to right.
- Never lift the router when it's spinning; wait until the router comes to a complete stop before moving it. This is a good practice for any power tool but especially important for a tool such as the router where the cutting edge is hidden from view.
- Unplug the router for bit changes and when making any adjustments.
- Make sure your cutting path is clear of staples, nails, screws, and other obstructions.

- When flush cutting, make sure the bearing's path is also clear of obstructions.
- Also make sure the path under the workpiece is clear when you are doing any flush or through cutting.
- Make sure the face of your workpiece plate is free from obstructions as well. Your router's sole plate travels on this face, and a misplaced screw or staple could jump your router off its cutting path.
- When you need to remove a lot of material, do it in several passes to minimize stress on the motor and the bit.

> **TIP** When flush cutting flat skins, make sure the glue is dry. Wet glue gets into the bearings and mixes with the sawdust. Add heat from friction, and the glue and sawdust mixture bakes solid and freezes the bearing. Once the bearing freezes, it gets hot, the bit gets hot, the bit burns, the wood burns, and eventually the bearing and the nut holding it fly off. Without the bearing to guide the bit, the bit can easily take too large of a bite into the work-piece and kick back. When you install the bit, check the bearing to make sure it rotates freely. Periodically unplug the router, and check the bearing's rotation when you have a lot of flush trimming to do.

Chapter 4

How Does It Go Together?

Construction Tips and Techniques

In this chapter, we talk about how to read designer plates and working drawings as well as how to cut-list the parts, lay them out, assemble them, move them around, and connect them to each other.

Designer Plates

Everybody likes nice things. And while you could eat off of designer plates, these are not the types of plates that you use to impress somebody when you invite them to dinner or put on a shelf to show you have excellent taste. The designer plates we are speaking of are actually the scenic designer's plans for how the set goes together, drawn on large sheets of paper, or *plates*. You may be more familiar with the term *blueprints*.

Actually, not all blueprints are blue these days. Blueprinting was an inexpensive way of reproducing the designer's original pencil sketches on photosensitive paper that left the background blue and the designer's lines white. These were replaced by the *Diazo process,* or *blue line,* where the background stays white and the designer's lines turn blue. But with the advent of the digital age, those machines are being replaced by large-format scanners and printers. These new machines can quickly reproduce drawings from the designer's pencil sketches (Figure 4.1) or digital information from a computer-aided design, or CAD, program. In this case, the lines can be any color the designer wishes them to be, but for clarity they are most often black.

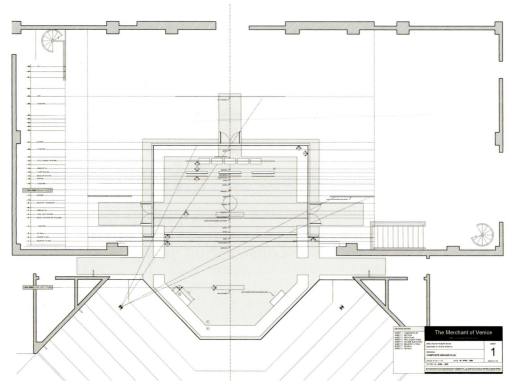

Figure 4.1: *Floor plan from the Pennsylvania Shakespeare Festival's* Merchant of Venice, *designed by Steve Teneyck. (Courtesy of Steve Teneyck.)*

Types of Plates

The *floor plan* or *plan view* is the designer plate that most people are familiar with. It's an aerial view of the stage's setting, including flats, platforms, staircases, legs, borders, cycs, scrims, show curtains, main curtains—basically anything that's going to be on the stage when the audience shows up the night the show opens.

Platform elevations are listed on the floor plans. *Platform elevation* is just a fancy way of saying how high the platform is from the stage floor. Designers will represent this by a little circle that has a number with a "+" in front of it. So, for example, if a platform is 8 inches from the floor, there will be a little circle with a +8″ written in it, drawn on top of the platform. If it is below stage elevation, a "−" will precede the measurement. This dimension is usually written in inches. But whether written in inches or feet, the style stays consistent throughout the floor plan.

Flat labels are also found on the floor plan. Most designers use letters drawn inside of little triangles whose points point to the flat it is labeling. These labels will show up later to identify the flat on other plates that will give you more information about that particular flat than you can find on the floor plan.

Sight Lines

In addition to what is on the stage, the designer will often include the position of the house's seats on a floor plan. By looking at the seats in relation to the set, the designer can figure out the audience's sight lines. *Sight lines* refer to everything an audience can see when they look at the stage. (Imagine little dotted lines coming out of the audience members' eyes toward the stage, to help you remember this term). We want the audience to see only what we want them to see. Therefore, we need to close sight lines to anything we don't want them to see. For example, the backstage areas where the actors rush to make their entrances or stagehands playing cards between their cues would be good sight lines to close. A piece of masking or a well-placed flat will close the sight line from the audience's view. *Extreme sight lines* are the sight lines from the furthest seats, and often these are the most critical ones to pay attention to since they are often forgotten. After all, they are usually lousy seats.

Scale

As you can imagine, to fit all of this on one plate, you cannot draw anything to its actual size. How can you figure out where anything goes or how large it is supposed to be? To solve this problem, designers use *scaled drawings*. For example, one of the most common scales we use in theatre is a ½″ = 1′, which means for every half-inch you move on the drawing in real life you move 1 foot. So, for example, if something on the drawing was an inch long, it would actually be 2 feet long in real life. Quarter-inch scale (¼″ = 1′) is also very popular, especially since it works really well on quad graph paper; each square in this case equals 1′. Both of these scales work very well for the shop carpenter since she can use her tape measure to scale objects on the drawings. Ultimately, it's up to the designer and whatever scale he or she is comfortable working in.

Elevations

Elevations are another type of plate (Figure 4.2). An elevation drawing looks like you took the floor plan, grabbed the top of one of the flats, and then pulled it straight up and out of the floor plan like a drawer. You elevated it so you could see what the face of the flat looked like. With these plates, the designer gives you the idea of what the finished piece's size and shape should look like. To help you in this process, designers add dimensions in addition to drawing things in scale. The amount of dimensioning is subjects to the designer's taste; some feel a few key dimensions are sufficient while others feel that the carpenter should never have to pick up the scale ruler to measure anything.

Dissection to Cross Section

The *cross section* is just that, a section of how the set would look if you sliced the theatre from the top to the bottom, opened it up, and viewed it from the side. Since you'll

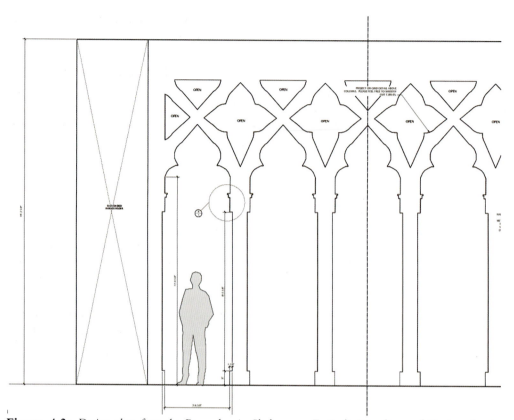

Figure 4.2: *Design plate from the Pennsylvania Shakespeare Festival's* Merchant of Venice *showing scenery elevations.*

never work at that theatre again if you actually do this, designers use these plates instead to illustrate the relationship of scenic units to each other as well as to the maskings, drapes, fly space, and even the architectural features of the theatre itself.

A *platform schedule* is a plan view that shows just the platforms and their relationship to each other. Quite often there will be a list at the bottom of the page, with each platform represented, that acts as a key to explain the drawing.

Parts of a Plate

To navigate around the designer plans, you should have some idea of what information you can find on a plate. So far, we've talked about platform elevations, flat labels, and sight lines, just to name a few things, and these are all found within the main border, or the *body*, of the plate. Over to the right side of the drawing you'll find the *title block*. Written sideways along the width of the paper, the title block has information that will tell you the name of the show, the show's director, the date the drawing was made, what type of plate it is, who designed it, which plate out of how many total plates that particular plate is, and what scale the plate was drawn in.

Notes can be found within the title block or underneath individual drawings on an elevation or anywhere on a design plate. These notes are just another way the designer can communicate design information, including specific materials, floor treatments, and design concerns, to the technical director, who will incorporate these notes into his engineering of the scenic unit.

Working Drawings

The designer gives you an idea of how the scenic units are supposed to look and how they fit together. Rarely will he or she give you an idea of how these pieces are actually constructed. This is where the *technical director* comes in. She will create a drawing that will contain the actual instructions for building the scenic piece. These working drawings will utilize the several different views: plan views, side views, bottom views, cross sections, or any other particular view that will give you enough information to build the piece. These drawings will have more detailed dimensions than you'll find on the design plates. Working drawings may also contain notes as to how materials will be used and fastened together (Figure 4.3).

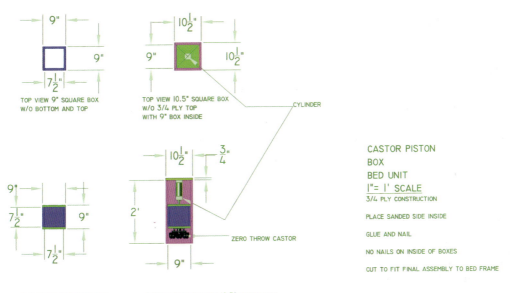

Figure 4.3: *Working drawings showing multiple views of the raked bed wagon's castor piston from DeSales University's* A Christmas Carol.

Table 4.1: *Example Cut List for a 4' × 8' Platform*

Unit: PLATFORM A Show: MUSICAL REVIEW		Prepared by: E. DELANEY Cut by: M. SMOLA	
Quantity	Material	Size	Notes
1	¾" plywood	4'-0" × 8'-0"	Skin
2	2 × 4	7'-9"	Stiles
2	2 × 4	4'-0"	Rails
2	2 × 4	3'-9"	Toggles 2'-8" OC
6	2 × 4	12"	½ Hog trough legs
6	2 × 6	11"	½ Hog trough legs
12	1 × 3	CTF	X braces

The Cut List

Many people, while in college, had an informal list of classes they liked to cut. This isn't that kind of list. This cut list is a list of the materials needed for a scenic unit (such as a platform or flat) and the sizes and quantities of each piece.

Table 4.1 presents an example of a cut list. It contains all the basic information you can gather from the TD's working drawings. There are columns for quantity, material, and the size of the material. As you can see, under "Size" for ¾" plywood, you get width (4'-0") and length (8'-0") dimensions, but thickness is omitted. Since we know the material is ¾" thick we don't need to write it again. Sheet goods dimensions will usually appear this way. The same thing goes for the 2 × 4's or other stick lumber: We know the thickness and width (1½" × 3½"), so all we need to know is the length.

The headers on the cut list need our attention. Of course, the "Unit" name makes sense; you need to know what these pieces are meant to build. You are free to name it whatever you like (Fred still hasn't been used since we decided on Chuck instead). But most TD's will want to use the same name as the designer does on his plates so that we can find it on the ground plan and eventually give it a home. The "Show" name also makes sense, especially in shops where you have more than one show being built. Why include information on who prepared the list and who cut the list? Basically, if there any special concerns or discrepancies between what pieces are cut and what pieces are on the list or working drawings, whoever assembles this unit will know who to talk to.

As you cut each piece, you should place a tally mark, an "x," checkmark, or whatever makes sense to you, next to the item you've cut on the list. This will help you keep track of what you're cutting. In addition, it gives an idea of where you left off in case you are interrupted in the middle of finishing the cut list. You should also clearly label the size of each piece directly on the piece of material you just cut. Many pieces can be within fractions of an inch of each other, differences so small you couldn't see them with your naked eye. You could also have scrapped pieces lying next to the pieces you cut-listed and not be able to tell them apart. It's just a good idea to label them.

> **TIP**   When you have many pieces to cut that are the same size, you should set up a stop block on your crosscut saw. This is anything that's perpendicular to your fence and stops you from sliding the workpiece past the measurement you need. To set one up, take an inside measurement from the blade along one side of the fence and mark it. If your table is made of something you can screw into, you can screw down a block perpendicular to the fence, right on that mark. If you can't screw into your table, then clamp a block to your fence. Slide your workpiece up to the stop block and hold it tight to the fence, keeping your hands clear as you make your cut. Take this piece out, check its measurement, and then make any necessary adjustments. Check every five pieces or so just to make sure you are still on the mark.

> **TIP**   Once all the pieces are cut, bundle them together until they can be assembled. Shrink-wrap twine or, as it is known by its brand name, Flat Twine, is great for bundling cut-listed materials. It's plastic wrap on a roll. The advantage to this clear film is that you can take your cut list and working drawings, wrap them around the cut-listed materials, and shrink-wrap over them. This gives you a handy label as well as a little package ready for assembly.

Building Flats and Platforms

So you reach for your little bundle of cut-listed goodness, peel off the shrink-wrap, and take out the working drawings. What do you do now? Well, one of the first things you need to do is make sure you understand the working drawings. The TD would rather take the time to explain the drawing to you than watch you waste time rebuilding the flat, so don't be afraid to ask questions. As you look at the drawing make sure you understand how the piece is oriented on the page. Is it a rear elevation you're looking at? A *rear elevation* is an elevation that you're looking at from the back. This is generally how we lay flats out to build them, and rear elevations can more easily show you the structure of the flat. Designers draw front elevations because they don't care how you build them as long as they look like what they drew (Figure 4.4).

Let's assume we're building a standard 1 × 3 soft-cover flat. One of the best ways to start is to lay down the bottom rail and square everything from that. If your shop's layout floor is made of wood, screw the rail down to the floor. If there are any lines on the floor you can use to help with your alignment, for instance, an edge of the sheet of Masonite floor covering, then feel free to use them as a baseline to line your rail up against.

> **TIP**   If you don't have a wooden shop floor, you can create a layout floor with a few sheets of 4′ × 8′ plywood, some 1 × 3 frames, and a few sheets of Masonite or luaun.

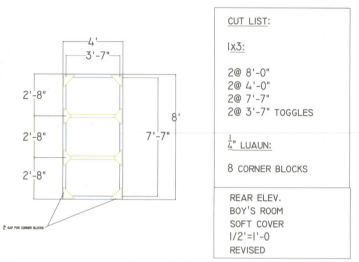

Figure 4.4: *Working drawings of the soft-cover flat frame with its cut list.*

Let's say you want to create a 16′ × 16′ layout floor (Figure 4.5).

- You could just drop four sheets of ¾″ plywood on the floor and work from that. But kneeling on the plywood over a hard cement floor hurts your knees after a while, even with kneepads. In addition, since we are going to screw into this floor, we will need a little more thickness for the screws to bite into. By adding 1 × 3 *sleepers* under the floor we solve both problems. The sleepers raise the plywood up another ¾″. And while the floor doesn't sag, it does give a bit where it's suspended between the sleepers and that's easier on your knees.
- We want the plywood supported at its seams and every 24–32″. Cut the materials on the cut list and follow the layout on the working drawing.
- Screw down the ¾″ deck about every foot around each edge. Measure and snap lines to find the toggle locations, and screw them down as well.
- Take your sheets of Masonite or luaun and lay them perpendicular to the plywood sheets. This is a good practice for any flooring you lay down. It helps to smooth the floor surface by bridging over the seams of the previous layer.
- Snap chalk lines perpendicular to each other and create a 2′ grid on the floor. If you trace over the lines with permanent marker and coat the floor with polyurethane they'll last longer.
- After a while of heavy use, inspect the floor. If it seems beaten up, replace it or just flip the decking over, snap new lines, and use that side until it needs to be replaced. If you use Masonite, make sure it's *dual tempered*, that is, hardened on both sides.

➢ **TIP**   If you have a series of similarly shaped scenic pieces, you can screw down jig blocks to help you set up faster. Square your first frame. Before you pull it

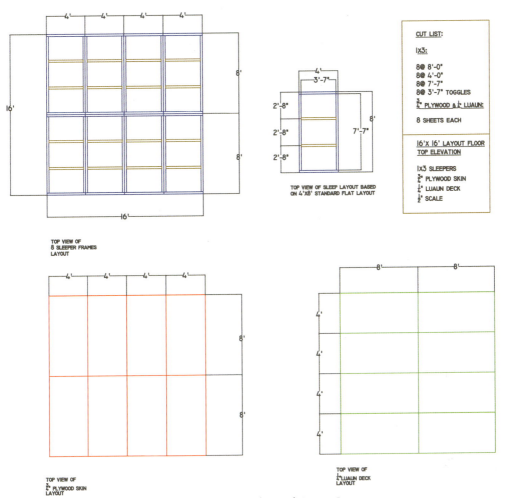

Figure 4.5: *Cut list and working drawing of a 16′ × 16′ layout floor.*

up, screw small chunks of scrap every foot or so into the floor, staggered on either side of each framing member. Pull the frame up and drop the next pieces in place inside the jig block. As with the stop block, check the jig's square every five frames or so just to make sure it's still accurate. You can apply this method to many scenic units, including jigs for welding steel frames.

Getting the Rails in Stile

Let's bring the stiles over. Take your framing square and use it to check for square against the rail. Once it's square, screw this down because we'll move over to the other stiles and repeat the process. Next add the bottom rail and check it for square to the stiles. Measure from the bottom rail to mark the center position of each of the

Figure 4.6: *Wide-crowned joint.*

toggles on the inside edge of both stiles. Bring your toggles over, line them up on their center marks, and screw them down.

Crowning the Joints, or Do I Have Crow's Feet?

Here's where the wide-crown stapler comes in handy. Using three wide-crown staples in a crow's-foot pattern, staple across each of the joints; then remove the screws that were holding the frame square (Figure 4.6). Don't forget to do this. You won't believe how angry you'll get at yourself when you go to move the flat and you've corner-blocked over the screws.

Now check the flat for square again, but this time take out your tape measure and measure from one corner diagonally to the other. Now do the same with the other corner. If they don't match, the flat is out of square. Tweak the flat frame until they read the same.

Corner Block

Now we are ready for corner blocks. Corner blocks should be indented at least the thickness of the flat frame, in this case ¾″, from the outside edge of the frame. This is so you can butt two flats together at right angles to each other without the corner blocks getting in the way. Make marks ¾″ away from the outside edge of the flat frame, and line the corner blocks up as laid out on the drawing.

> ➤ **TIP** The cardinal rule of corner blocks is that the grain must not be parallel to the joint. Traditional corner blocks are cut with the grain parallel to one of the right angle sides. You have to make sure you place the grain perpendicular

to the joint. If the grain runs parallel to the joint and the joint twists, the corner block can easily snap.

The *Backstage Handbook*,[1] on page 277 of the third edition, has the directions for making goof-proof corner blocks: "Rip six ½″ strips along the 8′ side, then crosscut at 45° angles." Simple yet beautiful instructions because the beauty of these corner blocks is that the grain is running diagonally. It's parallel to the hypotenuse of the triangle. The upshot of this is that no matter which way you turn it or which corner you put it in, the grain won't be parallel to the joint.

> **TIP** When you use narrow-crown staples you must definitely make sure they don't go parallel to the grain; if they do, they'll just separate the wood fibers instead of trapping them underneath their crown. Yes, they just hold the block until the glue dries, but that's until the glue dries. There's no point in taking chances. Since the grain runs diagonally on a goof-proof corner block, there is less chance of putting a staple in the wrong direction.

> **TIP** You can make a corner block layout jig easily from scrap materials. Take a couple of scraps of 1 × 3 and a scrap of luaun from your scrap pile. Lay one 1 × 3 face down on your work table and place the other 1 × 3 on edge perpendicular to one side of the first 1 × 3. Now take the luaun and spread glue on one of the faces except for 1″ of the bottom edge. Place the glued face flush to the face of the second 1 × 3, with the unglued side flush to the bottom edge of the first 1 × 3, resting on the table. Staple the luaun to the 1 × 3. Now you can hold your jig flush to the outside edge of the flat frame and trace the inside edge of the jig. This will give you a quick ¾″ marking without measuring.

Stapling the Blocks: It's All in the Glue

At this point you switch out your wide-crown stapler for your narrow-crown stapler with ¾″ staples in it. The corner blocks are ¼″; a rule of thumb for fasteners is that you fasten through the thinnest material into the thickest, and the fastener should be at least twice the thickness of the thinnest material. In this case we have a quarter inch to spare, and even if the narrow-crown staple blows through the thickness of the corner block bit, we still have room before it goes all the way through the 1 × 3. But before we get too far into the stapling, we need to remember that the staples don't hold corner blocks onto the flat—what really holds the corner blocks on is the glue. The staples only hold the blocks until the glue dries. We need only enough staples to keep the corner block down flat against the face of the 1 × 3's and their joint. The best way to do this is to start right at the joint.

Spread your glue out on the face of your flat frame inside the ¾″ guidelines. Many people take the glue bottle and just squirt glue on like they were decorating a cake.

---

[1] Carter, P. *Backstage Handbook: An Illustrated Almanac of Information*, 3rd ed., New York: Broadway Press, 1999.

It's really fun to do, but the problem is that the glue will dry that way and not form a good bond. The more the glue is spread out over the surface of the corner block, the better bond you will have. You can spread the glue out with another corner block, a scrap of luaun, your fingers, or a putty knife. Now lay the corner block inside your ¾″ markings at the corner of the flat frame.

> **TIP** If you just got a new credit card, recycle the cut-up old one as a glue spreader. Plastic cards such as old credit cards or supermarket discount cards make great glue spreaders. The advantage to a plastic glue spreader is that the most common wood glue, aliphatic glue, won't stick to most plastics. Once the glue is dry, you simply flex the plastic and peel the glue off.

Hold the corner block down and put two staples on either side of the joint, making sure, as always, that the staples aren't parallel with the grain. From each side of the joint, add four more staples to make a pattern of five (Figure 4.7), with one staple in the middle. Basically you are hitting all the corners and the middle to suck the corner block down flat and get a nice glue bond. Overall there should be 11 staples (there are two next to each other at one side of the joint, technically making it a pattern of six); you don't need any more.

Stretching the Flat

Now, if you haven't forgotten to remove those screws and accidentally corner-blocked over the top of them, you should be able to pick the flat up. Place it on two sawhorses, pull out your muslin cover, and lay it over the flat frame. Most often we use *non–flame retardant*, or *NFR*, heavyweight muslin for painted flats, but your designer may specify

Figure 4.7: *Corner block staple pattern showing the joints and ¾″ lineup markings for the corner block.*

a specific fabric. When you pull the fabric and stretch it over the flat frame we call it *stretching the flat*—and yes, it has nothing to do with changing the size of the flat.

The most common mistake people make when covering soft-cover flats is to place the flat frame in the middle of the cover stock. This wastes a tremendous amount of fabric. The most overhang you'll ever need is just enough to wrap around the backside of the flat—approximately 2–3″. So slide the fabric over closer to the edge and cut from there.

> ➤ **TIP** It is easier to cut a notch in the muslin and rip it to the size you want whenever possible. Not only is it faster, but since you follow the grain of the fabric, you'll get a straighter line.

With this bit done, we are now at a delicate point and a decision must be made for (dum, da dum dum) there are two styles of stretching the flat!

Traditional Flat-Covering Method

In this method, you take a glue-and-water solution and glue the muslin to the outside members of the flat. There are no staples involved. You take your muslin and cut it to the size of the frame with the 2–3″ overhang we spoke of. Lay it roughly in place over your flat frame. At this point you want to roll back one side and coat the stile underneath with glue. According to Bill Raoul in his excellent *Stock Scenery Construction Handbook*,[2] you want the glue to "tack through," that is, make it thin enough that it just soaks through the muslin but still feels tacky. The best way to formulate this mixture is to use some scrap muslin and test it out; then you need to roll back the muslin and press it into the glue until the fabric is stretched smooth but not tight. Repeat this process with the other side and then the rails. The next step asks you to cut the overhang off with a sharp mat knife ⅛″ into the frame. This protects the edges of the covering from peeling off due to mishandling. Then the flat is set aside to dry for several hours or overnight.

There is really nothing wrong with this method. It has been used for years and years—because it works. The only real drawbacks, and the reason there is another method, is that it takes time and space for the glue to dry. We sometimes have one of these and we strive to have both, but we don't always succeed. Smaller theatres can seldom afford the real estate needed to keep drying flats around.

The Other Way: Stapling the Cover

The second method is closer to the way an artist covers canvas frames. Again you cut your cover closer to the edge, not the center of the cover stock, leaving 2–3″

[2] Baoul, B. *Stock Scenery Construction: A Handbook,* 2nd ed., New York: Broadway Press, 1999.

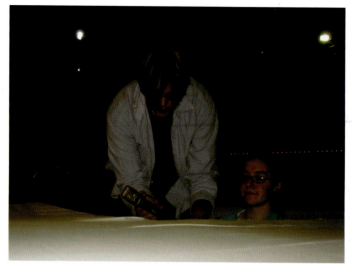

Figure 4.8: *Stretching a flat.*

overhang, and carefully fold up that remnant so that you can use it again for other flats on other days. Next, starting from the center of one side with a friend on the other, pull some of the overhang under the flat and staple it to the back side (Figure 4.8). Your friend, who would benefit from having a stapler himself, pulls directly across from you and pops a staple in his side. You rush him to the hospital, where they pull the staple out and get a more careful friend to help you finish. This new friend actually puts the staple into the flat, inside the first ¾″ of the back edge. Then you work your way from the center and out to the edges, pulling and stapling across from each other. Pull the fabric just tight enough that you don't have wrinkles but not so tight that the frame bows. When the flat is painted, the muslin will shrink and tighten on the frame. If you pull it too tight, it will shrink and bow the frame itself. Once you stretch all the sides, tuck the corners in and staple them down (Figure 4.9). Whichever method you choose, this is a good way to learn. You can't glue every fabric to a frame like muslin, especially some synthetic blends or thicker fabrics that won't absorb the glue the same way.

Sizing and Basing

The next step in both processes is to *size* the flat. In this case we don't mean measuring the flat. Sizing is shrinking the flat's cover. A 75% glue-to-water mixture will size a flat, as will commercial wall sizing. Another good method is simply to apply a base coat of latex paint; this will size the flats and gives all the flats a neutral base color to start from. If you have to repaint stock flats, basing over them is a good way to start. Primers are high-hiding paints that can cover over previous paint treatments. These act as good base coats as well.

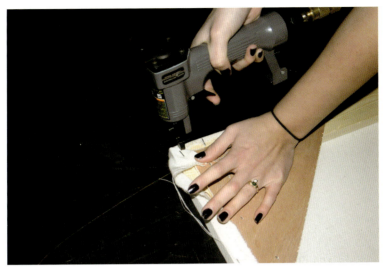

Figure 4.9: *Stapling the corners.*

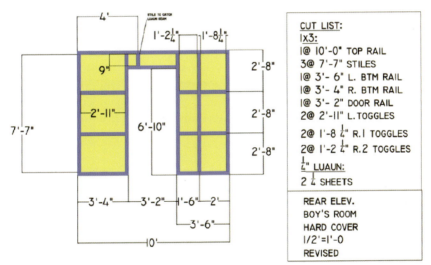

Figure 4.10: *Cut list and the technical drawings of a window-and-door flat showing the structure around the portals.*

Door and Window Flats

Door and window flats are built much the same as other flats, but with a hole built into them (Figure 4.10). When you frame them, you start from the basic outline the designer gave you and add structure around the opening.

When you cover these flats you can just simply cover them as you would a solid flat and then cut out the hole. Alternatively, you can cut individual pieces of covering and cover sections, placing your seams on the frame's members as support.

With a soft-cover flat it is difficult to cover sections without creating some kind of visible seam. You can seam the flat on a toggle or a stile and cover it the traditional way, without staples. You'll need to plan your seams to fall in the center of either a stile or a toggle and glue them and press them down carefully, smoothing the frayed edges of fabric into each other. If you can plan these seams around lines that will be painted on the flat, you'll have a better chance of hiding them.

> ➤ **TIP** On the outside edge of every piece of fabric you'll find the *selvage*. Rip this off if it will be visible, since it forms a hard edge. Softer frayed edges of fabric are harder to read from the audience. You never want a selvage edge on a seam.

> ➤ **TIP** You can also sew a cover's seams together and cover the flat with staples or glue it to the frame. As you can imagine, this take a little more time, but sometimes it's the only way to cover a wide, large flat.

The Hard Way: Hard Covering a Standard Flat

Actually it isn't hard at all. It's basically the same assembly process as soft covering a flat, except when you get to the corner blocking step you have two options. Some TDs argue that the corner block is an unnecessary step in a hard-cover standard flat since the skin actually does the same job as a corner block. Others want the corner block's extra structural support since ¼″ luaun, the most common and affordable hard cover, varies in strength from sheet to sheet. Also, if you don't hard cover the frame right away, the corner blocks keep the flat square until you do. Of course, if you are building a Hollywood flat, the corner block question is moot.

When attaching a hard cover to a standard frame, start by removing the screws you used to square the flat. It helps to lift the frame just to make sure it's free from the floor. You'll hate yourself if you hard cover the flat to the floor; a flat skin is harder to take off than a corner block, especially if you have glued it well. And this brings us back to the point that the glue is what really holds a flat together.

Spread the glue along the face of the flat and smooth it out, as discussed before. Then lay your flat cover over the flat and line it up with the bottom rail and one corner of the flat. Staple the rail every 10″ or so, working toward the squared corner. Put a staple into the stile (staying perpendicular to the grain), and take a look at the cover. Is it all lined up? If it isn't, you need to get a helper to tweak the luaun square with the frame as you staple. Continue around the flat edges. Then snap chalk lines across the luaun skin at the center point of the flat's toggles (measure from the bottom rail) and staple across the chalk line into them as well.

> ➤ **TIP** If you are working by yourself on a 4′–6′ wide to up to a 12′ tall flat and you corner-blocked the frame, you can still square up the sides. Staple the rail

and then put a staple into the stile as before. Now slowly lift the frame up onto whichever side the skin underhangs. The skin will shift with the frame and pull itself into alignment with the flat. Slowly tweak the flat back and forth until you have the proper alignment, and then staple the top side to lock it in.

Plugging the Staple Holes and the Little Dutchman

When you look at your finished flat you'll notice that it has a series of neat holes right where you stapled. As proud as you are of your stapling job, there is an excellent chance the designer doesn't want the audience to see them. There are a couple of ways to hide them.

First, you could cover your flat with a layer of muslin. Some designers specify this because of the nice paint surface the muslin gives them. Another method is to JC (joint-compound) the holes or fill them, using joint compound or spackle. Other choices include water putties, wood fillers, and auto body filler. Joint compound used in drywall joints is by far the most economical. This is a common method to hide fastener holes or any surface imperfections. What you need to remember as you apply the filler is that you are filling a hole, not building up the surface. Whatever stays on the surface will just have to be sanded off. Our goal is a flat, smooth surface.

> **TIP**   Take your putty knife with some joint compound on the underside, place it just above the staple hole, press down, and pull back sharply. The joint compound will fill the hole without building up on the surface. Scrape off as much joint compound from the surface as you can with the putty knife, and you've saved yourself some sanding time.

> **TIP**   When you have to hard cover a flat that is larger than $4' \times 8'$, you will need to place your sheet seam on a toggle or stile to give the sheet support and something to staple to. In a Hollywood flat you can turn this piece on its face instead of on edge to give yourself a nice wide seam support. You can also double the thickness of an on-edge toggle by adding scrap pieces to the top face. Make sure you place the sheet seams in the center of the toggle to give you equal support on either side. Of course if you have a flat that is wider than $4'$, all of the same techniques for placing seams apply to stiles as well as toggles.

> **TIP**   If you aren't going to muslin-cover this hard flat you'll need to hide the seam somehow. One method is by using a Dutchman. But if he can't stand in front of the seam all day, then you need to use a *dutchman* instead. Traditionally, a dutchman is a strip of muslin back-painted or glued and spread across the joint. It bridges the seam gap and creates the look of a smooth, continuous surface. These work well on soft-cover flats. By slowly smoothing out the glued back-side against the flat face and feathering out the frayed edges with your paint brush, you can create a nearly invisible line.

> **TIP**   Because the fabric's texture is different from that of smooth luaun, sometimes cloth dutchmans actually do more harm than good by creating a top

and bottom seam line with a middle section of a different texture. You can make a thinner dutchman out of wallpaper or newsprint and carefully spread it across the joint. An even better method of hiding seams is to plan them to fall behind moldings or other architectural features.

Irregular-Shaped Scenery and the Full-Scale Layout: A Story of a Designer, Some Technicians, and Their Quest to Take Something Little and Make Something Big Look Like It

Designers like funky shapes. We'd love it if they just designed $4' \times 8'$ flats and platforms. We could bang those out like mad, then sit around and complain about how slow the electricians are. But the reality is they don't design that way; we have to make them the way they draw them and find something else to pick on the sparkies for. So how do we turn the designer's little squiggles into giant squiggles?

CAD technology has made this a lot easier. We can actually print out CAD or scanned pencil design shapes into full-scale sections, piece them together on our workpieces, and cut them out. But if you don't have this technology available, you may want to learn the old-school method of *gridding* a layout.

A Scale Ruler, a Chalk Line, a Squiggly Design, and Thou

The first thing is to see what scale the design is in. Then you take a scale ruler and go to work. Draw a horizontal baseline, making sure it touches the bottom of the unit. Draw a line perpendicular to the baseline at the extreme left or right of the unit, making sure you have all of the shape behind the line. We'll call this the *y*-axis (Figure 4.11). Measure up this line, starting at the baseline, marking it at regular intervals in the appropriate scale with the scale ruler. Do the same thing along the baseline, starting from the corner and working toward the other end of the line.

Now draw a perpendicular line up and out from the last mark on the baseline, parallel to the *y*-axis so you enclose the drawing. Make the same marks at the same intervals up this line as well. Draw another line at the top of the elevation, parallel to the baseline so the entire thing is boxed in, and mark it the same as the baseline. Now connect lines at the opposite sides, completing the grid. Make sure the lines are all square and you've gridded the entire shape.

> ➤ **TIP**   If you don't have drafting equipment at hand, in a pinch you can use your framing square to draw perpendicular lines. If this is too big, use it to check the square on a corner block and use its right angle instead.
> ➤ **TIP**   If your elevation is in ½″ or ¼″ scale, you can speed the gridding process up considerably by using a quad graph paper jig. Prep a piece of quad graph

Figure 4.11: *Gridded elevation from the Pennsylvania Shakespeare Festival's* Merchant of Venice.

paper (four squares to an inch) by darkening over the lines in marker. Trace every line for ¼″ and every other for ½″ until you have a grid the size you need. You can save this grid jig for other drawings. Tape this jig to the window, and then line up and tape your elevation to a baseline on the grid and tape it over. Of course this only works if there is light coming through the window.

➤ **TIP**   If you have a copy machine at your disposal, you can take your grid jig and copy it to a transparency. Then you can tape this over your elevation.

Here's where the chalk line comes in. You now want to go to your workpiece and draw a baseline and a *y*-axis just as you did before, but this time in full scale. Make marks at the same intervals going in the same directions as you did to draw the grid on the elevation. Snap these lines with a friend, making sure you are directly across from each other, and create the grid in full scale.

Figure 4.12: *Full-scale layout for the Pennsylvania Shakespeare Festival's production of* A Little Mermaid. *In this photo the sea floor is gridded using string to avoid marking the carpet.*

Now look at your gridded elevation. Start at the baseline and look at a specific grid square. Find that square on your full-scale layout. Using the grid square on your elevation as a guide, draw the shapes inside that little grid square in your big grid square. Continue until you have transferred over all of the grid squares on the elevation to your full-scale drawing. Gigantic layouts can be made this way (Figure 4.12).

> ➤ **TIP** Don't throw out that ancient opaque projector; if you still have it you can project your layouts. Start by marking your workpiece to the general size you want the projection to be. Stand it up so it can become a projection screen for the opaque projector. Then darken the room, put your drawing in the projector, and move the projector back and forth until the projection fits inside of the outline you marked. Trace the projection and you are finished.

Irregular Frames

For the most part the standard flat frame construction method best fits an irregular flat, since it's on-face frame can be more easily adapted to an outline and corner-blocked in place at odd angles. Now that you have the outline made, you're halfway home when it comes to framing the irregularly shaped unit. Cut out the outline and any inside voids or windows. Mark the face "face," and mark the back "back." Flip it over on its top so that the bottom is face up. "Why? I won't forget." If you don't do this and build the entire thing wrong, you will hate yourself even worse than when you corner-blocked the flat to the floor.

Now try to imagine the standard rectangular flat that lives inside this shape. Keep in mind that rails run on top and stiles are in between them. Take some 1 × 3 scrap and trace in the framing outline in full scale on the back. Place toggles every 30″ from each other, and make sure you catch the seam lines. With these irregular shapes it is a good idea to corner-block even though you have a hard skin. This corner block will undoubt-edly have an irregular shape, so you will have to custom cut each one. If this flat doesn't mate to another flat, don't worry about the ¾″ indent; take it all the way to the edge.

> ➤ **TIP**   A quick way to get these shapes is to lift the frame a bit, slide the poten-tial corner block under it, and trace its outline. Slide it out and cut it. Chances are it will be too steep an angle for your miter saw, so cut it on the band saw, jigsaw, or scroll saw. Make sure the grain isn't parallel to the joint. When you go to staple the block, follow the same basic rules, two on either side of the joint and a few others to hold the end down, always placing them across the grain.

One problem with 1 × 3 framing is that there isn't an easy way to bend it to a curved shape to support an irregular outline. Instead we can cut sweeps of plywood and wide-crown them to the 1 × 3's to give the curved shape support. When you are planning your frame, take the 1 × 3 rails and stiles as close to the edges as you can without breaking through the outline with the 1 × 3's straight lines. Whatever is left hanging over may be ¾″ plywood. You may trace the shape by laying a square edge of the plywood flush to the edge of the rail or stile, lifting the frame and outlined skin a bit and tracing the shape on the plywood. Cut this shape out, and glue and wide-crown it on. Once you have the entire outline framed out, flip the unit on its face, line the outlined skin up to its frame, and glue and narrow-crown it down.

This method also works well for the irregular platform. Lay out the shape on the plat-form skin and cut it out. Look for the square platform shape inside the irregular shape. Mark the top "top," and mark the bottom "bottom." Flip it over on its top so that the bottom is face up. Take a piece of framing stock, 2 × 4, for example (though you could just as easily use 2 × 6 or 1 × 6), and place it on edge as it would be in the finished platform. Use this as a jig to trace the outline of the platform frame on the back in full scale. Lay out the frame as you did with the irregular flat, following the basic rules.

> ➤ **TIP**   Where you need to cut odd angles, take your t bevel and copy the angle from the full-scale outline you drew and cut it. If the angle is too extreme to cut on the miter saw, use a band saw or clamp the workpiece down and a use a reciprocating saw; or if you're having someone else cut it, use a hand saw.
> ➤ **TIP**   You may also trace the angle from the skin the same way you did with the corner block, but platform materials are heavier than 1 × 3 and luaun. Line up your 2 × 4's to the full-scale outline. When you have a joint that has a sharp angle, stack up the 2 × 4's of the surrounding members to copy that angle, and trace the places it intersects on the 2 × 4's (Figure 4.13).

Figure 4.13: *Tracing the 2 × 4 angles for a platform.*

Platform Leg Types

We've talked about the legs on a platform, but we haven't talked about the types of leg styles available. Before we talk about leg styles, we should talk about how legs work. Legs are most effective when they support the frame of a platform, not the skin. If the leg is attached to the skin, it's quite likely that the frame will separate from the skin. This leaves you standing on a piece of ¾″ plywood with nothing to keep it rigid. You'd better step off it.

The leg's main goal in life is to bring the platform up to a finished height. A platform's finished height is the height of the platform from the stage floor with any additional decking, such as painted Masonite, on it. Therefore a platform with a finished height of 8″ would need a 7″ leg: 7″ leg + ¾″ plywood skin + ¼″ painted Masonite deck = 8″. Leg heights are finished height − skin + decking.

Here's a list of some common leg types (Figure 4.14).

- *Straight leg*: This is the most common leg. It's usually a piece of 2 × 4. You can also make it from 1× material. You will need to cross-brace the heck out of these things once you get past 7″. They are also subject to the twists and turns of the lumber itself.
- *Hog trough leg*: This improves on the straight leg by adding another perpendicular to it. Both sides help to straighten each other.
- *Step leg*: This leg is a little different from the other two. You cut one leg to the standard leg height and then cut a second leg (the *step*) the same thickness as the

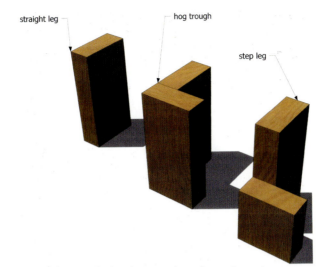

Figure 4.14: *Drawing of the straight leg, hog trough, and step leg styles.*

platform's frame, to the height of the bottom of the frame to the floor. (Step length = frame face thickness + skin + deck − finished height). Then you glue and fasten the step to the other leg, flushing the bottoms. Once you've bolted this leg to the frame, the step sits under the frame and fully supports it.

- *Pipe legs* (Figure 4.15): These are usually made of black iron schedule 40 water pipe, and they can hold a lot of weight. Used at a low height they can be screwed into a pipe flange connected to the frame by a mounting plate. This is usually a piece of ¾″ plywood or 2 × 4 screwed and glued on face to the frame and parallel to the skin. The mounting plate connects the leg to the frame, which, as we said, is how you keep from standing on a teetering piece of ¾″ plywood. You may also U-bolt the legs to the outside of a platform or create a scaffold structure with pipe hardware such as Kee clamps or Rota pipe locks when creating taller structures. This isn't any easier than conventional legging, but it gives the structure a definite industrial look your designer may want.
- *Platform jacks:* Platform jacks are legs connected together to form a frame. This may be as simple as taking a long 2 × 4 or 1 × 3 and fastening it across a set of legs at their base and just below the platform frame. When you assemble the legs in this fashion, you have effectively made a long step leg.
- *Folding parallels:* These are actually a leg–and–platform unit that folds and disassembles. Basically you make 1 × 3 platform jacks that hinge together to fold and a ¾″ plywood skin that locks the unit together (Figure 4.16).

Building the Stressed-Skin Platform

As we said in Chapter 1, there are many ways of building the stressed-skin platform. The most common method consists of building a standard platform frame and

179

Figure 4.15: *Photo of a pipe-legged structure from DeSales University's production of* Cabaret. *In this photo, the student TD is pointing so that it looks like he is doing something important.*

Figure 4.16: *Tech drawing of a folding parallel platform.*

covering both sides with a skin. The problem we have with this method is that it makes attaching the legs difficult, because you can't get inside the platform. The following construction style, which we've used, takes care of this problem. The inset allows legs to be attached to the frame and stay flush to the outside dimension of the platform, which would be impossible with a traditional stressed–skin platform. This is handy since it allows you to attach any facing directly to the platform and the legs and have it be nice and flat like a big box side. The platform is inset 1½" around the perimeter of the frame for the 2 × 4 style leg. If you prefer the 1 × 3 or 1 × 4 style of leg, you can easily adapt the inset to match the width of your legs.

Inset Leg Stressed–Skin Platform

The cut list for the platform is as follows:

Fasteners, Hardware, and Other Supplies

There are a variety of fasteners needed for the project.

- 1⅝" #6 drywall screws may be used to fasten the ¾" skin to the frame.
  - 1¾" medium-crown staples can be substituted for 1⅝" drywall screws if you have pneumatic staplers on hand, or 1½" pneumatic nails will work.
- The frame may also be joined with 3" #6 or, even better, #8 drywall screws (easier to drive because of their beefier thickness).
  - 16d nails, 3" pneumatic framing nails.
- The second skin can be fastened with ¾" narrow-crown staples, 4d nails, or 1¼" drywall screws.

Glue! Glue! Glue! It's Always About Glue!

As you can see, a variety of choices are available to you. There is one fastener you can't do without, and that is glue. As we said, there are many styles of stressed-skin platforms; however, the one thing that everyone agrees on is that stressed-skin platforms must be glued at every joint. Many types of glues are available, but one of the most versatile glues to have in your shop is the old-fashioned white, water-soluble glue, or *aliphatic glue*. The advantage to this glue in this instance is that you can thin it out enough to pour it into a roller pan and roll it along the faces of the frame and other long joints. Any of these fasteners is holding the lumber together only long enough for the glue to dry.

Coffin Locks and Other Fasteners

Two fasteners that should be included actually do nothing to hold the platform together but do make the platform easier to use. Rota-locks (coffin locks) allow the platform to be tightly joined while one is standing on the platform deck. We will also need 2¼" × 1¾" to 2" stove bolts per coffin lock to attach it to the platform. And ⅜" tee nuts allow the platform legs to be bolted to the platform without having to get under the second skin to get inside the frame. The tee nut will slide into the hole and provide a ⅜" thread for the bolt to thread onto. It's held into the hole by its base, which is a

Figure 4.17: *Tee nut.*

fierce-looking circle with three to four prongs sticking out of it (Figure 4.17). It's these prongs that bite into the inside of the 2 × 4 frame and prevent the tee nut from rotating.

Also depending on the leg style we choose, we will need two to four ⅜″ × 3″ hex head or stove bolts per leg.

Noise Versus Art and Eric Clapton

If you take a frame and add surface to both sides, you have created a large sound box. You're only a hole, some strings, a neck, and a fret board away from a really big guitar.

The best way to stop the platform from sounding hollow when walked on is to fill that void with some kind of insulation. Test this out by borrowing a friend's guitar, filling the insides with some old rags, and then asking him or her to play a selection from one of Eric Clapton's albums. Don't do this with your own guitar, but that goes without saying. White polystyrene or beadboard or blue foam insulation cut and placed in the empty bays created by the toggles can help eliminate a lot of the noise produced by the platform's vibration.

Construction

The added advantage of this platform is the inset of the frame. For this example, we will build a 4′ × 8′ platform.

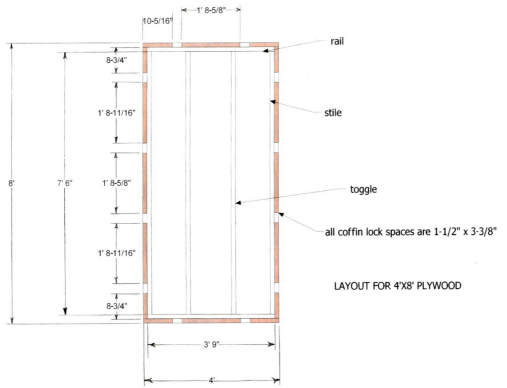

Figure 4.18: *Full-scale stressed-skin pattern layout.*

Layout

We'll begin by creating a large full-scale pattern on the skin of the platform. This pattern is extremely helpful with the first few platforms you build. As you become more accustomed to the construction methods you can simplify this layout and use only the lines you feel you need.

- Starting with a 4′ × 8′ sheet of plywood, draw guidelines at 1½″ in from and along each edge. This will be the inset for the platform frame (Figure 4.18).
  - ➤ **TIP**   A simple jig to draw these lines is a straight 2 × 4 stood on its 1½″ edge and placed flush to the plywood's edge
- Along the 4′ edge continue the 1½″ guideline until it touches both 8′ sides of the plywood; now you have a line that goes straight along the plywood at the top and bottom. This line will serve as the guidelines for the ¾″ × 1½″ thickness that will be added to the platform edges.
- The next layout step is to place marks on both 4′ edges every 16″ from the outside of one of the 8′ edges of the plywood. The two marks closest to the center are the midpoint location of the toggles. Connect these lines with a framing square and a straightedge, or snap a chalk line between the points.

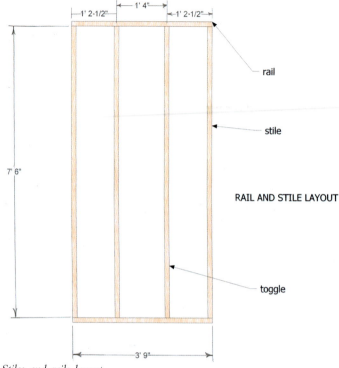

Figure 4.19: *Stiles and rails layout.*

Framing

Once the prep work is done you can begin framing the platform.

- Start by laying the frame rails perpendicular to the stiles. Add glue to the end of each stile and attach the rail to the stile using screws or nails. Check the joints for squareness with a framing square (Figure 4.19).

  ➤ **TIP** Working with warped or bowed 2 × 4 can be very frustrating, but it's a universal problem. In fact, there are a few commercial devices, such as the *bow wrench*, designed to pull the 2 × 4 back into shape. You can also do a fair job with a pipe wrench. Clamp the jaws over the edge of the 2 × 4 and pull it into place; have a friend fasten it while you hold it. If you add bowed lumber into your project, the toggles will force the frame into alignment and make attaching the skin to the structure easier.

- Lay the frame inside the layout you drew on the sheet of plywood, making sure the frame is nestled inside the 1½″ lines. Locate the toggle lines; using the framing square, transfer the lines up onto the inside of the frame face and over the top and across the edge.

- Add glue to the toggle ends and attach to the frame again, checking for square.

Edge Thickness

The added ¾″ thickness on the edge of the platform keeps the skin from bowing at the inset. This is also the part of the platform that will hold the coffin locks. The width of the coffin lock we are using is approximately 3⅜″, and its thickness is approximately ⅝″. If we were cutting a dado or a hole in the frame to fit the coffin lock into, we would need to worry about the width. In this case we don't have to. The coffin locks will sit between the thickness pieces and bolt onto the skin with the ¼″ × 1½″ stove bolts we spoke of, and they will be "snugged up" flush to the top of the skin.

For this project we are going to construct a coffin-locked platform with locks spaced every 1′ from every corner and 1′ from the 4′ point or midpoint on the 8′ sides. The coffin-lock dimensions are based on a Safeco standard coffin lock's dimensions, but you can use the principles to adapt the dimensions to the type of lock you are using. Cut a piece of 1½″ scrap to 3⅜″, and mark it "coffin-lock spacer jig." Set it aside and don't lose it (Figure 4.20).

Four-Foot Side of the Skin

Starting at one of the 4′ edges of the plywood:

- Take one of the 10⁵⁄₁₆″ pieces of edge thickness and roll glue on its face. We're going to place this piece flush to one of the outside corners of the plywood—let's say the corner to your left, and we'll call this the *starting point*. Place the piece glue side up underneath the platform skin, where you drew your

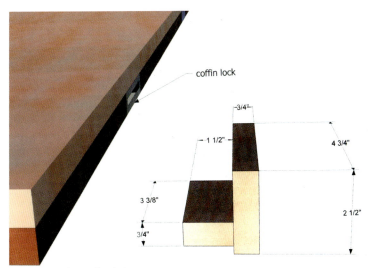

Figure 4.20: *Drawing of a coffin-lock jig.*

guideline for the thickness. The outside corner of the piece should now be flush to the outside corner of the plywood. Staple, screw, or nail this piece in place, with one fastener at either end and one in the middle, so we pull the piece nice and snug against the plywood. Wipe any oozing glue with a wet rag.

- Grab another 10⁵/₁₆″ and do the same thing to the right side.
- Take one of the 1′-8⅝″ pieces and mark its center at 10⁵/₁₆″. Mark the center of the 4′ side of the plywood near the bottom edge. Match these two marks and flush your piece up. Place a coffin lock in the gap to the left side and check to see if the fit is good; it should have just a tiny bit of wiggle room. Check the gap to the right in the same way. Trim if necessary.
- Attach this piece in the same way you attached the smaller pieces, making sure you glue the joint.

Eight-Foot Side of the Skin
Go back to the starting point and turn left to the 8′ side of the plywood.

- Take one of the 8¾″ pieces of edge thickness and roll glue onto its face. Place it perpendicular to the first piece you put on, with its 1½″ face flush to the 10⁵/₁₆″ piece and the edge of the 8′ side. It should look like an L is hiding under the platform. Attach it as before.
- Run some glue across a 1′-8¹¹/₁₆″ piece. Take the coffin-lock jig and place it to the left of the piece you just put in. Using it as a spacer, place the next piece to the left of the jig and attach it.
- Moving the jig to the left edge of this piece you should now be able to place the 1′-8⅝″ piece to the left of the jig. Attach this piece and the remaining pieces in the same way, making sure to glue the joints.
- If everything has lined up, the pieces should fit just like in the drawing, with the 8¾″ piece sitting nicely 1½″ from the corner.

From here you can just repeat the process for each length of side continuing from this point.

Drilling the Holes
There are two ways you can drill the holes for the coffin locks.

- If you're making only one, clamp the coffin lock in place and drill through the bolt holes. It's quick and dirty, but the drill bit may scuff the lock.
- Drill the holes for the male ends. Make these holes with a half-inch bit to give yourself a little wiggle room.
- The bolt holes can be drilled with ¼″ bits. They are needed for both types of locks.

Finish the process by bolting the locks into place. Make sure you snug the stove bolt so that it *countersinks* itself and that you put the male lock in the places where you have drilled the hole.

Adding the Frame

- Roll glue on the top edge of the platform frame. Make sure you get all the top edges coated, including the toggles.
- Lift the skin and lay it over the frame. It should snuggle right inside the edge thicknesses you just added.
- Using the lines you lay out on top of the skin as a guide, attach the frame to the skin with staples, nails, or screws. Space them about every 10″ or so. Make sure you grab the toggles as well as the rails and stiles. If you use the centerlines of the toggle, you shouldn't have any trouble. Remember, these fasteners aren't the primary holding force—the glue is. The screws, nails, or staples pull the pieces together and get the proper bond. You could achieve the same effect with a whole lot of clamps, but that's not as practical when you have more than one platform to build.

Adding the Legs

There are three leg styles you can use: *straight*, *hog trough*, and *step leg*. Remember, the inset in the platform is geared toward the 2 × 4 dimensions. The important thing about the choice at this point is the number of holes you will need to drill into the frame while you still have access to the inside of it. Whichever style you use, it is best to create a hole-drilling jig (Figure 4.21) to keep the hole spacing consistent, especially if you are going to keep the legs in stock.

Just to make things interesting we will use a variation on two styles, combining the step leg and the hog trough. This combines the stability of the hog trough leg with the extra support the step leg gives. For this example we will want our platform to have a finished height of 12″. The finished height of a platform is the height of the platform with any additional decking.

Step/Hog Trough Combo, or the "Stepped Hog" Leg

- Cut one 2 × 4 and one 2 × 6, for each leg, to the height you need the legs to be. It sounds simple, but keep in mind that you have just added ¾″ thickness to the bottom of the skin. You'll need to subtract that amount from the length of your leg. This will make the 2 × 4 leg 1½″ smaller than the total height you want the platform to be (skin + thickness). Also, if you are going to add any

187

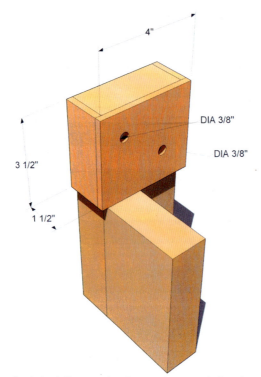

Figure 4.21: *Drawing of a hole-drilling jig for the step hog trough leg showing the leg.*

additional decking material, such as ¼″ luaun or Masonite, tile, or wooden planks, you'll need to subtract its thickness from the leg length as well.

- Cut the 2 × 6 to 4¼″ − the thickness of the platform + the thickness of any additional decking material you added. Cut another piece of 2 × 4 to 4½″ (the thickness of the platform) less than the finished height of the platform, making sure the bottom edges are flush and to glue the joint. It should look like an L.
- Spread glue on one of the faces of the new piece. Put this face inside the L piece mated to one of the faces and with bottom edges together.
- Take your leg-drilling jig and drill holes into the top part of the legs, that is, the opposite side of the leg that doesn't have the little 2 × 4 step on it.

Drilling and Installing the "Tee" Nuts

The best-size bolts for the job are ⅜″ × 3″ hex head or stove bolts. Ordinarily, you would use at least a 3½″ bolt (the two 2 × 4's are 3″ thick plus the extra ½″ to get the nut and washer on the end of the bolt), but we won't be using a traditional nut. The tee nut fits inside the hole we will drill, and we don't need additional length for a nut and a washer. The hole size will have to be larger than you would normally drill for a ⅜″ bolt to allow for the sides of the tee nut to fit into the hole. You should check the size of the nut you are using, but on average a $^{29}\!/_{64}''$ bit should work for this size tee nut.

- Just to be consistent, go back to the corner we began with when we did the edge thickness. Clamp your drilling jig onto this corner, and drill into the frame with the $^{29}\!/_{64}''$ drill bits at the jig's guide holes.
- Take a tee nut and place it into a hole from the backside. With a hammer tap the nut until it is seated. If you're carrying around a lot of aggression you could just whack the nut until you seat the base and the prongs flush to the 2 × 4's face. It's a lot easier to tap it just enough that the bolt can catch the nut's threads and let the tightening of the bolt suck the tee nut into the hole. However, if you aren't going to be legging the platform in the foreseeable future, whack away.
- If you'd like extra added assurance—if you're the kind of person who triple knots your shoes—you can dab some epoxy on the back of the tee nut's base. Be careful to avoid getting epoxy on the threads, and make sure to seat the tee nut before the epoxy dries.

Finishing with the Second Skin

- Take a 4′ × 8′ sheet of plywood and trim it to 3′9″ × 7′9″.
- Roll glue over the edge of the frame that's looking at you.
- Go back to our favorite corner with the sheet of ¼″ plywood and fit it over the frame, flushing it to this corner.
- Start with one fastener in the corner and work toward you right along the 3′9″ side of the frame.
- As you continue up the 7′9″ side of the platform to your right, check the "flush-ness" of the second skin to the frame.
  - ➤ **TIP**   If the skin is hanging over one side more than the other, you can "tweak" the frame and skin into square.
- Stop fastening the skin at the point where the skin just starts to veer away from the frame.
- Get a pipe or bar clamp that can open wide enough to fit over the platform's width. Make sure that the screw handle is run all the way down so that you have room to tighten.
- Put the clamp over the platform a few inches away from the point where you stopped fastening, with the screw handle side opposite the point where the skin hangs over. The opposite side of the clamp should be on the skin. (You can place a scrap block of plywood on the edge of the skin to prevent the clamp from digging into the skin too much.)
- Tighten the screw. You should see the skin shift over and sort of pivot on the last fastener you put in. Stop tightening when you see the skin is flush with the frame.

Figure 4.22: *Finished platform shown with legs added.*

- Put another fastener into the skin to hold this in place.
- Loosen the pipe clamp and repeat the process as necessary.
- If you are tweaking often, you should look at your build process. Is the lumber substandard? Are your joints square? Are all your pieces the correct length?
- If everything is flush, continue around the platform, tweaking as necessary. Don't rush, but don't let the glue dry before you have fastened it either. Once again, the fasteners only hold the wood together until the glue dries (Figure 4.22).

Rakes, Ramps, and Stairs

A *raked* stage is not a neatly landscaped platform. *Rakes* are sloped platforms that are higher on one side, the upstage side, and lower on the other, the downstage side. There are a couple ways to do this but they all benefit from a full-scale drawing.

Raked Stock Platforms

- This is the most direct way to make a raked stage. The legs are cut at an angle to the floor and bolted to its frame. This allows you to use standard legging positions and existing bolt holes in the platforms. You can adapt this to any leg style you choose
- To draw a full-scale pattern of these platforms, you need to know the rake's *rise* and *run*. A typical rake will rise ½″ to 1′ of run (but your designer will specify a specific rise and run for you). On a ½″-to-1′ rake, for every 1′ you move back the rake moves up ½″. The designer will no doubt draw a cross section of the stage rake, and you can use this as a reference for your drawing. This cross section will be just the basic outline; you'll need to draw in platform thicknesses, rails, and leg positions.
- Start as we did before, with a baseline. Then draw a *y*-axis to the length of the rake's downstage height. Move over to each platform edge and draw in the platform's rail.
- Now take a 2 × 4 and draw in a leg position perpendicular to the platform and extending down to the baseline. A typical 4′ × 8′ 2 × 4 framed platform will

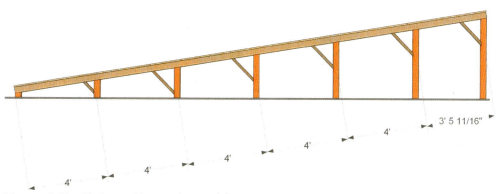

Figure 4.23: *Platform with correctly spaced legs.*

need a leg every 4′, making for six legs per platform; one at the downstage rail, one at a middle toggle, and one at the upstage rail on both sides (Figure 4.23). Mark the leg lengths with numerical or alphabetical labels, or name them after your favorite pets.

- Using the full-scale drawing take, your T bevel and trace the angle of the rake. Set your miter saw to this angle. Now look at each leg position, count how many units you'll need for each size leg, and make a cut list. Label each leg as you cut it.
- Bolt the legs in ascending order to keep from confusing them. It helps to label the leg positions on the actual platforms.
- Cross-brace any leg over 7″ from two directions.
- At this point, your rake looks like a lot of upside-down bugs. Get a few people together and flip them over. Then move them in place, and lock them together with ⅜″ carriage bolts through the platform frames.
- Go around to all the outside legs and *toe* them down. This doesn't mean adding appendages to these lucky outside legs. Toeing is actually the process of locking the platform legs to the floor. You toe a leg by tilting a nail or screw at a bit of an angle to the leg and nailing or screwing it in.

Raked–Platform Jacks

Using your full-scale layout, you may connect your straight rake legs to each other by making a raked platform jack. The top of the jack slopes at the same angle as the rake and sits directly under the platform frames. The advantage of this method is that you can make them in 16′ lengths and lock platforms together.

Stud Wall Construction

Another variation on this method is to make a series of on-edge framed 2 × 4 jacks that resemble the structure of house walls or studs. Going back to your full-scale drawing, you simply create the shape of the rake under the platform's frame 2 × 4's

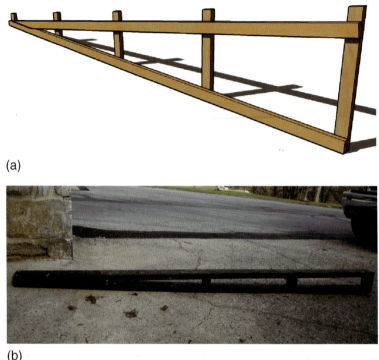

(a)

(b)

Figure 4.24: *Drawings comparing (a) platform jack rakes and (b) stud wall.*

(Figure 4.24). The wide face of the 2 × 4 gives you plenty of space to lay your platforms on it and a nice surface to screw it down to the floor without having to toe the legs. (If you really miss doing this, you can draw little toes on the stud walls).

Ramps

Ramps are small rakes. We use them as stair alternatives or as a front piece to a rake where the rake needs to smoothly transition into the stage floor. When you need this, you can easily make a full-stage layout on a piece of ¾″ plywood and cut triangular sweeps to use as legs. You're creating a sloped plywood platform frame that's open on the low side. If it doesn't need to go to zero, then rake a platform in one of the methods described earlier.

Stairs

Stairs have a rise and run as well. A common rise and run found on stage is an 8″ rise and an 11″ run. There are three main parts to a staircase: the riser, the tread, and the carriage, also known as a *stair jack* or *stringer*.

Carriages

A carriage is the zigzag frame that gives the staircase its shape. There are two types of carriages: open and closed.

An *open* carriage is usually made of 2 × 12, 1 × 12, or ¾" plywood ripped to width and length. You literally cut the rise and run out of the carriage at an angle to the edge.

> ➤ **TIP** One of the features of the framing square is its use for laying out stair-cases. Hold the square on the edge of the lumber and set the square's edge on the measurement for the rise, in this case 8". The measurement for the run is next. Swing the other leg of the framing square around to the measurement on the same side of the square, in this case 11". Trace the inside of the framing square and slide it over for the next tread. Stair gauges clamped onto the framing square hold the measurement so that you can use your square like a jig (Figure 4.25).

You then cut this layout with a circular saw or a band saw. Band saws are nice because you can get right into the corners and cut the scrap piece out in one operation. However, the depth of the band saw's neck can make it difficult to cut long carriages. A circ saw can cut the carriage as well, but you need to stop short of the corner and finish the cut with a handsaw or a jigsaw to avoid overcutting the corner. Never use a jigsaw to cut the entire carriage; the thin blade of the jigsaw will flex on thicker materials, giving you a wobbly cut.

Closed carriages require less precision cutting. You can actually construct a closed carriage from the same materials and lay it out the same way with a framing square, but

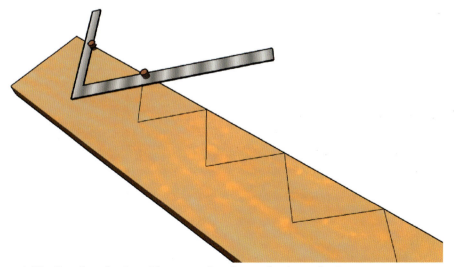

Figure 4.25: *Drawing of a 2 × 12 open carriage layout showing a framing square.*

Figure 4.26: *Steel-framed closed-carriage staircase.*

instead of cutting it out, you can just fasten nailing blocks to the layout's outlines (Figure 4.26).

Treads are the part of the stair you walk on. Their width is determined by the run of the stair. On an open carriage, the tread length is determined by the total width of the stair-case. Closed-carriage treads are the width of the staircase minus the thickness of the car-riages. *Risers* are the facing that covers the rise on the carriage. Their length is determined the same way as the tread's length, and their height is the same as the stair's run.

Moving Scenery

While scenery can be quite moving, especially if those darn actors would stop stand-ing in front of it, we're talking about moving scenery from one place to another. There are a few basic techniques: walking, running, footing, tabling, on edge, and floating.

Walking Scenery

Walking a flat is easier than walking a dog because you don't have to carry that little plastic bag around with you; you're just taking the flat from a horizontal position to a

Figure 4.27: *Two people walking a flat up.*

vertical one. Basically, to walk a flat up, you lay the flat on its face, lift the flat off the floor from its top rail, and have someone foot the other side (Figure 4.27). In this case, the foot goes in front of the bottom rail and keeps the flat from shifting forward as the top rail is lifted up. Now that the top of the flat is in the air and the bottom can't go anywhere, you simply continue walking forward, letting your hands slide down the face of the flat as you gently push up until the flat is vertical.

This is easy with a soft-cover flat because they weigh next to nothing, but you have to be careful to place your hands on the framing since the muslin gives under pressure. Hard-cover flats and platforms can be lifted this way too; they weigh more, but you don't need to worry about hand placement. Four-foot-wide flats even up to 16′ tall can be walked by one person, but any wider is best done with two walking and two footing (Figure 4.28).

Calling All Walking Platforms: Walking Platforms Safely

Platforms, because of their weight, can always use as many people as you can get around them. But this causes another problem: When more than one person lifts anything, someone has to be in charge to make sure communication is clear and that people are

195

Figure 4.28: *Walking the fireplace unit up for DeSales University's production of* The Diary of Anne Frank.

working safely. This person is the *caller*. The caller is the one voice that people are to listen to for instructions and counts; he tells you by his count when you're going to lift the piece, reminds you to bend your knees and lift with your legs, not your back; and before you drop the piece on his count, he'll make sure everyone's fingers, toes, and other body parts are clear.

> ➤ **TIP**   When lowering a large piece of scenery, such as a heavy platform, from vertical to horizontal, you can walk it *down*; it's the same process in reverse. The part that people get hung up on is the very end, when you are inches from the ground and you have to get your fingers out. Usually the caller says, "Watch your feet. On my count—one, two, three—drop. Watch your eyes." Everyone lets go at once and the platform falls to the ground, pushing the air underneath it out along with all the dust. "Eyes" is a call to remind you to look away; even with safety glasses on, the high volume of dust can kick right into your eyes. You can avoid this with a little forethought and preparation and some 2 × 4 scraps. By placing the 2 × 4's where the top of the platform will come down, you can lower the scenery onto the 2 × 4's instead of dropping it. The 2 × 4's lift the platform edge off the ground, giving you enough room to easily get your fingers out from under the platform without crushing them.

Floating Scenery

While inflatable scenery is becoming popular, that's not what this term refers to. *Floating* a flat is simply letting a flat drop from a vertical position to a horizontal position. Flats are ideal candidates to float since their large surface area and low weight make them act like a sail. Remember what we said about the air under a platform when it's dropped? In this case the displaced air actually slows the flat's descent, creating a cushion of air for the flat to fall on. It's really cool to watch, since you see this large object fall with hardly a sound. Soft-cover flats float best; platforms aren't good candidates for floating. The heavier an object is compared to its surface area, the faster it will fall and the more likely it will sustain damage.

Low-Impact Running

Running a flat is actually controlled *dragging*. Remember when we spoke of the anatomy of a flat and pointed out that the rails run the width of the flat? One of the main reasons it looks that way is that the easiest way to move a vertical flat is to run it, and the full width makes the flat easier to slide.

Two people face each other, with one hand as high as they can comfortably reach and one hand as low as they can reach. We call this position, oddly enough, *one hand high and one hand low*. When you face your partner and she's not doing it, you say, "One hand high and one hand low" until she does. You have every right to insist on safe practices; in fact, it's an obligation. Then slightly tipping the flat back so it's on one edge, you drag the flat in the direction you want to go.

Overtipping Doesn't Get You a Good Table

You can run a platform a short distance, but usually the easiest way to move a platform is to *table* it. Just like the name implies, you hold the platform between you and a partner so that it looks like a table. Keep it as flat as possible, and let the person walking backwards know if he or she is going to walk into something, since if that person falls, you and the platform will fall too.

> ➤ **TIP**   The easiest way to carry anything heavy is to keep your arms straight instead of bending them. Old-timers used to say, "Carry it with your bones, not your muscles." What they meant was that you expend extra energy bending your arms by keeping that muscle flexed.

Even a Good Table Won't Get You Through the Door

If you ever have to carry a scenic piece though a door that's too wide to table through, what will you do? You'll tip the piece on edge. To get from horizontal to vertical you'll need to set the piece down on one edge. Then you'll stand at opposite ends from your partner, bend your knees, and lift. You'll keep one hand high and one hand low, with the bottom arm straight, the hand holding underneath the platform, and the top hand behind the top edge steadying the platform's balance. Make sure that you and your partner are on the same side of the platform, or you'll be fighting each other to keep balance.

When carrying or moving scenery, good communication is just as important as good planning. Don't carry anything farther than you have to; if you can put something on a wheeled dolly, use it. If something is too heavy for you, let your partner know and get an additional person to help.

Connecting Different Types of Scenery

Connecting Flats

Everybody wants to make a connection. Everybody wants to stand upright. So do flats. Oddly enough, if you take two flats and fasten them together, they will hold each other upright, like some kind of scenery support group. There are times when, just like us, scenery needs a little help from its friends. Here are a few examples of a flat's support group. To begin with, there are two types of scenery installations: permanent and shifting, or touring.

Permanent Installation

When we say *permanent* we mean it as permanent as anything gets in the theatre. These pieces aren't going to move as long as the show is open. Since that's the case, we can attach them with some pretty standard fasteners. Let's start by talking about self-supporting scenery.

Hollywood Can Rest on Its Fame . . . Err . . . Make That Frame

One of the attractive qualities of a Hollywood flat is that the on-edge construction allows you to screw right down through the bottom rail into the stage floor. Flats up to 10′ tall stand by themselves when screwed to the floor, without any other support at all. (Of course if you lean against it or even walk by it fast there is a good chance it will fall over; but it's a good start). The on-edge construction style allows you to easily join one flat next to another; for quick setups you can even clamp flats together. If you throw a flat into the mix set at 90° to the other flats every 6 feet or so, you may not need any additional vertical bracing since it will help support the others. But as we said before, Murphy's Law rules theatre; we need to be prepared for the worst-case scenario.

Hollywood, Brace Yourself

That's where stage braces come in. *Stage braces*, or *flat jacks*, look like a right triangle on a long stick (Figure 4.29). These devices have been are around as long as we have had flats, and they are used in conjunction with Hollywood and theatrical flats. They are easy to use: The stile of the stage brace connects to a stile on the flat, and the stage brace's bottom rail connects to the floor. Most often stage braces are made to stock scenery sizes, such as 8′, 10′, 12′, and 16′. The stage brace's structure takes advantage of

Figure 4.29: *Stage braces and the infamous Yonkers flat that appeared in numerous DeSales University productions.*

one of the strongest geometric forms, the triangle. By adding the little diagonal brace or corner brace piece in the stage brace, we keep the stage brace from flexing and it prevents a flat from flexing backwards. Stiles are most effective when they reach the top of the flat. A rule of thumb for rail length is approximately one-fourth the stiles' height and the diagonal corner brace anywhere from two-thirds to three-quarters. Corner-block the wood joints as you would a standard flat frame, maintaining the ¾″ to 1″ inset from the outside edges.

There is even an *adjustable stage brace* you may find kicking around older theatres. This is a contraption with two pieces of wood that slide back and forth until you get the length you want, and then a little clamp on the brace holds them in place. The metal ends provide attachment points to the floor and flat by sliding into specialized cleats on the flats and pinned by stage screws (see later) into the floor.

You Dirty Rat! You Can't Pin That on Me. Oh, You Did. Well, I Guess I'm Stuck

Stage braces may be connected to the flats in various ways. One of the most common methods is, believe it or not, hinging. Yes, hinges bend, but only if the object they are connected to isn't attached to anything. So, for example, if you attach three evenly spaced fixed-pin hinges to a stage brace, attach the other blade of each hinge to the stile of a flat, and then hinge the bottom rail of the stage brace to the floor; you've created a rigid structure. The nice thing about hinging is that the hinge will bend to the shape you need it to and not lose any strength.

You can also hinge the faces of flats together to form an inside corner. Once you dutchman over the faces of the hinges, you have two flats that are now one self-supporting unit. These flats conveniently fold together for storage. We call these *booking flats*, and they are notoriously famous as masking flats.

Hinging isn't the only way to attach the brace to the floor. Sometimes you may not be able to fasten to a stage floor; the management may not let you or you may be on cement or steel plate. To avoid using any kind of fancy fastener, you can simply weight down the bottom rail of the stage brace. Sandbags and pig iron weights from your fly system are two common choices.

A 2 × 4-able Solution

If you can screw into the floor, you can always toe through the stage brace's rail or, even better, screw a scrap 2 × 4 block alongside the rail, screw that to the floor, and screw the rail to the scrap 2 × 4. Blocking the rail is possibly the most economical form of securing it; everybody seems to have scrap 2 × 4. This method also works for flats and securing the bottom of platform facings. So whenever possible you need to save those scrap 2 × 4's; it will break your heart to cut up a full stick into little blocks.

> **TIP** You can make an extremely low-tech brace yourself that works the same way as the adjusting stage brace, with some 1× scrap. Pick a piece that reaches from about the flat's midpoint to about 3 feet behind it. Screw the 1× into the inside of one of the flat's stiles and then diagonally block it into the floor. These 1× braces also work to brace the top of flats to each other or (with permission) to the theatre's walls for the extra support you'd need to keep hard-cover flats from shaking when a door is closed (Figure 4.30). The key to this bracing is to pick solid scraps without cracks or loose knots and to make sure the audience can't see them once they are in place. You should also confer with the lighting designer on their placement before she spazzes on you for blocking her lights. Trust us, it's not pretty.

Theatrical Flats: Why Do They Have to Be So Dramatic?

Seriously, why do they? They're always walking, floating, or running, and they can't stand still by themselves like their Hollywood siblings. The on-face construction method doesn't give them as wide of a base as a Hollywood flat. So you could say it's genetic.

Figure 4.30: *1× Bracing from the backstage perspective.*

Aside from screwing them down through their bottom rail, you basically use the same methods to secure these flats as with their better-behaved siblings. If you attach two theatrical flats at a 90° angle to each other, they will self-support; you just have to block or hinge them to the stage floor.

Stage braces were invented for theatrical flats. The on-edge stile of the stage brace and the on-face stile of the theatrical flat form a rigid structure not unlike the hog trough leg. You can hinge the stage brace on or simply screw through the face of the flat into the stage brace. (If you're going to keep the flat around for some time, hinging is the less invasive method.) Next you need to block or hinge the brace's rail to the floor.

Fasteners—Rhymes with Fascinating, Doesn't It?

While we're talking about screws (we were, weren't we?), let's look at the basic types. We'll start with drive heads. There are three main types that you'll run into but there are countless more.

That Dang Screw!

The old standby type of screw is the slotted screw. You always seem to have more than a handful of these in the bottom of your hardware bins. That's because they're the most

Figure 4.31: *The author's father's original Yankee ratcheting screwdriver, complete with the straight slotted drive head that left the scar across his palm. These were designed for the assembly line, just like the Phillips head screw. (Courtesy of Bob and Theresa Napoli.)*

aggravating and difficult to use. The slotted screwdriver, or straight-bladed screwdriver, was never intended to be turned quickly. Whenever it is, it jumps out of the slot and heads right for your free hand. These screws are fine for softer woods and for use as adjustment screws, but they are freakishly dangerous for power drivers. The slotted screwdriver, however, is a very useful tool, and we like it.

Around 1933 the Phillips-head screw was invented for use in powered screw drivers to speed up production (Figure 4.31). The cross-shaped slot matches the cross-shaped driver head. These are designed not to slip at high speeds. They are designed to cam-out, though, and this can cause a problem when you're first learning how to drive screws.

Too Fast, Too Furious: A Story of Cam-Out and What You Can Do to Prevent It

The edges of the driver are slightly rounded, so when the screw is tightened too much, the drive head will slip out to prevent overtightening. This is *camming out*. When this happens, the driver head tends to chew up the little slots in the screw head, making the screw almost impossible to remove. Experience with a screw gun helps you avoid this, but we can give you a few tips. When the drive bit starts to cam out you'll hear a "brrrup! brrrup!" noise. This is your cue to readjust the driver head right or left, up or down until it is in a straight line with the shaft of the screw. You'll also need to press a little harder to overcome cam-out. Whenever the driving gets difficult, drive the screw in short pulses. This tends to defeat the camming nature of the drive head.

Again, It's Hip to Be Square

People who have trouble with the Phillips-head cam-out will be overjoyed with a Robertson, recess, or square-drive screw. The screw heads have a square hole in them that fits a square driver. These things hold onto the drive head so well you'd swear they were magnetic. In fact the biggest criticism of them is that they tend to pull the drive bit out of your screw gun when you pull it away from the inserted screw. They are becoming very popular in the United States, although they've been around for quite some time in other countries, such as Canada.

Basic Screw Types

There are three main screw types you'll run across in a theatre's hardware bin: wood screws, drywall screws, and self-tapping screws.

Wood Versus Drywall: An Epic Contest of Screw Champions

Drywall screws are the most familiar screws to the modern shop carpenter. Their manufacturing process rolls them between ridged plates, forming the threads, and this work hardens them as well. Wood screw threads are cut; this makes them softer than drywall screws, and they have duller points. They are also conical in shape, not round. If you don't predrill, you can easily split the wood.

Most people find drywall screws easier to use, since their sharp points and thread style zip right into wood, and they have abandoned the wood screw completely. But the work-hardening of drywall screws also makes them brittle; you can easily snap the head off of a drywall screw if the torque on your screw gun is too high. (Always drive screws in first gear, and don't crank the torque if you don't need to.) You can also cam-out and destroy the head faster than you can do anything about it. The brittle metal gives the screw lower shear strength; you can easily snap the end off a drywall screw with a hammer. This is a plus sometimes because of drywall screw sizing.

Drywall screws are limited in size. The selection ranges from the most common #6 1″, 1¼″, 1⅝″, 2, 2½″, and 3″ screws to some selections in the wider-diameter #8, including the longer 2½″ and 3″ screws. Wood screws come in multiple sizes and diameters.

So why use drywall screws? Well, they are fast, cheap, and available anywhere. The size limitation doesn't hinder us too much, for we use a limited amount of materials. The common thickness of materials we use (¼″, ¾″, ½″, and 1½″) work around the drywall screw's sizes. The major limitation is fastening ¼″ skins or corner blocks to 1× stock. The 1″ screw is the smallest drywall screw, and it's actually just a bit longer than 1″, depending on the manufacturer. Since most shops use ¾″ narrow-crown staples to fasten their ¼″ skins or corner blocks, this size limitation hasn't been that big of a setback.

➤ **TIP**   A rule of thumb when using a fastener is that the fastener should be twice the length of the material it's going through. Therefore, if you are fastening ¾″ on-face to ¾″ on-edge, you should have a 1½″ screw, which in drywall terms would be a 1⅝″ screw. A 2× to 2× would require a 3″ screw. If you need to fasten ¾″ face to face and can't have the screw stick through (and for safety's sake you shouldn't), you'll have to use 1¼″ screws. Also, it seems common sense, but always fasten through the thinner material into the thicker material.

Square-Drive Versus Drywall and Wood Screws

If you want to know anything about *square-drive screws*, follow this link to http://www.mcfeelys.com/sdscrews.asp. McFeely's square-drive screws are the self-proclaimed "square-drive authority." The newest generation of these screws is fast becoming the choice of woodworkers worldwide. They combine the sharp point and fast thread of drywall screws with the size varieties of the wood screw, and as we said before, there is virtually no cam-out. They are also heat treated, which makes them harder than the other two types. So why doesn't everyone use them? They are a better screw. Change is difficult, especially when you have a lot of scenery made with Phillips-head screws. But the ease with which these screws go in and their potential reusability make them a serious consideration, especially if you are just setting up shop.

Pocket screws are another type of screw, with a square drive specifically designed for face frame construction. If you reach inside your kitchen cabinet and feel behind the stiles of the cabinet frame you may discover two oblong holes. These are pocket screw holes. They are made with a special jig called a *pocket screw jig*. This jig adjusts for that funky angle you have to hold the screw at to toe it in. It also adjusts for the thickness of the material and puts the hole right in the center of the board, giving you optimum board penetration and little splitting. With glue, these screws form a very tough joint. For us, these can potentially replace wide-crown staples and corrugated fasteners. They also make very nice toe holes for stock platform legs. Everything you ever wanted to know about pocket screws can be found at http://www.kregtool.com/education_center/index.php.

Bolts

Bolts form a very tight compression joint and are the fastener you need if the joint will be under a lot of stress, as with a leg joint or anything that may be hanging overhead. There are three main types of bolts we use.

- *Lag bolts*: These bolts actually look like screws with a hex-shaped head. We use these bolts in applications where we can't get to the back of the fastener to put a nut on, like fastening a floor flange to the floor. You turn these bolts in by placing a wrench or a socket of the proper size over the head and tightening it down.

> **TIP** olt-and-screw mantra: "Righty tighty, lefty loosey." The majority of threads you'll run into for common fastening applications will be right-handed threads. (Unlike the reverse arbor thread on the table saw, which would be loosey righty, tighty lefty, and that just doesn't sound right.)

- *Hex-head bolts*: This bolt has the same kind of head as the lag screw, but the other side is flat and the thread is pitched to receive a nut. When you tighten a hex-head bolt, you grab the hex head with a wrench or socket to keep it from rotating and tighten the nut side.

  > **TIP** Yes, in a pinch you can hold a bolt head or nut with a pair of pliers (or pinch the head with a pair of pliers), but it isn't the best tool for the job. The teeth in the pliers' jaws will chew up the head of the bolt, which we want to avoid; rounded bolt heads and nuts are hard to turn. Washers are used with hex-head bolts and other bolts to keep the head or nut from biting into soft materials, such as plastic and wood, or bending tube steel, and they disperse the holding power of the bolt over a wider area. *Rated* bolts are bolts that have been tested to hold a specific load without failing. We like to work with a safety factor of 10 to 1 for anything that goes overhead (it's not just the actors that walk under flying scenery; we do too). This means that whatever you are holding up, the rating for the hardware and other rigging holding the object should be designed to hold 10 times the amount of weight. Here's where we give the Murphy's Law speech again and realize that what we do requires diligent safeguards, since flying scenery often moves quickly and in relatively tight spaces. To see if a bolt is rated, look at its box. If you've lost the box, you can find the rating written in code on the top of the bolt. There are lines on the bolt head, and when you add 2 to their number, the resulting sum will give you the bolt's rating (Figure 4.32). We refer to this rating as the bolt's *grade*. Common grades we use are grade 5 and grade 8. To learn more about rated bolts, look at http://www.mcmaster.com/.

- *Carriage bolts*: These bolts have a rounded head like a big dome. So how do you hold them to tighten them? Carriage bolts are primarily used for wood-to-wood or wood-to-metal fastening. Key here is the hole in the wood. Underneath the head is a little square collar or neck that locks into the round hole you drill for the bolt's shaft and keeps the bolt from turning as you tighten it. It won't work well if that square neck doesn't bite into the wood; occasionally you have to rap the bolt head with a hammer to seat it, and then you tighten the nut. Because you are using these bolts in soft materials you will need to use a washer on the nut side; the head is actually designed like a washer and doesn't need or want one. The carriage bolt is great for mounting legs on platforms and bolting platforms together, since these are wood-to-wood situations.

  > **TIP** The domed head does cause some problems when facing the platform. But if you drill a hole slightly larger than the size and depth of the head, you can eliminate that problem. We call this technique *counterboring*.

Figure 4.32: *Rated grade 5 bolt head.*

- *Framing nails and staples*: Yes, you may use nails and staples to connect scenery. Here's why most people don't. Nails are the cheapest and most common fastener around, and they hold things together pretty well. Nails also have good shear strength. Pneumatic nails and staples shot through their respective guns go into wood really fast. So why not use them? Nails and staples work by forcing the fibers of the wood apart, and their head, or *crown*, provides the surface area to hold the pieces together. Pneumatic nails and staples have glue on them that hold them together in the clip. When they are fired, the glue reheats and reactivates; this helps hold the fasteners in the wood. All this adds up to a one-way trip for nails and staple. They don't come out easily, and when they do the wood is never the same. So these fasteners are great for construction. But when you are connecting scenery that will be disassembled for stock use, you want to use a removable fastener like a screw or bolt.

  ➤ **TIP** There is a nail called a *duplex* or *toe* nail that was designed for easy removal and temporary construction. The duplex name comes from its two heads, one below the other. The lower head does the holding; the upper head is for driving, but it also gives you a place to hook your hammer's claw so that you can pull the nail out. These aren't that common anymore since pneumatics and screw guns became popular, but you can still find them.

Shifting (Touring) Installations

One of the illusions theatre is so good at creating is the illusion of permanence. We create things that appear to have greater depth and solidity than they actually do. Then we pack them up and store them away, sometimes in the course of an act. When we unhook a piece of scenery and move it offstage, we call this *shifting*. We discuss some of the tools for doing this next.

Loose-Pin Hinge

If you thought a hinge was a handy item, you'll love the loose-pin hinge. It's a hinge. The pin is loose. "Big deal," you say. "Fix it and let's move on with our lives." The reality is that the hinge pin is supposed to be that way. Loose-pin hinges, or loose pins, as we call them, have little 90° bends on the ends of the pin. These bends act as a handle for pulling the pin out. By hinging two flats together and later removing the pin, you have made it possible to quickly shift that piece of scenery offstage and even replace it with a second flat by matching the hinge pieces and dropping the pin back in. The possibilities are endless; you can use them for stage braces, folding parallel platforms, props, and any other item you want to quickly shift.

There are two halves to the loose pin: the male and the female (Figure 4.33). Just like there are never enough men around your theatre department when you want to do a production of *Henry V*, you always seem to lose the male ends of the hinge. It's one of the grand mysteries of theatre.

> **TIP** In a pinch you can cast a female in a male role in *Henry V*. You can also do that with a loose-pin hinge. The female side has two ears that stick above its blade like a cartoon mouse's. (The male side lives between these.) If you put one set of these ears inside another set, you can drop a pin through them. But more than likely, you've lost the pin as well. It's gone to that black hole where the male ends, your missing right sock, and no ATM fees have disappeared to. Run out to the lobby and, when no one is looking, grab a few wire coat hangers, cut them into short sections long enough to serve as replacement pins, and put the little 90° bends on the ends of the wire. Then blame the missing hangers on the electricians.

Figure 4.33: *Loose-pin hinge.*

Folding Foot Irons and the Stage Screw

Although it sounds like a compact medieval torture device, the folding foot iron is basically a modified hinge. The part that makes it unique is the large hole at the end of one of the hinge blades. This hole is made to hold a *stage screw*. The stage screw is another one of those pieces of stage hardware that have been around forever. The original stage screws looked like a lag bolt with a handle on top. You found your foot iron, put the point inside the hole, and tightened it down. The wide neck just under the handle acts as a washer and holds the blade down.

The improved stage screw is actually two pieces of hardware used together: the improved stage screw and the threaded insert. It's actually called the *improved stage screw* in most hardware catalogs, even though most people don't use the original type anymore. The insert is essentially a hollow lag bolt; it has lag threads on its outside, and boltlike threads in the hollow inside, similar to a nut. The threads on the improved stage screw are made to fit inside these threads. The original stage screw holes were hard to find once you removed the screw; and you always had the danger of the wood stripping out from repeated use. The metal insert's threads have increased holding power and have the additional benefit of making a metal clink when you're searching around in the dark for them.

Coffin Locks (Rota-Locks)

The coffin lock, also known by the brand name Rota-lock, is a grim enough term to follow the folding foot iron. Like the loose-pin hinge, this fastening device is made up of a male and a female side. The male side has a hex-shaped hole in it that an Allen key fits into. By turning the key in this hole, a cam turns and rotates into slots on the female side (Figure 4.34). This ratcheting action actually pulls two pieces of scenery together, making it an ideal fastener for joining stock platforming together. If you carefully lay out the coffin positions, alternating male and female sides around a platform, and do this in uniform fashion to all your stock platforms, you'll speed up your setup time astronomically.

Lash Cleats

This is another piece of hardware that's been around forever. And although there are specialized pieces of hardware to serve as lash cleats, you can temporarily make do with anything you can hook a piece of rope around. They function the same way as those little hooks at the top of your hiking boots grab your shoelaces so that you can pull your boots extra tight. By alternating the lash cleats in a zigzag fashion between two flats, you can lace them tightly as well. The tie line may be anchored at the top of one of the flats so that you can quickly run the cleats and tie the rope off. For some reason these aren't in wide use anymore.

Figure 4.34: *Coffin lock showing the cam extended and the mating female slots.*

Stiffeners

Remember those sci fi fantasy movies where some unspeakable terror is chasing the heroes into their castle and they bar the castle gate with a heavy timber dropped into metal brackets found on either side of the doors? That timber is a *stiffener*. If you line up a series of flats with stiffener brackets on their upstage side, a stiffener will prevent the flats from opening up and letting some unspeakable terror get at the actors.

Stiffeners, or *battens* (not to be confused with drop battens, though they are both just sticks of lumber), are a good way of joining smaller flat walls to make one large flat wall. This helps to utilize smaller stock or to join flats that were designed to fit inside the tour truck. The stiffener can be as simple as a piece of 1 × 3 screwed or bolted across the top rail of a series of flats, a loose-pin-hinged unit, or even a swinging batten bolted on one side that lowers into batten hooks.

These aren't the only ways to join flats and other scenery. One of the wonderful things about this profession is that if it is safe, fast, and inexpensive it's a usable idea. Don't let your own creativity be limited because your idea isn't in a book. Run it past a few people, test it on a small scale, and then, when you're ready, revolutionize the industry with the new, more improved stage screw.

Shifting Scenery

Shifting Flats

Flying scenery is one of the most potentially dangerous things we do in theatre. That's why we work with the 10-1 safety ratio mentioned in the last section. That's not just for the bolts; that's for any part of the flying rig, the cables, the connectors that hold the cables to the scenery and to the fly lines, the chain and connectors that hold the rigging to its batten, and on up the entire system. Let's look at the hardware first.

Flying Hardware

If you are looking in your rigging box and aren't sure if a piece of hardware is rated, the best thing to do is not use it. One of the easiest ways to make sure you have the piece of hardware you need for the job at hand is to order it from a reputable supplier and start fresh. This isn't cheap. Nothing about rigging should be done on the cheap. Your first step in assuring your crew's safety and that of the actors is to know your hardware.

Rated Hardware

This is hardware that is rated for a particular load. If it shouldn't be used for overhead lifting, most likely it will say, "Not for overhead lifting." So don't use it for that.

Hanging Irons

These are pieces of steel bent around D-shaped welded steel rings. The D-rings are what you connect the line to, and the steel is perforated to allow you to bolt it to the flat with rated bolts. (With wooden flats there are two schools of thought: (1) Always go with rated hardware; (2) the wood will fail before the rated hardware.) There are two basic types of hanging irons: top and bottom hangers. The bottom hangers are J shaped and the hook of the J sits under the bottom rail of a standard flat. The top hangers are flat and bolt to the rear face of the flat, D-ring side up (Figure 4.35).

D-Rings and Keepers

D-rings and keepers are basically the same idea as handing irons but are meant to be attached to the ground.

Quick Links

A quick link is a link of chain with a threaded, sliding nut on it. This allows you to add chain to lengthen it. There is a great debate as to what the quick link can hold in an overhead–lifting situation. Unlike a forged shackle, quick links aren't rated. The threaded nut slides over the threads in a collarlike fashion, so on visual inspection you can't tell if they're completely closed or not. Also, they aren't made of the same hardened alloy as the trim chain. As you may have heard, a chain is only as strong as its weakest link.

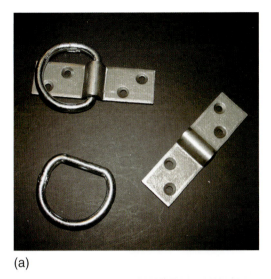

(a)

(b)

(c)

Figure 4.35: *(a) D-rings and keepers; (b) hanging irons; (c) quick links.*

Forged Anchor Shackles

Forged anchor shackles are used to connect scenery to the fly lines. It's important to note the distinction of being forged. These are made of hard steel that is rated for overhead lifting. Malleable steel shackles are considerably cheaper and aren't rated. Shackles are made in a U shape with a pin that threads into the side of the U. You can theoretically hang several lines off one shackle in a rigging technique known as *bridling*. Bridling allows you to branch off of one pickup line to two or more pickup lines on your piece, giving it more support. This of course reduces the load each individual line can hold, since the total load cannot exceed the rated load capacity. Also, the *fleet angle* listed on the product's information sheet or website for each piece can't be exceeded.

211

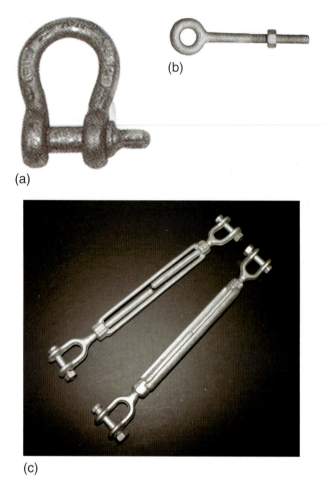

Figure 4.36: *Forged and rated hanging hardware: (a) Screw pin type anchor shackle; (b) eye bolts; and (c) turn buckles.*

The fleet angle in this case is the maximum angle the bridle can extend from the shackle. The most common type of shackle used in theatrical applications is the *screw-pin shackle* (Figure 4.36a).

Forged Eye Bolts

Forged eye bolts look like regular bolts, but the top is looped around to form an eye that you can pass a shackle through. These are cast in one piece and rated for a particular load. Just as with forged shackles, you should only use forged eye bolts for overhead lifting. (Common eyebolts are just bent into shape, and when a load is placed on them they can easily open up and cause a bad situation. They aren't rated for overhead lifting; don't use them.) These should be used with a rated nut and preferably with a rated nylon insert nut. Grades 5 to 8 are commonly used, but look at your specific application and calculate the load based on the 10:1 ratio (Figure 4.36b).

Forged Turnbuckle

The forged turnbuckle looks like a couple of forged eye bolts end to end in a threaded "0." These are used for tightening and adjusting trim on lines. Same story as the other rated forged hardware (Figure 4.36c).

Copper Oval Swages

Copper oval swages are used to create terminations on wire rope assemblies. (Aluminum swages aren't approved for overhead lifting and should not be used.) They are the most secure way of terminating the ends of aircraft cable. Swages must be applied with a matching swaging tool. (We've all heard horror stories of people smashing them down with a hammer—that's not good; don't do it.) For example, Nicopress swages, Nicopress swaging tools, and Nicopress press Go No Go gauges all go together. Operated using the correct swaging groove in the tool, with the proper number and pattern of swage compressions (how many times the swage is squeezed), and with the tool in proper calibration, a properly swaged wire rope termination with a thimble can be as strong as the cable itself (unlike knotted fiber or synthetic ropes, which may lose up to 50% of their safe work load, or SWL, with each knot). We call this 100% efficiency for a wire rope termination. If you see a wire rope termination with more than one oval swage, it's not really doing anything but putting the swage manufacturer's kids through college; only one properly applied swage is needed. The most common sizes in operation are ⅛″ and ³⁄₁₆″. To see a video of proper swage application, check out www.jrclancy.com (Figure 4.37).

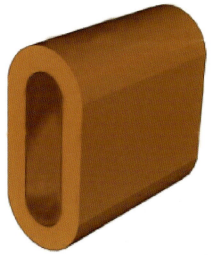

Figure 4.37: *Drawing of a copper oval swage.*

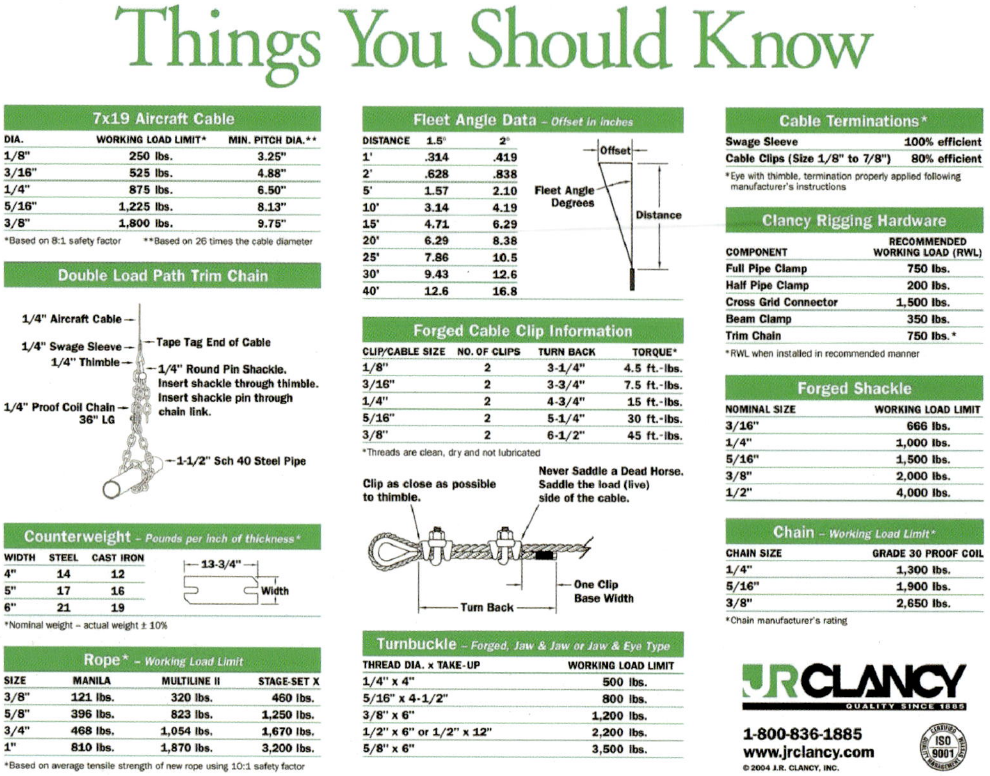

Things You Should Know

7x19 Aircraft Cable

DIA.	WORKING LOAD LIMIT*	MIN. PITCH DIA.**
1/8"	250 lbs.	3.25"
3/16"	525 lbs.	4.88"
1/4"	875 lbs.	6.50"
5/16"	1,225 lbs.	8.13"
3/8"	1,800 lbs.	9.75"

*Based on 8:1 safety factor   **Based on 26 times the cable diameter

Double Load Path Trim Chain

1/4" Aircraft Cable —
1/4" Swage Sleeve — — Tape Tag End of Cable
1/4" Thimble — — 1/4" Round Pin Shackle. Insert shackle through thimble. Insert shackle pin through chain link.
1/4" Proof Coil Chain — 36" LG
— 1-1/2" Sch 40 Steel Pipe

Counterweight – Pounds per inch of thickness*

WIDTH	STEEL	CAST IRON
4"	14	12
5"	17	16
6"	21	19

13-3/4" — Width

*Nominal weight – actual weight ± 10%

Rope* – Working Load Limit

SIZE	MANILA	MULTILINE II	STAGE-SET X
3/8"	121 lbs.	320 lbs.	460 lbs.
5/8"	396 lbs.	823 lbs.	1,250 lbs.
3/4"	468 lbs.	1,054 lbs.	1,670 lbs.
1"	810 lbs.	1,870 lbs.	3,200 lbs.

*Based on average tensile strength of new rope using 10:1 safety factor

Fleet Angle Data – Offset in inches

DISTANCE	1.5°	2°
1'	.314	.419
2'	.628	.838
5'	1.57	2.10
10'	3.14	4.19
15'	4.71	6.29
20'	6.29	8.38
25'	7.86	10.5
30'	9.43	12.6
40'	12.6	16.8

Offset
Fleet Angle Degrees
Distance

Forged Cable Clip Information

CLIP/CABLE SIZE	NO. OF CLIPS	TURN BACK	TORQUE*
1/8"	2	3-1/4"	4.5 ft.-lbs.
3/16"	2	3-3/4"	7.5 ft.-lbs.
1/4"	2	4-3/4"	15 ft.-lbs.
5/16"	2	5-1/4"	30 ft.-lbs.
3/8"	2	6-1/2"	45 ft.-lbs.

*Threads are clean, dry and not lubricated

Clip as close as possible to thimble.

Never Saddle a Dead Horse. Saddle the load (live) side of the cable.

One Clip Base Width

Turn Back

Turnbuckle – Forged, Jaw & Jaw or Jaw & Eye Type

THREAD DIA. x TAKE-UP	WORKING LOAD LIMIT
1/4" x 4"	500 lbs.
5/16" x 4-1/2"	800 lbs.
3/8" x 6"	1,200 lbs.
1/2" x 6" or 1/2" x 12"	2,200 lbs.
5/8" x 6"	3,500 lbs.

Cable Terminations*

Swage Sleeve	100% efficient
Cable Clips (Size 1/8" to 7/8")	80% efficient

*Eye with thimble, termination properly applied following manufacturer's instructions

Clancy Rigging Hardware

COMPONENT	RECOMMENDED WORKING LOAD (RWL)
Full Pipe Clamp	750 lbs.
Half Pipe Clamp	200 lbs.
Cross Grid Connector	1,500 lbs.
Beam Clamp	350 lbs.
Trim Chain	750 lbs. *

*RWL when installed in recommended manner

Forged Shackle

NOMINAL SIZE	WORKING LOAD LIMIT
3/16"	666 lbs.
1/4"	1,000 lbs.
5/16"	1,500 lbs.
3/8"	2,000 lbs.
1/2"	4,000 lbs.

Chain – Working Load Limit*

CHAIN SIZE	GRADE 30 PROOF COIL
1/4"	1,300 lbs.
5/16"	1,900 lbs.
3/8"	2,650 lbs.

*Chain manufacturer's rating

JRCLANCY
QUALITY SINCE 1885
1-800-836-1885
www.jrclancy.com
ISO 9001
© 2004 J.R. CLANCY, INC.

Figure 4.38: *JR Clancy's "Things You Should Know Guide" showing load limits, aircraft cable and swages, fleet angle, and wire rope clip info. (Courtesy of JR Clancy.)*

Thimbles

Thimbles are used to wrap the *aircraft cable* around to prevent it from kinking and to prevent it from wearing against its connection point. Thimbles should be used in all overhead lifting applications. Their proper installation allows them to rotate slightly (Figure 4.38).

Wire Rope Clips

These are sometimes known under the trade name Crosbys (but so are shackles and just about every other thing that Crosby makes). They are a removable method of terminating the ends of wire rope. Used with a thimble and torqued to the correct tension, they have 80% efficiency when compared to a swage. The mantra "Never saddle a dead horse" helps you remember their proper installation. The saddle-shaped part of the clip (called the *saddle*) goes under the *live* end of the wire rope, or the part that holds the load. The *dead* end is the end of the wire rope that goes nowhere. Once you apply the load to these clips you should check them and retighten them. When placed in a permanent or semipermanent application, it's a good idea to check the torque on these connectors regularly. These connectors should be used with thimbles, just like swages.

Span Set, or Round Slings

A span set, or round slings, are loops of chain with a web mesh over them used for lifting and other temporary hanging applications. Each sling is tagged for capacity by color: purple, green, yellow, and tan (Figure 4.39).

Grade 30 Chains

Grade 30 chains are commonly used for rigging. See the chain table in Figure 4.38 for information on WLL (working load limit).

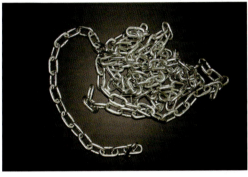

(a)

(b)

(c)

Figure 4.39: *Various chains and slings: (a) Grade 30; (b) S.T.A.C.; (c) round slings in use.*

Grade 80 Chains

Grade 80 chains are a hardened chain suitable for overhead lifting. The grading is governed by the NACM (National Association of Chain Manufacturers). Grade 80 is considered high strength.

Deck Chain, or STAC (Special Theatrical Alloy Chain)

Deck chain (special theatrical alloy chain, or STAC) has longer links than most grade 80 chain. These links are made larger, to allow a shackle to pass through. This longer link allows for easier trim adjustment. This material is usually sold by theatrical suppliers in short lengths, from 10″ to 6′, and each link has been tested for proper welds and strength and tagged for reference with grade, reach, size, and working load limit. These chains are especially nice for bridles.

A Few Lines About Rope

Rope is the name of a movie made by Alfred Hitchcock that was shot in one continuous take—basically, the camera cut only when it ran out of film. That's not the *rope* we are talking about here. *Rope* is a series of fibers that are twisted or braided together to form a single line we use to pull or connect objects together. You can't push a rope. Really you can't; try it. While hemp or manila natural fiber rope is certainly one of the most economical control lines available, there are a few disadvantages. One major disadvantage is that it is susceptible to atmospheric conditions. When the humidity changes, the rope will either shrink or grow. It doesn't hold up to long-term abrasion well, and the fibers are murder on bare hands.

If you unraveled the end of a manila rope, you would see that it is made of what looks like smaller ropes that are made of smaller ropes that are made of little fibers (Figure 4.40). Working backwards, the first smaller ropelike group that unravels is a *strand* (also a movie theatre in most larger towns). The strands are wound around each other in the opposite way they themselves are twisted together. The littler ropelike things that strand is made of are *yarns,* which are twisted together opposite to the way the strands are twisted. The yarns are made of *fibers,* which are brought together and twisted the opposite way of the yarns. This method produces a rope that holds itself together, holds knots well, and is easy to splice. However, the ends of the rope tend to unravel, and when under load twisted ropes want to untwist and spin.

Synthetic Rope: Unraveling the New Line on an Uplifting Subject

There are many newer alternatives to natural fiber rope. *Synthetic* rope is made primarily from polyester fibers. After using natural fiber rope, this will seem like a walk in the park; it's very easy on the hands. They are also very abrasion resistant and they are

Figure 4.40: *Twisted rope showing the various parts.*

impervious to atmospheric conditions. (This was an excuse to use the word *impervious*—they won't shrink or grow with humidity.) And they cost a lot more than natural rope. A ⅜″-diameter double-braided polyester rope will cost somewhere in the neighborhood of five times the price of its manila counterpart. But they last a lot longer.

The synthetic rope we use in theatre comes in a few basic types.

- *Single-braid rope*: This is made by braiding 12 or more fibers together to create a strong, kink-resistant rope that is slow to unravel. Braided rope can be hollow or solid. The "single" in single braid means there is no core inside of the rope. This rope is often used as a purchase line in counterweight rigging systems since it is strong and abrasion resistant and easy on the hands. Also, braided rope doesn't want to spin the way twisted rope does when it is under a load (Figure 4.41).
- *Composite ropes*: These are made by weaving a hollow braid around a separate core of fibers. The core fibers may be braided (we call it a *double braid*), twisted, or laid out straight. Double braid is a good all-purpose hauling rope and is often the substitute for manila in a rope house. Composite ropes are extremely strong, and they may be spliced. Yet we don't use them for counterweight systems. The inner core can slip inside the outer layer. This is a big problem with a counterweight rigging system's rope lock since it clamps down on the rope to hold scenery from moving. This movement of the inner core inside the outer layer is called *milking*—just imagine a cow's udder in the rope lock and you won't soon forget the term.
- *Three-strand twisted braid* (sounds like a heavy metal group): The yarns of synthetic fiber are twisted around the core. The core doesn't move in this rope, so the rope won't milk like other composites. It's also a lot cheaper than single-braid rope, but its safe work load is less than half that of a comparable single braid.

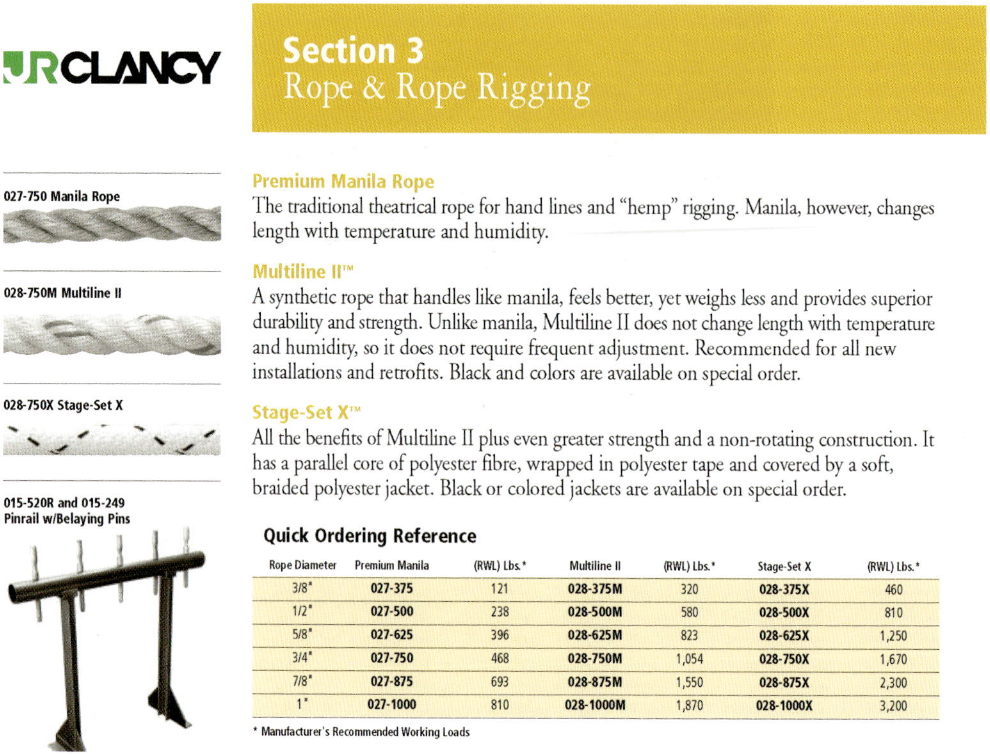

Section 3
Rope & Rope Rigging

027-750 Manila Rope

028-750M Multiline II

028-750X Stage-Set X

**015-520R and 015-249
Pinrail w/Belaying Pins**

Premium Manila Rope
The traditional theatrical rope for hand lines and "hemp" rigging. Manila, however, changes length with temperature and humidity.

Multiline II™
A synthetic rope that handles like manila, feels better, yet weighs less and provides superior durability and strength. Unlike manila, Multiline II does not change length with temperature and humidity, so it does not require frequent adjustment. Recommended for all new installations and retrofits. Black and colors are available on special order.

Stage-Set X™
All the benefits of Multiline II plus even greater strength and a non-rotating construction. It has a parallel core of polyester fibre, wrapped in polyester tape and covered by a soft, braided polyester jacket. Black or colored jackets are available on special order.

Quick Ordering Reference

Rope Diameter	Premium Manila	(RWL) Lbs.*	Multiline II	(RWL) Lbs.*	Stage-Set X	(RWL) Lbs.*
3/8"	027-375	121	028-375M	320	028-375X	460
1/2"	027-500	238	028-500M	580	028-500X	810
5/8"	027-625	396	028-625M	823	028-625X	1,250
3/4"	027-750	468	028-750M	1,054	028-750X	1,670
7/8"	027-875	693	028-875M	1,550	028-875X	2,300
1"	027-1000	810	028-1000M	1,870	028-1000X	3,200

* Manufacturer's Recommended Working Loads

Figure 4.41: *Manila and synthetic ropes shown in the 2005 JR Clancy Product Catalogue. (Courtesy of JR Clancy.)*

Wire Rope? Why Not?
By taking the regular twisted rope idea and making the fibers out of long wire strands you considerably increased the *tensile strength*, or the strength the rope may be stretched without breaking. *Aircraft cable* (AC or ⁷⁄₁₉) is the wire rope that's most commonly used in theatre. The wire is made of seven strands of 19 wire fibers; that's where the name ⁷⁄₁₉ comes from. Six strands are twisted around a center core of the seventh strand. As we said, it has great tensile strength, and its size is small in relation to synthetic and natural fiber ropes of similar SWL. This makes it ideal for lift lines in a counterweight system since its smaller size is harder to read or see from the audience (Figure 4.42).

Hardware and the Single Flat: How They Got Together and Why They Hang Around Each Other
There are a few basic material types we use for flats and each type has its own rigging solution.

Figure 4.42: *Cross-section of ⁷/₁₉ aircraft cable.*

Standard Wood-Framed Flat

The best way to hang a wooden flat is to bolt the hanging irons to the bottom of the flat. Think about it. The rail runs the entire width of the flat. The stiles run in between them. If you lift up from the bottom, the bottom rail is less likely to pull off than if you lifted from the top. The idea is not unlike holding the bottom of a paper bag when you carry it; if you held it from the top, the top would rip off. This is called a *compression lift*. Your next question is "If it's attached from the bottom, what keeps it from falling forward?" Attach a D-ring keeper with the D-ring removed or a top hanging iron to the top of the flat for each line. Then pass the cable through it on its way to your batten. This holds the flat loosely to the fly line and prevents it from falling forward (Figure 4.43).

Wooden Hollywood Flat

You still want to bottom hang these units. Bottom hangers won't work the same way on these units, however, because of the face frame construction. If you turn the hanger with the D-ring facing the outside rail and bolt the strap iron to the bottom rail, you achieve the same thing. Another method is to bolt it to the inside and center of the face of an outside stile. The cable then runs up the inside of the unit and you drill a hole in the top rail for the cable to come out of, eliminating the need for a top iron or a D-ring (Figure 4.44).

Metal-Framed Flats

The theory behind welding is that the welded joints are actually stronger than the surrounding steel. Therefore, the steel-framed flat may be easily top hung with rated bolts

219

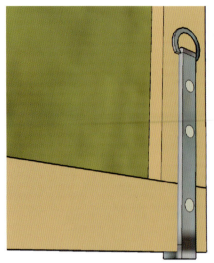

Figure 4.43: *Bottom-hung standard flat with hanging irons and D-rings.*

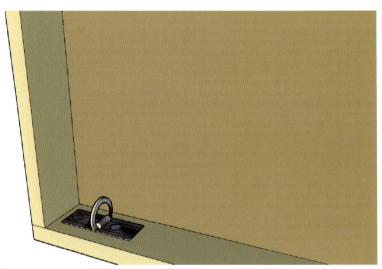

Figure 4.44: *Bottom-hung Hollywood flat with hanging irons and D-rings.*

and hanging irons. Because of the nature of the steel frame, other options exist. You can easily drill through the top of the flat and insert rated forged eye bolts into the holes and tighten them down with rated nylon insert nuts. These nuts are designed to resist vibration. *Forged eye nuts* are another type of fastener that can be used to top hang. When you drill your hole to top hang, you insert the rated bolt upside down through the top rail so that the threads are coming out of the top of the flat. The eye nuts are attached to these threads and the rest is history (Figure 4.45).

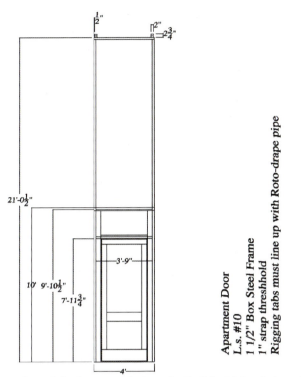

Figure 4.45: *Drawing of metal-flat-hanging techniques for DeSales University's production of* West Side Story. *(Drawing by Mike Smola.)*

Rope Rigging and Pirate Movies

In theatre, during a show, if we want to move something up in the air, we don't want to be seen moving it. Therefore we need to *fly* it up somehow from offstage. The oldest method of doing this is by a rope line system or hemp line system (the confusing thing is that hemp hasn't been used in years; the natural fiber rope in use in this country is predominately manila rope). This system involves rope attached to the batten that travels up to a pulley that changes the rope's direction, allowing it to run offstage, where it can be operated out of sight of the audience. The rope is then secured to the pin rail that is securely fastened to the floor. The rope is fastened to the rail by wrapping it around a *belaying pin*, which you may have seen in a pirate movie. They are the pins that the pirates pull out of the mast rigging to use as clubs when the bad pirates board their ship. The rope gets wrapped around them in figure-eight fashion, just like in the pirate movie, and the last coil gets flipped so that it cinches on itself.

There is a reason those pirates always looked so unhappy. This method of rigging is very difficult and somewhat dangerous. That is why they tried to board each other's ships. They were hoping the other ship had a better system of rigging. Sandbags may be used to counterweight these lines, which more or less means adding a similar amount

Figure 4.46: *Rope wrapped around a belaying pin and pin rail and an unhappy pirate.*

of weight to your end of the line as is on the batten. Since the load is balanced, a smaller amount of energy is needed on your part to move the batten. The *sandbag* is a canvas bag filled with sand and connected to a trim clamp or rope clew on the operating lines (Figure 4.46).

Clewing You in on Controlling Lines

Controlling lines travel up from the pin rail through a *head block* that directs them towards the *loft blocks* that hang above the battens. Then each line descends through an individual loft block to its place on the batten. These blocks are essentially housings for *sheaves*, grooved wheels that hold the lines and turn as the line passes through them. By the time the lines all come to you from the batten, you will have one line for every place a rope is attached to the batten. At the very least you will have two. If you want to eliminate sag or deflection in the batten you may have to add additional lines. Bridles may cut down on the number of lines and still prevent deflection, but no matter what, one line is easier to control than more than one. That's when you have to suck it up and get a clew. *Clews* are devices that join the various lines together on one end and send a single line out the other end (Figure 4.47). (Clues are: Colonel Mustard, with a rope, in the library.)

Figure 4.47: *Rope clew and Colonel Mustard.*

Here Spot—Drop Me a Line

All in all it's not the easiest system to operate, but it is essentially easy to rig. That is why almost every stage house you go into will have a pin rail of some kind, even if the rope line system isn't the major method of flying. Sometimes it's the best method of dropping a control line where you don't have one. We call these auxiliary lines *spot lines*: You've dropped into a spot where you didn't have a line.

Counterweight Systems

The most common method of flying scenery is by counterweight. That is, the object you are flying is balanced by an object of equal weight at the other end of your control line. This allows you to raise and lower the object at a controlled speed and with little effort.

Single and Double Purchase

If you have a double-purchase system in your theatre it doesn't mean you buy everything twice or have it rougher than those techies in single-purchase theatres, who only have to buy things once. These terms are, as you have guessed, types of counterweight systems. There are manual and motorized counterweight systems, but both types operate on the same basic principles. *Motorized* systems are extra expensive, and the technology differs from company to company. Basically, your energy is replaced with that of a motor. *Manual* systems are quite common, and once you understand their concepts it will be easier to adapt to any other kind of system.

Most of the terminology we have learned still applies because these systems are an improvement on the rope or hemp system and the terms were just brought along. The batten in most single- and double-purchase systems is made of 1½″-diameter black iron schedule 40 pipe. (However, there are systems that use 2½″-diameter schedule 40 or even schedule 80 pipes. It's all about keeping the weight down and having the stiffest batten possible that won't sag under weight.) Counterweight systems are designed to handle a lot more weight than you will find in most hemp systems. Black iron pipe is stiffer than a wooden batten and also a lot stronger.

Journey to the Center of a Single-Purchase System

Around the pipe batten, hanging upwards, are the *trim chains*. These are hardened rated chains, usually proof coil connected with rated shackles and rated safety bolts. This hardware, just like the rest of the components in the system, must be able to hold the weight of the pipe batten and whatever is hung on the pipe, or the *load* (Figure 4.48).

The trim chains are connected to the lift lines. These lines connect the batten and load to the rest of the counterweight system. They are made of aircraft cable terminated with a thimble and swages on both ends. These lines are spaced evenly along the batten and adjusted with the trim chains to prevent it from sagging at any point. When you place a load on the pipe, it is best to spread the load out along the pipe whenever possible to prevent strain on any one lift line.

The lift lines, on their way offstage, travel up to the *grid iron,* or *grid*. The grid is a steel framework of beams and channel steel that hangs below the ceiling of your fly tower. It gives you an access point you can walk across to reach the rigging below you.

> **SAFETY TIP** Whenever you walk on a grid, remove anything from your pockets and attach any tools securely to your belt. Anything dropped will become a lethal weapon. Also, cordon off the area below you and give hard hats to anyone still on the ground. It is common courtesy and good practice to shout, "Person on the grid!" whenever you are grid walking. The people on the floor will acknowledge you by saying, "Thank you!" This is also a common rigging safety practice and part of theatrical tradition. People should respond "Thank you" to every called warning. If they don't, they are rude or they didn't hear you. Repeat it until they respond. It's important that everyone is aware of what is going on in the theatre environment for everyone's safety.

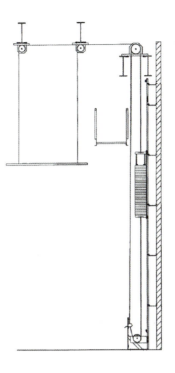

Single Purchase Set

Figure 4.48: *JR Clancy drawing of a single-purchase set. (Courtesy of JR Clancy.)*

The grid supports the *loft blocks*. These blocks are steel pulleys that change the lift lines' direction and mule them offstage, just like the pulleys in the rope system. The *sheaves* (grooved wheels that the cable travels through) on these blocks are made of hardened steel. Why? Remember the rod saw? A piece of aircraft cable under load works exactly like one as it travels through the groove in the sheave. (PVC pipe saws are often pieces of steel cable between two handles).

From there, the lines travel through a *head block*, just like in the rope system, but then they connect to the counterweight arbor. *Arbors* are also called *carriages,* and this name gives you a better idea of what they do. The arbor travels up and down vertically in a T-shaped track (*T track*) or wire-guided system carrying the counterweights, just like passengers in a carriage. As the arbor lowers on the track, the batten will rise onstage. The arbors hold the counterweights for each line set in one place, stacked on top of each other. This weight should be roughly the same weight as the batten and the load. We say roughly, because it is next to impossible to get the weight perfectly right. When the batten is heavier than the arbor, we call this *batten heavy,* and *arbor heavy* is the term for the reverse situation. If a load cannot be balanced perfectly, the safest thing is to make it arbor heavy to prevent the batten from coming in too quickly (Figure 4.49).

225

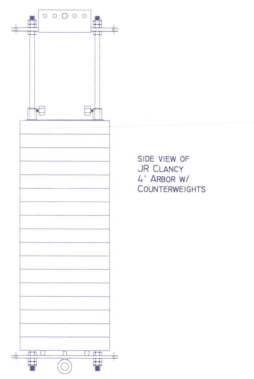

SIDE VIEW OF
JR CLANCY
4' ARBOR W/
COUNTERWEIGHTS

Figure 4.49: *Arbor and counterweights. (Courtesy of JR Clancy.)*

The *operating lines,* or *hand lines,* are what we pull to operate the counterweight system. In a single-purchase system, it travels from the bottom of the arbor around the tension block located at the bottom of the counterweight system. (The tension block is made to shift to take up slack in natural fiber ropes when they react to atmospheric changes.) Then the line travels back up to the head block and back down around to the arbor's top. This creates a continuous loop, so when you pull down the line closest to you, the arbor will fly up and the batten and scenery will fly in. If you pull on the side of the hand line furthest from you, the arbor will lower and the scenery will fly out. When you fly the batten to its maximum height, we call that *full out* or *gridding the line set,* since it stops just below the grid. The opposite we call *bringing in the line set* or *full in.*

> **TIP** We do not always want a piece of scenery to fly full in or full out. To get the line to this proper location we can *spike* the hand lines. (This is not like the other meaning of spiking something, and alcohol has no place backstage.) First, fly the scenery to the height you want it to be. Then at eye level mark the hand line in front of you. Then mark the line behind it at the same level. You will *reach spike* when you are moving the purchase lines and these two marks come together. The preferred method of marking is to *jab* a spike. (Tape spikes wear off and leave a sticky residue when removed, and the tape adhesive attracts dirt

that gums your rope locks and causes rope abrasion.) Twisted manila or hemp hand lines, although hard on the hands, are easy to mark by twisting the rope a bit and inserting a piece of ribbon as a spike between the strands of the rope. An easy method of jabbing a spike uses a crochet hook to jab between the strands, grab the ribbon, and then pull the ribbon through to the other side of the rope. This method works well with braided synthetic ropes as well.

➤ **TIP** If you have several different spike positions for the same line set, mark each set of spikes with a different color. As part of your preshow prep, you should check each line set, test its weight, run it to its spikes, and basically make sure that nothing has changed since you last used it. This was common practice in hemp houses because of the atmospheric changes the natural fiber rope was subjected to. It is still good practice in synthetic rope houses since you have no idea what could have happened to your line sets while you were gone and should not expect that someone has not screwed around with them in your absence.

Once we fly the scenery to the height we need it to be, we tighten it down to the locking rail with a rope lock. The locking rail is anchored down to the building's framework and runs the length of the fly system. Each line set has its own lock number and a card holder that may hold a reference card for the scenery on the line set. The *rope lock* is a lever that forces two clamps, or *dogs*, to grab the rope but not crush it. The lock is just that, a lock. It is not intended to slow or brake an out-of-weight load (Figure 4.50).

➤ **SAFETY TIP** Every time you move a line set you need to call it. For example, if you were moving line set 3, you would call out, "Unlocking line set 3," and the people onstage would respond by saying "Thank you." This call will give them the time needed to look up to see where the line set is and to move if they are near it. You don't unlock the line until they say "Thank you." Repeat until they respond. Once they do and before you move the line you call, "Line set 3 coming in—downstage." The upstage–downstage location is critical, because if they don't know that line sets are numbered from upstage to downstage, they at least know the general location. At this point the people onstage will again respond "Thank you" and you can fly your line. Then you will lock the line set, and call, "Line set 3 locked." The people onstage will say "Thank you" again and move back to their former positions knowing that the flys are secure and safe.

The *load rail* is a gallery above the locking rail used to weight the line sets. This is the maximum height the arbor travels when the scenery is full in. While the batten is on the ground, the scenery is attached and the counterweights are added to the arbor from the load rail to balance the load. The counterweights used to balance the line set are stored on the load rail floor. Remember the batten, trim lines, lift lines, and all the hardware that connects them? They all weigh something, and we have to account for their weight on the arbor to balance the line set even before we put a scenic load on

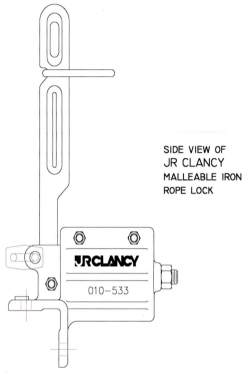

SIDE VIEW OF
JR CLANCY
MALLEABLE IRON
ROPE LOCK

Figure 4.50: *Drawing of a standard rope lock. (Courtesy of JR Clancy.)*

it. We call this weight *line weight, pipe weight,* or *house* or *balance load.* These weights are usually marked in some way so that they do not get removed from the arbor, and the most common way to mark them is to paint them.

Spreader plates are also an effective way of marking the pipe weight. When weight is added to the arbor, the slots in the counterweight are fitted around the arbor rods. These rods stretch from the top of the arbor to the bottom, with the weight riding in between; and as the arbor travels, the rods prevent the weights from falling out. If, however, the arbor comes to a sudden stop, the weights will want to keep moving and could fly off of the arbor rods. Spreader plates fit around the arbor rods and hold the counterweights down. The plates are secured down by clamps known as *stop collars* that sit above each spreader plate on the arbor rods and tighten down with a thumb screw. By placing a spreader plate above the pipe weight, you have a clear marking for your scenic load, which will live under a second plate topped with a stop collar (see Figure 4.49).

> ➤ **TIP** Stacking weights on an arbor is a pain. When the top spreader plate keeps smacking your hand as you load, it is a bigger pain. If you bring a set of spring clamps with you, you can quickly clip each clamp under the top plate, holding

228

it up while you stack. After you finish, remove the clamps and tighten the stop collars.

➤ **SAFETY TIP** Whenever you load weight, make sure that no one is under you. And whoever is in the vicinity should wear a hard hat. You may not believe this, but a dropped counterweight will bounce around as it drops causing all kinds of havoc. It is not a pretty sight. As you load you should also call, "Loading line set 3," and you will get the "Thank you" response as people move to safe positions. Again, anyone on the locking rail should move out from under you, and they should also wear hard hats.

Double Your Purchase, Double Your Loading Fun

Double-purchase systems create a 2-to-1 mechanical advantage. That means for every pound of weight on the batten you need two pounds of counterweight on the arbor. But for each foot of arbor movement, the batten moves two feet. This can come in handy in stage houses without the vertical space for a single-purchase system to operate. Another advantage is that the locking rail is lifted off the floor, freeing up valuable real estate and giving the operator a clearer view of the stage floor. Some disadvantages are that you have to have twice the weight around and the system is more difficult to install and operate (Figure 4.51).

Hanging Track, or Your Scenery Is Getting Carried Away

A common method for shifting flown scenery on and offstage is by tracking it. Hanging tracks and carriers are used to suspend the flat or drape, and pull lines or operating lines are used to move it on- and offstage. To get an idea of how they work, go back to your living room curtains. Are you there? Good. The cord that dangles down on one side, when pulled, opens and closes the curtains. The end of this cord runs up through some pulleys to a master carrier that rides with little wheels on the curtain track. The curtain track in this case is connected to your wall. When you pull the cord, the master carrier moves back and forth on the track following the direction of your pull.

In a *single-pull* operation, the other end of the cord is connected to the other side of the master carrier, as is the end of the curtain. When you pull the string, the curtain will slide all the way over to one side or the other. If you have two curtains that part in the center and travel to either side, you have a *center-pull* curtain. It is actually made of two curtains and has two master carriers; one acts as the *master master carrier*, and the other is the *slave master carrier*. Just as with the single pull, the cord starts at the master carrier, but in this case it takes a small detour to get clamped off at the slave master carrier before getting terminated at the other side of the master carrier. Both halves of the curtain attach to their respective master carriers, but when the operating line is pulled, the halves will run to opposite sides or meet in the center, depending on the pull.

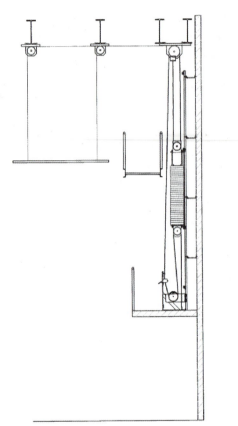

Figure 4.51: *JR Clancy drawing of a double-purchase set. (Courtesy of JR Clancy.)*

Stage track rigging is not all that different from your living room curtains. The cord in this case is called an *operating line*, just like in the fly systems. Most often it's made out of a soft braided cotton rope called *sash cord*. The sash cord may be spiked, similar to the way we spike operating lines, but you can't jab a spike into sash cord. In this instance we resort to paint, marker, or spike tape to make spike markings.

The track isn't connected to the wall, as it is in your house. It may be dead hung from the ceiling or grid or attached to a batten so that it can be flown out (Figure 4.52). Also, the operating line doesn't dangle the way your living room curtain's cord dangles. The slack is taken up by a *tension pulley* that is anchored or weighted to the floor. This pulley is similar to the tension block in the fly system; a spring-mounted pulley takes up the slack in the lines, and it also prevents the operating lines from tangling around each other. (There may not be anything like this in your living room.) These lines go up to the *live-end pulley*, which changes their direction from straight up to horizontal, just like the head blocks in the fly systems.

Figure 4.52: *Track and carriers for the main rag of the Perkins Auditorium on Penn State Berks Campus.*

From there it depends on what type of scenery you are carrying. In *curtain rigging,* the lines pass through single carriers, each of which has a trim chain that drops down to each curtain grommet. The number of carriers you need is the same as the number of grommets in your curtain, minus one for each end of the curtain. The curtain ends are attached to the end of your master carriers and the other end to the end of your track.

In *flat rigging* or *scenery rigging*, the carriers are a little different. Unlike a traveling curtain, which pulls itself across as it unfurls, a traveling flat or scenic unit just moves across the stage. Also, since it is most often rigid, the type of carrier is different, and the number of carriers depends more on the weight of the flat than on the number of grommets. Flat carriers are bolted directly to the flat instead of chained, and the least number of carriers you will use is two, one for each end. The control line is connected to the onstage carrier, which acts like a master carrier does in a curtain rig (Figure 4.53).

> ➤ **TIP** Often designers may want to mask behind a unit as it travels on. If you hang and rig a masking black on the track, you can trail it behind the scenic unit as it travels onstage. In this case, once you connect the curtain to the scenic unit, you do not need a master carrier for it; just tie off the offstage edge and it will follow the unit like Mary's little lamb.

Wagons Ho!

What is a wagon? Any scenic unit that rolls or slides may be considered a wagon. Wheeled platforms are the most common, but any piece of three-dimensional scenery may be treated as a wagon. What are the advantages? If you do not have fly space, an

Figure 4.53: *Scenic carrier. (Courtesy of BMI Supply Catalogue.)*

Figure 4.54: *Wagon from DeSales University's production of* An O. Henry Christmas.

entire setting can roll onstage for one scene and roll off for another. There are three concerns with a wagon: how to make it move, how to direct its movement, and how to get it to stop (Figure 4.54).

A Moving Subject: Castors

Wheels are the most common method of moving a wagon, and castors are the most common wheel. Castors come in all shapes and sizes. But when it comes to functionality there are two basic types: straight and swivel (or smart) castors. *Straight* castors only go in a straight line, whereas *swivel* castors will travel in any direction they are pushed. For scenic purposes we use both. Swivel castors, in spite of their other name, are not that smart. If you castor a wagon with only swivel castors you will have a hard time

Figure 4.55: *Straight and swivel castors.*

steering it. The combination of straight and swivel castors is easier to maneuver. For example, think of your average shopping cart. There are wheels on the front that swivel to steer (sometimes) and straight castors on the back that keep it from fishtailing out of control.

Good castors make all the difference in making a wagon move. In general, the harder the wheel material, the easier it is to move the castor. However, hard wheels are noisy, do not work as well on smooth surfaces, and may mar the floor. The best castor for our purposes has a medium-hard wheel that allows it to move across the stage with minimal noise. Hard synthetic rubber and neoprene are two materials used for castor wheels. The hard synthetic rubber tires are good for smooth stage surfaces and wear well. Neoprene wheels are a bit more expensive, don't pick up floor debris like rubber wheels, and are extremely quiet (Figure 4.55).

Good castors are also rated for weight. That means not only that it will support the weight of the platform, but that it will roll easily under that weight. Two factors contribute to a castor's weight capacity: the bearings and the frame material. The frame may be hot forged or cold formed. The *hot-forged frame* will support heavy-duty loads, and the *cold-formed frames* are in the medium-duty range. In a swivel castor, the weakest part of the frame's construction is the *kingpin*, the pivot that sticks through the castor's plate and allows the frame to turn. The heavier the pin, the more shock the castor will be able to take. A shock load could be as violent as the platform's being dropped on its castors, jamming on a broken screw head sticking out of the floor, or a lot of actors jumping and dancing. *Bearings* are possibly the most important part of the castor, next to the wheel. A bearing is any device that helps the castor turn. Light-duty castors may just have a piece of plastic or brass between the axle and the wheel. Medium- to heavy-duty castors use some kind of ball bearing.

If One Castor Is Good, Tri More: Zero-Throw Castors

Think about an 18-wheeled tractor trailer truck. Many of the weight-bearing wheels are doubled up to spread out the load. If you could invent a castor to do that it would

Figure 4.56: *Zero-throw castors.*

make your wagons easier to push and they could carry more weight. Too late, someone beat you to it. Zero-throw castors double the wheels like tractor trailers and then go one step further. Under their top plate lies a heavy kingpin that holds a triangular yoke. At each corner of the triangle lies another kingpin that holds a castor with double wheels (you can also find these under the name *tri-wheel castors*). Heavy plate steel makes up the frame, and ball bearings keep everything that turns rolling smoothly. The result is an easy to push and steer castor that may hold as much as 300–1100 lbs (Figure 4.56).

> ➤ **TIP** Zero-throw castors are great fun to use, but they have a large footprint under your wagon. Make sure that wherever you place one of these or any swivel castors they have enough room to spin without hitting the frame. Place the castor in its potential location and spin it to see if it clears. The tri-wheel design of the zero throw may be a bit more problematic than other swivels when test spun; centrifugal force in combination with really slippery bearings may tuck the three castors toward the inside when they are not under load. Make sure you have clearance with these castors in their fully extended positions. Chances are if you are using this type of castor, it is a very heavy wagon, and you do not want to lift it twice.

Hello, Dollies? or Mount Up

Castor placements on your wagon will basically be the same as the leg positions if you were to make it a stationary platform, but you also have to balance that idea with the load rating of the castor. The total weight of the wagon is divided up between all of the castors, and that weight cannot surpass any individual castor's load capacity or rating.

It is always a good idea to place castors in all of the corners and close to any platform joints if you are using multiple castors. Attaching the castor may take a couple of forms: Castor plates, castor brackets, and castor dollies may be used as castor mounts, depending on your preference and the size of the wagon.

A *castor plate* is a piece of wood that the castor is attached to, and that plate is in turn attached to the wagon's frame. Castor plates work best on small wagons where the castor does not have to raise the finished height much above 4–6 inches. As with platform legs, the castor is attached to the frame of the wagon (not the skin), and it should be bolted on through its top plate to withstand any shock. The trick with the castor plate is to figure out the height of the castor and to lag-bolt the plate into the frame so that you have at least ½″ of clearance from the floor. This amount of clearance should let the platform travel easily over any irregularities in your stage floor, prevent the audience from seeing the castor, and prevent any actors' toes from getting under the platform (Figure 4.57). (If you have a floor as smooth as glass, you can go even lower, but ½″ is a good standard to work from.)

> **TIP** In metal-framed wagon construction, the castor plates may be as simple as pieces of plate steel drilled to match the bolt holes in the castor's top plate that are then welded to the wagon's frame.

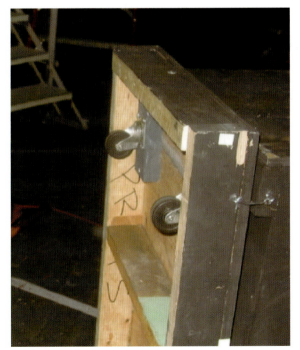

Figure 4.57: *Wagon with castor plates.*

Figure 4.58: *Metal zero-throw castor brackets for periactoi used in DeSales University's Production of* Carousel.

Castor brackets actually use castor plates in their construction, and they support the wagon from its frame as well, but they attach underneath the wagon, usually in a corner, instead of into the side of the frame like a castor plate. There are as many ways of making these brackets as there are of making platform legs, but the basic idea involves a piece of steel bent like an L or a Z that's connected to a castor plate. The steel bracket connects to the bottom of the platform and is long enough to raise the castor plate so that it can sit above the castor where it's bolted on. Another bracket does the same thing on the other side of the corner. A well-designed bracket allows the ½″ clearance from the floor and is removable so that it can be kept for stock. These brackets work especially well on plywood-framed platforms and steel-framed platforms since their frames extend to the total height of the platform (Figure 4.58).

> ➤ **TIP** Castor brackets also have another advantage over other styles of castor mounts. If you plan to use them on a very heavy wagon, you don't have to flip the wagon upside down like a bug to attach the castors. If you do not face or skin the wagon right away, you may drop the castor inside the frame, lift its designated corner, and slide the castored bracket underneath. Once you have all of the castors slid in place, roll the wagon to the edge of the stage or over an open trap and attach each bracket from underneath.

Castor dollies are used when the wagon has no means of attaching a castor plate or bracket. Legged platforms are a good example. In this case you would place a castor under each leg of the platform on a castor plate and connect all of the castor plates into a rigid structure. The finished height of the wagon would need to include the castored dolly's height, so the platform legs would need to be shortened accordingly (Figure 4.59).

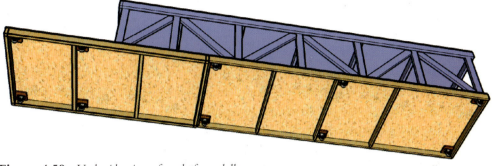

Figure 4.59: *Underside view of a platform dolly.*

➤ **TIP**   A phenomenally easy way of making a castor dolly involves castoring a stock platform with castor plates or brackets and mounting the rest of the wagon on top of the new platform/dolly.

Castor Alternatives, or Moving Platforms on Dead Men's Parts

We often call low-riding wagons *pallets*. These things are used to move small scenic pieces, like a side chair or a small settee, onstage quickly. They do not have to move heavy loads and often they are just sheets of plywood. Quite often the plywood is scrolled out so that it is just big enough to carry the scenic piece. Since your wagon is not big, heavy, or high off the ground, there are a couple of alternatives to castors to make it move.

- *Rollers*: Remember dead men and how well they worked handling the outfeed from the table saw? The top part of a dead man is called a *roller*. Placed side by side, rollers have been used for years as conveyors to move objects in factories. If you place these under a pallet and connect them to its bottom with a bracket, you have a *roller pallet*. Just like castors, the rollers have a load rating and are available from industrial supply companies.
- *Furniture slides*: These handy doodads come in a lot of shapes and sizes, but the most familiar are the types that look like nails with wide, thick heads often made of metal. As we said earlier, the harder the wheel, the less effort it takes to push something. The metal or nylon heads these slides use work in the same way. If you tap these big nails under an armchair, you may push it across a smooth floor with relative ease. You can do the same thing with a pallet; just place them under the load as you would with castor dolly.
- *UHMW Polyethylene*: Ultra-high-molecular-weight polyethylene may be used in strips under the pallet like furniture glides. In fact, some furniture glides are made of UHMW polyethylene. You can buy it from industrial supply companies in bar stock or sheets, and it can be cut to size using regular woodworking tools. When you attach it, be sure to countersink the screws to avoid marring your stage floor.

Tracking the Wagon

Wagon tracking does not involve a radio collar or an ear tag, which is fortunate since a lot of wagons do not have necks or ears. Instead it is a method of getting the wagon to roll where you want it to. There are many methods but the following are a few examples.

Straight Castor Tracking

As we said, castor placement is very critical, especially when straight castor tracking a wagon. If the castors are not perfectly lined up in the same plane the wagon will be really hard to move. One of the advantages to getting all the castors perfectly lined up is that the wagon will more or less run true when pushed in a straight line.

> ➤ **TIP**   If you make up uniform castor plates with the castors perpendicular to the plate and mount them square to the frame, you may easily true up a wagon since the castors should all be in the same relationship to the frame. Castor brackets can also be used in this fashion, but since they mount diagonally to a corner, special care must be used to make sure the straight castor is traveling in the proper direction.

Bump, Force, and Rub Tracking (Sounds Like a Disco Song)

One of the hardest things about straight castor tracking is getting the wagon back on track once it begins to stray off course. Each time you roll a wagon out, its course varies just a bit. That is why this method is best for moving wagons that do not move very often. Still, there is a low-tech solution. Bumpers made of 2 × 2 or 2 × 4 screwed into the floor just offstage may corral the edge of the wheel as it comes in contact with it and force it like a stray neoprene steer back into its offstage position. These bumpers will even guide the castors onstage until the wagon clears the onstage edge (Figure 4.60).

Now, if we take that idea one step further and trap the wagon's straight castors on the outside of either side of the wagon with some sort of bumper, you may easily keep a wagon on track. 2× material works well for the track, but you may substitute box steel tube or angle iron as well. The steel track has advantages since it comes in 20′ lengths and long seamless runs can be made; angle iron has a very low profile from the house, so it reads less than 2×. The disadvantage to this tracking method is that you may see the bumper tracks on the floor, and actors will trip over them if they are in major traffic areas. If they are dancing in that area, you can just forget about it (Figure 4.61).

If a wagon moves in between two stationary platforms of the same height, we call this a *slip stage*. You may track this wagon by facing the insides of the two stationary

Figure 4.60: *Rub track wagon used in DeSales University's production of* Oliver, *shown in front view.*

Figure 4.61: *Angle iron track used in DeSales University's production of* Hello, Dolly.

platforms with a hard, slick surface such as Masonite or hardboard and letting the wagon rub against the platforms, which act as bumpers. If you are moving this wagon a lot, mount straight castors inside the stationary platforms so that the wheels are just flush with the surface of the Masonite facing. As the slip stage slides between the platform rub tracks, the castor wheels will roll and force the wagon back to true as they come in contact with them (Figure 4.62).

Figure 4.62: *Pennsylvania Shakespeare Festival's slip stage, partially slipped, showing castor locations.*

Going Under the Knife

If you do not want to see visible tracks on the floor, you may *knife* your wagon. *Knifing a wagon* is a method of tracking that involves using a piece of metal attached to the wagon that rides in a slot in the floor; it does not mean that you are literally going to stab the wagon (if you must knife the wagon, wait until you strike the set). It functions the same way as a bumper track: When the wagon wants to swerve off course, the edges of the knife rub the edges of the slot and force it back on track (Figure 4.63).

> ➤ **TIP** The slot in the floor may be as simple as the joint between two rows of platforms lined with Masonite, and the knife a 1–2″ × ⅛″-thick piece of flat steel strap that is about long enough to connect to the wagon frame and sink into the slot about 2–3″ inches deep. Start by lining up and bolting platforms together to form one side of the slot, and then face them on the side the knife will ride against. The facing need only be as wide as the depth of the knife, and you should make sure you overlap platform edges to prevent the knife from catching on them. The seams of the facing should be looked at as well and sanded down if necessary, and all of your fasteners should be countersunk to prevent knife snags. Face the platforms for the other side the same way. Create a ¼″ gap jig by taking scrap ¼″ Masonite or luaun strips and screwing a 1 × 3 to the top of them. You may use one long jig or several smaller jigs that you space along the slot. The 1 × 3 will rest on the platform top, and the ¼″ will extend down into the slot over the facing. Push the other side of the platforms up to the first side and against the spacing jigs, and toe down the platforms. Grab the jigs by the 1 × 3 and pull them out of the slot. Now you can drop your knifed wagon into the

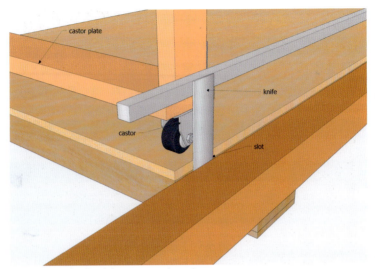

Figure 4.63: *Drawing of a knifed wagon and track.*

slot and test drive it. The knife needs to fit in the slot snugly so that the platform stays on track, but with enough room to move freely without binding. If necessary, you may wrap the knife with UHMW skid tape (available at most theatrical supply websites) to reduce friction on the blade. The ¼″ gap is small enough to prevent tripping, and spike heels won't get stuck into it. It is also wide enough to allow for any irregularities in the platforms' frames that might bind the knife. Once you have the platforms set and the wagon running smoothly, you should deck the platforms with Masonite. Decking over the facing on the inside of the platforms will add a little extra insurance that the facing won't get kicked loose and jam the knife in the slot.

Knifing Dogs and Other Forms of Entertainment

The knifing technique opens a realm of possibilities for tracking your wagons. Once you have a knife and a slot, you may attach just about anything to it. One fun thing to do is to *knife a dog*. Don't call the ASPCA—a dog in this case is a series of castors connected by a frame that ride under a platform to guide a knife down a track slot (Figure 4.64).

It's Curtains for Your Knifed Dog

Once you have dogged the knife, you may then connect it to a cable that is run to an offstage position. By pulling the cable you can move the wagon unseen. If you connect both ends of the cable to either side of the dog, you can pull the wagon forward or backward according to the direction you tug the cable.

241

Figure 4.64: *Working drawing of a dogged wagon in a slot. (Courtesy of Bob Mond.)*

Figure 4.65: *Revolve for DeSales University's production of* Carousel.

Since you brought this subject up, yes, this is the same way a curtain track works. If you pull on the curtain track in your home, you may get the idea of how a cable-run dogged track works. Go ahead, we will wait. Okay? Yeah, we saw you stop by the TV; don't think we didn't. Just as with a motorized fly system, you can add a motor or a hand-turned winch into the system to reduce the effort on your part. The larger the wagon, the more likely you will want to motorize, not just because of the effort needed (you could always get a rookie stagehand to operate it), but for the smoothness of movement a motor can provide.

Revolves and Jackknifes

If you take a wagon and add a stationary pivot point to it, you have created a *revolve*. Revolves are handy to quickly change from one scene to another, such as from an interior scene to an exterior. By placing the pivot in the center of a circular wagon, you can make the wagon rotate around the pivot and the scenery on the wagon rotate in a circle. These wagons may be hand-turned at the base, or you can belt drive them with aircraft cable and a winch or motor. Again the larger the revolve, the more you'll want a motor (Figure 4.65).

Jackknifed wagons are also a type of a revolve, but one that does not rotate 360°. A *jackknife* opens like the folding pocketknife that it is named for, usually around 90°. In this

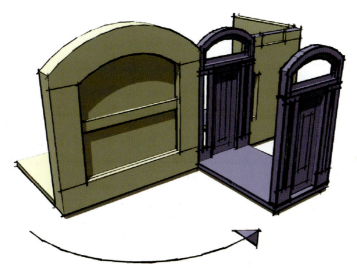

Figure 4.66: *Drawing of a jackknifed wagon.*

way a piece of scenery that was in the wings may be swung onstage like an opening door and then swung off. Zero-throw castors are great for this kind of operation, and although they may be cable driven, they most often are pushed by hand (Figure 4.66).

This brings us to two even lower-tech solutions to operating wagons: the push stick and the push bar. *Push sticks* are everything their name promises: sticks with which you push the platform from offstage. The end is loose-pinned and hooked under the frame or tight-pinned to the wagon's frame, and it is long enough so the pusher cannot be seen from offstage. Where traffic patterns are an issue, the removable stick becomes a plus, since you can push the wagon out, unhook it, and slide the stick away unseen. Where it is not an issue, a tight-pinned stick may be stood on, weighted, or stage screwed to the deck to act as a wagon brake (Figure 4.67).

The *push bar* is just as self-explanatory. This is a braced bar about hip height on the off-stage side of a wagon that the wagon movers may push against to get the wagon rolling onstage. Usually this is also the point to which the wagon gets spiked, since the operators are on the offstage side of the wagon and the wagon masks the spike marks on the floor from the audience's view. The brake for this wagon is also most often located by the push bar and usually right on the spike mark for easy alignment (Figure 4.68).

Gimme a Brake, or Stop Moving Already (I'm Warning You—If This Wagon Doesn't Stop, We're Turning This Book Around)

Wagon brakes, as we stated, can be as low tech as standing on a push stick or can get quite complicated, depending on the way the wagon travels. The following are a few examples.

Figure 4.67: *Wagon with a push stick.*

Barrel Bolts

If you take a barrel bolt (one of those sliding boltlike things with the little handle that acts as a lock) and mount it to the frame vertically, you may drop the bolt into a hole in the stage floor and stop the wagon's forward and backward movement. The nice thing about this method, besides its economy, is that the hole in the floor gives the operator a positive spike mark each time. This method is really just for straight-castored wagons, since the bolt may limit the movement in only one direction. The wagon will also wiggle slightly, depending on its weight and how carefully you drilled the bolt hole. It should be oversized for ease of operation but not sloppy big. The placement on the frame is also an issue since the bolt should drop down in the neighborhood of ½″. If you cannot drill into your stage floor, you will need another method (Figure 4.69).

Wagon Brakes

These are lever-action brakes that lower a bolt down to the stage floor, lifting the wagon off its castors. No holes are required and they are very quick. These brakes are available in a variety of styles and load ratings. As you might imagine, the higher the rating,

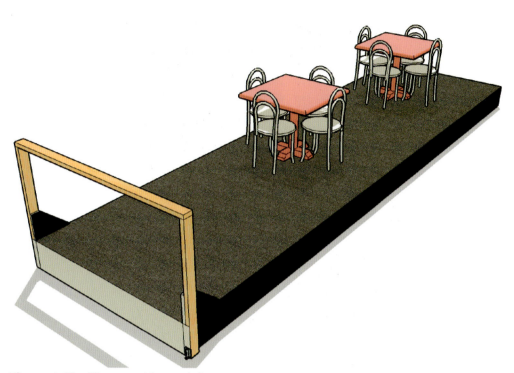

Figure 4.68: *Slip stage with a push bar.*

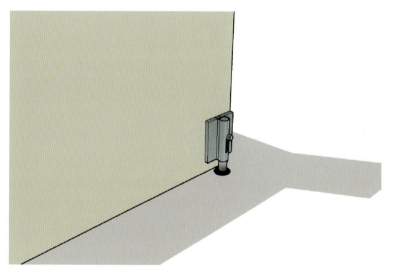

Figure 4.69: *Close-up of a wagon frame and a barrel-bolt brake.*

Figure 4.70: *Wagon brake.*

the more expensive the brake. Some people swear by these brakes, and our guess is that they are the people who have budgets for the really good ones. Other people feel the spindly little legs on the brakes are just too wobbly to be believed. It is another of the eternal tech debates, like who should buy the donuts (Figure 4.70).

Foot Irons and Stage Screws

A foot iron off the back of a wagon's frame has the advantage of locking the wagon tightly down to the floor, and the stage screw insert acts as the positive spike mark. The disadvantage here is the time it takes to screw down the stage screw through the foot iron and into the insert (Figure 4.71).

Scenery Jacks

These act in a similar manner to wagon brakes by lifting the scenery up, but they add an important difference: When they set the scenery down, they set it down on its frame and not on the castors. There are many styles of jacks, but the basic premise is the same. The wagon rests on the castors only when it's in motion; when it stops, the castors fold under the frame (Figure 4.72). There are any numbers of ways to move the castors up and down, from lift plates to folding tip jacks, but the sexiest version has to be the *pneumatic castor jack* (Figure 4.73). Pneumatic pressure from an air tank forces a piston to move down, lowering the castors and raising the wagon. When the air is released, the wagon sinks down onto its frame.

Figure 4.71: *Close-up of the folding foot iron.*

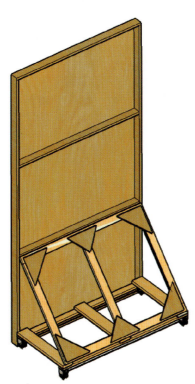

Figure 4.72: *Drawing of a tip jack.*

247

Figure 4.73: *Bed wagon from DeSales University's production of* A Christmas Carol *showing the pneumatic castor jacks and the jack-of-all-trades that rigged it.*

In the long run, how you move you scenery depends on what kind of stage you have. If you do not have fly space, you cannot fly; no wing space, no wagons. While these circumstances call for creativity, they can also cause a lot of frustration. The simplest, safest solution is usually the best; it leaves less room for mechanical and operator failure. Also, once you have the solution, make sure adequate training is provided at tech rehearsals for everyone who comes in contact with or is onstage while the scenery is in motion. Even if a technician or actor never comes in contact with a moving piece, strange things happen during a show that may cause someone to wind up in the path of a moving piece. Forewarned is forearmed.

Section 2
Creating the Environment

Chapter 5

What Do I Need?

Interpreting the Script for Its Basic Scenic Needs

You've been given the task of designing the set for a play. Whether this is something you've been yearning to do or you just drew the last straw, we can give you some basic guidelines to start. Theatre gives you the chance to create your own pocket universe with every production. The colors, the textures, the laws of nature are yours to decide. The trick is that you have to use this world to help tell the story of the play. "Whoa! Too many choices! So how do I do this?" Start with the script.

Words, Words, Words: Reading the Script

The first thing you need to do is read the script. Just read it. We'll wait.

Okay, you've read it over. What are your overall impressions of the story? What is the story about? Is there an image that you locked onto? Is there a central metaphor or theme you can come up with to describe the play? Jot these first impressions down.

Notebook Project

Start a notebook for your design ideas. A three-ring binder works well for holding the variety of materials you'll be gathering. Get some sheet protectors, a three-hole punch, colored pencils, blank paper, and loose-leaf paper. If you don't like carrying around a binder, try a sketchbook or one of those bound blank journals, whatever you feel you can work with. The most important thing is to have your ideas all in one place.

Read the script again, this time with your notebook nearby. With a highlighter, high-light every location or setting needed in the play. With a colored pencil, underline everything that relates directly to the setting, for example, mentions of doors, windows, or stairs. Every time someone refers to a prop, underline it in another color. Every time there is a reference to a sound or light cue, underline those in their own colors. Why do you care about lighting, sound, and props?

To start with, most scenic designers design the props as well, and with good reason. You are creating the look of the world of the play; these are the things in that world, so they define the look. There's another, more practical reason. They have to come from somewhere, and that affects your design. If a character brings an elephant onstage, you have to make sure that the doors are big enough for them to pass through, the plat-forms give the elephant easy access (they have bad knees, you know), and there is enough overhead clearance so the elephant's head isn't blocked by borders, lighting, or scenery. And make sure the carpets you choose are cleanable, because quite often ele-phants get stage fright, and accidents do happen.

The lighting and sound follow the same lines. The light comes from somewhere (for example, a window, a lamp), the sound comes from somewhere (a radio, a balcony open to a nearby band shell). At this point you just need to be aware of these effects. You can start thinking about where that somewhere is a little later. You can also change it later. You probably will.

Notebook Project

Play publishers generally permit a photocopy version of a play for production use as long as you buy a copy of the play. Check with the play publisher to be sure. By copying each page of the small acting edition to a larger, letter-size sheet, you give yourself lots of room for margin notes, underlinings, and coffee stains. Punch these with three holes and put them in your binder.

Play Scene Investigations: Who, What, Where, and When

Sometimes criminals leave obvious clues that are easy to find; other times you need to do fiber analysis to get clues. We need to answer three basic questions for every setting: who, what, and where and when?

- *Who belongs to this place?* What socioeconomic class to they belong to? Who would have had the most control over its contents? What kind of people are they? What are their interests? Who else spends time there, and what are they like?
- *Where and when does this take place?* Is it someone's home? Is it a public common area? Is it a private common area? Is it a secret inner sanctum? Is it a neutral area that takes on many locales? Is it a famous location? Does it have a specific geographic look? Is it a specific kind of building? Is it outdoors? What time of

year is it? What happened in that period of time that may have shaped ideas, customs, and styles?

- *What happens here?* What dramatic actions take place that will affect the settings? Where is the main entrance? How many other doors do you need? What is on the other side of the windows and doors? Where does most of the action take place in each scene (these are the major acting areas)? What furniture or props are needed?

Creating Breakdowns of Basic Scenic Needs

The first place to start is the stage directions. The majority of these are written by the playwright, and they give us an idea of how the playwright saw the character's environment. Your production will be unique and individual; you may not wind up with anything like these once you and the director talk. But they are a good place to start, and they flesh out the words of the play.

George Bernard Shaw was the king of stage directions; you'll rarely find a better example of a playwright knowing exactly what a room looks like. The marked-up page of Shaw's *Arms and the Man* in Figure 5.1 needs no fiber analysis; we know exactly what Shaw wants. And from reading these directions we know exactly what he wants us to think of the characters, based on the things he puts in the room. We know that Raina is a young girl of means and somewhat silly romantic tastes. Some of Shaw's clues include the paperback romance novels, the gorgeous tapestries, the "long mantle of furs, worth, on a moderate estimate, about three times the furniture of her room," and the "paltry wallpaper."

What Is a Prop and When Is It a Set Dressing?

What's Practical About It?

Some objects, like the portrait or the chocolate creams in the Shaw, will actually get used by the actors, and these, as you know, are called *props*. But when a prop does what it looks like it should do, we call this a *practical prop*. Lighting uses a similar term to describe a light fixture on stage that actually lights: a *practical light* or just a *practical*. Most often, the prop department will supply the lamp and the electricians will wire it into the system.

If your practical prop is food that gets eaten, that is what we call a *consumable prop* (go figure). The chocolates in the Shaw scene are consumable, and the stage manager and director will have to let you know how many will be consumed each night. The same goes for cigarettes, matches, and anything that gets used and is gone. These props tend to consume your budget. When it comes to food and anything that gets ingested,

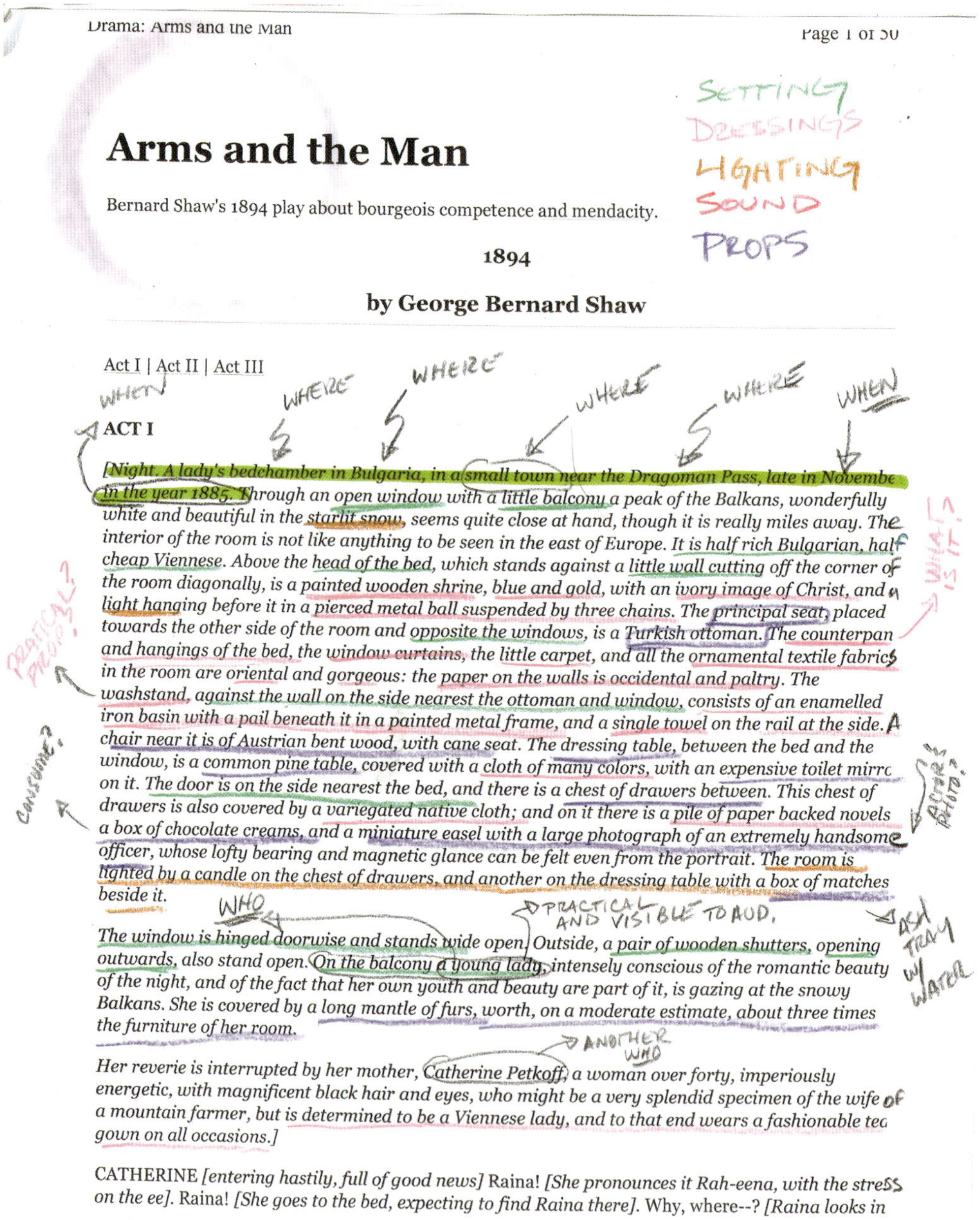

Arms and the Man

Bernard Shaw's 1894 play about bourgeois competence and mendacity.

SETTING
DRESSINGS
LIGHTING
SOUND
PROPS

1894

by George Bernard Shaw

Act I | Act II | Act III

WHEN   WHERE   WHERE   WHERE   WHERE   WHEN

ACT I

[Night. A lady's bedchamber in Bulgaria, in a small town near the Dragoman Pass, late in November in the year 1885. Through an open window with a little balcony a peak of the Balkans, wonderfully white and beautiful in the starlit snow, seems quite close at hand, though it is really miles away. The interior of the room is not like anything to be seen in the east of Europe. It is half rich Bulgarian, half cheap Viennese. Above the head of the bed, which stands against a little wall cutting off the corner of the room diagonally, is a painted wooden shrine, blue and gold, with an ivory image of Christ, and a light hanging before it in a pierced metal ball suspended by three chains. The principal seat, placed towards the other side of the room and opposite the windows, is a Turkish ottoman. The counterpane and hangings of the bed, the window curtains, the little carpet, and all the ornamental textile fabrics in the room are oriental and gorgeous: the paper on the walls is occidental and paltry. The washstand, against the wall on the side nearest the ottoman and window, consists of an enamelled iron basin with a pail beneath it in a painted metal frame, and a single towel on the rail at the side. A chair near it is of Austrian bent wood, with cane seat. The dressing table, between the bed and the window, is a common pine table, covered with a cloth of many colors, with an expensive toilet mirror on it. The door is on the side nearest the bed, and there is a chest of drawers between. This chest of drawers is also covered by a variegated native cloth; and on it there is a pile of paper backed novels, a box of chocolate creams, and a miniature easel with a large photograph of an extremely handsome officer, whose lofty bearing and magnetic glance can be felt even from the portrait. The room is lighted by a candle on the chest of drawers, and another on the dressing table with a box of matches beside it.

WHO

PRACTICAL AND VISIBLE TO AUD.

The window is hinged doorwise and stands wide open. Outside, a pair of wooden shutters, opening outwards, also stand open. On the balcony a young lady, intensely conscious of the romantic beauty of the night, and of the fact that her own youth and beauty are part of it, is gazing at the snowy Balkans. She is covered by a long mantle of furs, worth, on a moderate estimate, about three times the furniture of her room.

ANOTHER WHO

Her reverie is interrupted by her mother, Catherine Petkoff, a woman over forty, imperiously energetic, with magnificent black hair and eyes, who might be a very splendid specimen of the wife of a mountain farmer, but is determined to be a Viennese lady, and to that end wears a fashionable tea gown on all occasions.]

CATHERINE [entering hastily, full of good news] Raina! [She pronounces it Rah-eena, with the stress on the ee]. Raina! [She goes to the bed, expecting to find Raina there]. Why, where--? [Raina looks in

WHEN?   WHAT IS IT?   PRACTICAL PROP.?   CONSUME?   ACTOR PHOTO?   ASH TRAY w/ WATER

Figure 5.1: *First page of* Arms and the Man *showing Shaw's stage directions and underlined scenic clues with margin notes and coffee stains.*

254

you need to ask if the actors involved have any allergies before you give them the props.

Not Now—We're Dressing!

Some objects will never be never touched or referred to again; we call these *set dressings*. They set a mood and create atmosphere for the world the actors will inhabit. There's an old saying: "You can learn a lot about a woman from the contents of her purse." The same goes for the spaces the woman lives in (or a man's purse for that matter). The set isn't just a backdrop; it's another way to give the audience information about the characters and the world of the play.

Notebook Project

In your notebook (or on a spreadsheet in your notebook computer that you will print and put into your notebook), start lists of the lighting, sound, props, and dressings and scenic notes you come across, organized by act and scene (Tables 5.1–5.4).

Also start a list of all the actions in the play, called an *action sheet*; list every entrance and exit, every time a character sits, crosses, cooks, dances, or fights, and every action, all organized by act and scene (Table 5.5).

Table 5.1: *Lighting Breakdown*

Lighting Breakdown	*Arms and the Man*		Act I, Scene 1
Cue	Effect/Action	Page	Notes
Raina—revealed at top of act	Moonlight from window	1	Snowy Balkan peaks? Drop can't block moonlight. Need space for cyc lights?
Revealed at top of act	Practical candle	1	Electrify
Revealed at top of act	Practical candle	1	Electrify
Revealed at top of act	Practical candle in sphere	1	Electrify
Catherine	Enters through door	1	Practical hall light?
Raina	Enters through window	1	Do windows have shear curtains to let in light?
Louka	Crosses to window and closes shutters	3	Shutters practical
Raina	Crosses to candle— chest of drawers and dressing table—blows it out	4	Moonlight only light—what about lighted sphere?
Man	Opens shutters from balcony	4	Shutters let in light
Man	Closes shutters and lights match	4	Fakes lighting candle
Man	Blows out match	4	Ashtray near window
Raina	Lights candle	4	Fakes lighting candle

Table 5.2: *Sound Breakdown*

Sound Breakdown		*Arms and the Man*		Act I, Scene 1
	Page	Action	Effect	Notes
Raina	4	"My hero"	Gunshot	From balcony area
Raina	4	Same cue	2 gunshots	From balcony area closer
Man	4	Blows out candles	"Fusillade"	From balcony area quite close
Louka	5	Knocks on door	Knock	Live cue, actor on door
Raina	6	Stands in front of the curtains and throws open the shutters	2 shots	From under window
Offstage effect	6	Same cue	Bullet shatters glass	Breaking glass effect
Officer	6	Crosses to window to yell out	Crowd noise	Could be live sound

Table 5.3: *Prop Breakdown*

Prop Breakdown	*Arms and the Man*		Act I, Scene 1
Prop	Dressing	Practical	Notes
Bed		Raina, Man lie on it	See Shaw's notes about dressings
Wash basin		Towel and water	Man splashing water on his face at end of scene?
Bentwood chair		x	No notes. Do we need it?
Shrine	x		Do we want this? Adds period and geographical flavor.
Sphere		Electrify	See above. Create prop, electrics wire it.
Chocolates		Consumable	How many can he eat and still talk? New or partial box?
Ottoman		x	Hold at least two people
Counterpane	x		What the heck is a counterpane? Research!
Rug		x	Stock item?
Curtains		x	Man hides behind these. Large enough to hide him.
Dressing table		?	Not in stage directions, but does this need a chair?
Mirror		x	Tilt down and frost to avoid glare.
Toilet articles	x		Should be usable brush? Fake other items.
Chest of drawers	?		Do the drawers open?
Cloth	x		Pull from stock.
Candles		Electrify	What kind of holders? Electrics will wire.
Matches		Consumable	Put strike plate on box and on side of dressing table; water in ashtray or candle base.

Table 5.4: *Scenic Breakdown*

Scenic Breakdown	*Arms and the Man*	Act I, Scene 1
Major Units	**Action**	**Notes**
Door	Main entrance opens in, locks, knocked on	Paneled door? Check graphic resources for door locks, knobs, and plates.
Window	Opens in, handles both sides, glass panes; smashing panes	Effect needed for gunshot
Balcony	Man climbs onto it from offstage	Only one person on it at time, practical railings, down spout?
Shutters	Latch closed, need handles both sides	Don't actually lock.
Raised entrance or step up to window?	Raina, Man entrances; Officer yelling down	Allows balcony to be seen and Man somewhere to climb from.

Table 5.5: *Actions Sheet: A Summary of the Play by Actions*

Actions Sheet		*Arms and the Man*		Act I, Scene 1
Character	**Page**	**Page**	**Character Count**	**Notes**
Raina	1	Stands on balcony looking out	1	Must have backdrop: snowy Balkan peaks?
Catherine	1	Enters through door	2	What's on other side of door? Hall?
Raina	1	Enters through window		Do windows have shear curtains to let in light?
Raina & Catherine	2	Sit on ottoman		Big enough for two people
Raina	2	General pacing		How large is floor space?
Louka	3	Enters through door	3	
Louka	3	Crosses to window and closes shutters		Shutters practical
Louka	3	Locks shutters		Practical lock
Catherine	3	Exits through door	2	
Louka	3	Pushes shutters to prove they don't lock		Lock closes shutters but doesn't bolt them down
Louka	3	Relocks shutters		
Louka	3	Exits through door	1	
Raina	4	Crosses to portrait, picks it up, puts it back		Practical prop; get actor's picture
Raina	4	Takes book from chest of drawers and gets into bed with it		Practical book, make sure it doesn't read.
Raina	4	Crosses to candles on chest of drawers and dressing table, blows them out		Check on real flame, have ashtray with water in it.
Raina	4	Gets back in bed		
Man	4	Opens shutters from balcony	2	Must have entrance to balcony from outside. What floor are they on? Do we see him climb up?
Man	4	Closes shutters and lights match		Has them or finds them?

Table 5.5: *(Continued)*

| Actions Sheet | | *Arms and the Man* | | Act I, Scene 1 |
Character	Page	Page	Character Count	Notes
Man	4	Locks door		Door must have a period lock of some kind.
Man	4	Blows out match		Ashtray near window
Raina	4	Lights candle		Matches and ashtray
Man	4	Crosses to the ottoman and gets cloak		
Louka	5	Knocks on door		
Man	5	Tosses cloak to Raina, crosses to door, and pulls saber		
Raina	5	Pulls Man to window and hides him behind the curtain		Can't be curtains on window because they need to be sheer
Raina	5	Takes off cloak, crosses to door, and unlocks it		
Louka	6	Enters through door	3	
Catherine	6	Enters through door	4	Getting crowded at door
Officer	6	Enters through door	5	Must position door and window so that the curtain with the Man is seen
Raina	6	Stands in front of the curtains and throws open the shutters		Curtain and Man must be close to shutters.
Offstage effect	6	Bullet shatters glass		Can we afford FX? Need bullet FX, replaceable smash glass in window, and glass in each pane. When is broken glass struck?
Officer	6	Crosses to window to yell out		

Next, start three more lists, for who (Table 5.6), what (Table 5.7), where and when (Table 5.8). From the information you gathered from the previous lists, start answering these questions. These sheets will serve as a quick reference for design meetings.

A Stage Picture Is Worth a Thousand Words

You may find that in the course of filling in this information you need to revise your original impressions of the play. The more time an artist spends studying his subject, the more he learns about it. You need to become an expert. Audiences don't always get the chance to read a play before they see it, and some wouldn't anyway. The program notes may be great, but audiences don't always read them either (just look at how many

Table 5.6: *Who Sheet Breakdown: Shows Everyone Who Enters the Setting and the Influence on the Environment*

Who Sheet Breakdown	*Arms and the Man*		Act I, Scene 1
Character	Class	Interests	Influence
Raina	Upper	Romance	Primary
Catherine	Upper	Viennese culture/social status	Head of house—some influence (Viennese)
Louka	Servant	Ambitious	Cleans it
Man	Soldier	Survival	None
Officer	Soldier	Duty	None

are on the floor after a performance). Your set will jump-start them into the play's world by giving them visual information in addition to the characters' words. After all, they did come to see a play.

Questions for the Director: The First Concept Meeting

What Does the Director Want?

You've read the play again; you've decided for yourself the playwright's ideas of who, what, where, and when; you know the action inside and out; and you have a good idea of the lighting and sound environment and how that affects you. You're now ready for your first conversation with the director. There are some questions you need to ask her; they aren't that different from the ones you already have answers to. In fact, most of them are those same questions. But you need to know what the director is thinking. In this initial meeting you must ask her about her *concept*, or her impression of how the world of the play and its story interrelate.

What Does It Feel Like to You?

You may find that the director has a different take on it than you do or even the playwright does. For example, you've listed locations for every scene's setting you found in the play. The director may wish to cut those settings down or to set everything in a unit location. The director may want to set *Arms and the Man* at a colony on the moon in the 1930s. "Great—all that work I've done is down the drain." Well, it isn't. It's important information, even if it's used for contrast. It may be the information that proves to the director that the concept needs more work. As a member of the production team, you owe it to the production to share your insight into the play and ask provocative questions.

That's why it is important to get the director to talk about her concept and answer the three questions. You also need to ask her where she visualizes the major acting areas of

Table 5.7: *What Sheet Breakdown: A Reference to Major Actions, Lights, Sound, Scenic, and Prop Needs*

What Sheet								Act I, Scene 1	
				Arms and the Man					
Major Actions	Page	Lighting	Page	Sound	Page	Effects	Page	Scenic Needs	Page	Practical Props	Page
Stands on balcony looking out	1	Practical candles (2)	1	Gunshots	4	Shutters push open	3	Backdrop	1	Bed	1
Climbs onto balcony	1	Practical lighted sphere	1	Gunshots	6	Broken glass	6	Practical balcony	1	Chest of drawers	1
Locks shutters	3	Moonlight	1	Breaking glass?	6			Practical door	1	Dressing table	1
Pushes shutters open	3	Blows candles out		Crowd noise (inferred?)	6			Practical windows (French doors)	1	Ottoman	2
Opens shutters from outside	4							"Locking" shutters	3	Bentwood chair	1
Lights candles	s									Chocolates	7
Blows out candles	s									Novel	4
Lights matches	s									Portrait	4
										Ashtrays	s
										Lighted sphere	1
										Candle holders (2)	1

Table 5.8: *Where Sheet Breakdown: A Quick Reference for Research*

Where and When Sheet Breakdown	*Arms and the Man*	Act I, Scene 1
Where geographically	A small town near Dragoman Pass, Bulgaria	
Where location	Raina Petkoff's bedroom	
When year	1885	
When month	November	
When time of day	Night	

each scene. Find out if there is something the director feels she needs to create the environment of the play—a type of chair, a special Viennese postcard, a revolving stage—so that you can get that in the works. She may not be able give you all the answers at this time, but it's important to put the questions out there so that you can both start thinking about them.

Notebook Project

Take copious notes at your meetings and take the time to write everything down. Don't worry. People will give you the time and will expect you to do this. Date your notes so that you can refer back to them and keep them in a special section of your notebook.

Now that you know what the director wants, reread the play. See how this concept jives with your own. Start a new series of lists, and reanswer the questions if need be. How do you go on from here? Let's start with a where-and-when question.

Chapter 6

How Do I Get Them to Build It?

Communicating Your Ideas

Believe it or not, some people aren't as visually gifted as you are. You have to lay everything out for them in graphic detail. We call these people producers, directors, and actors.

Who, Where, and When Research, or Don't Reinvent the Wheel

Take a look at the time period during which you've agreed to set the play. Newspapers and periodicals can provide wonderful examples of the kinds of things that were going on at the time. Catalogues from the era are nice for props and dressings, to get an idea of the styles of items your character might have. Look at the popular art of the time. If your setting is an actual historical place, get as many graphic resources as you can. If it's a contemporary piece, go to the magazine rack at the bookstore and make copies of anything that seems applicable or that you just like. Sometimes an image may not be the right time period but have a shape or color or mood that speaks to you. Put them all in your notebook.

All of this research will help you get a look into the world of the characters. Research the types of things the characters might read, books they would own, or art they would like. See how this information might change what you think of the characters and who they are.

The Stock Floor Plan

Before we set this down on paper, we need to take a look at your particular theatre and discover its specific needs. What type of theatre do you have? Where are the audience's seats? What are the sightlines? You can answer these questions by walking into the theatre, or you can look at your theatre's stock floor plan and cross section. If a production has been held there, such a stock floor plan exists and the theatre should provide you with a copy. If they don't have a clean copy, then borrow a set of old designs and trace your own. While you are at it, it doesn't hurt to look at old production photos and see what's been done in your theatre. Sometimes these can give you a clue to potential sight line problems. Since you're in the archives, you should also get an inventory of stock scenery and masking. Do you have wing space? Is there flyspace? Do you have trap system?

> **TIP** At this point many theatres are storing their information digitally. If you aren't using CAD, this can be a problem. Have them print it out. If they can't, have them store it on disk for you as a PDF. Take this to a copy center with a large-format printer (most national chains have them) and have it printed out to its original paper size so that the PDF file preserves the scale of the drawing.

> **TIP** While you are out, pick up some *tracing paper* for your sketches and some *vellum* for your finished drawings. You'll need some other drafting supplies:

- *Drafting table:* a good investment. You need one that will hold paper up to 18″ × 24″ at the least. Make sure it has square sides. Adjustable legs are a plus. You can find a fancy one that has a parallel arm for drawing horizontal lines that are square to the paper or a drafting arm or drafting machine built into it that allows you to draw nice square lines and that tilts to any angle.

- *Drafting tape:* looks like masking tape. It holds your drawing on the table so you can square it to the board. Some people use it to pin their work down. This leaves bumpy little holes that catch your pencil.

- *T square:* You can do without the drafting machine if you buy one of these. This acts as square baseline and draws parallel horizontal lines when you hook it to the side of that square-sided drawing board. We know it's cool looking, but resist the urge to hook your boyfriend around his neck with it or torture your girlfriend's cat with it. These are useless if they go out of square.

- *Triangle:* This doesn't just draw triangles. Think of it as a *tri*-angle. They come in 30–60–90° and 45–45–90° styles (three angles, get it?) as well as an adjustable angle (yes, the tri-angle analogy falls apart there, thank you very much). When its 90° side is held square to the T-square, you can draw perpendicularly vertical lines and angled lines.

- *Scale ruler:* Get an architect's scale ruler. Engineer's scales are different and we don't like them. You can get the triangular style, which has two different scales on each side, or a flat scale that looks more like a ruler. But scales aren't like rulers. You don't draw lines with them. That could notch the edges and ruin their accuracy. You use them to mark points and connect those points with a T-square or triangle. Never throw them at the director either. That ruins their accuracy. What do you think hammers are for anyway? With the triangle kind of scale, place the scale you want to use in front of you, and put a binder clip on the side pointing its little apex at you (serves it right for doing that in public). This will remind you which side of the scale you are using. A piece of tape will do this for the flat scale.

- *Pencils:* This is another one of those touchy subjects. Some designers like wooden pencils (maybe it's the taste). Some like mechanical pencils that hold removable leads. Neither of these pencils is any good if you don't keep them sharp. As your pencil wears down, the lines get thicker, which can throw off scale measurements by several inches. You can never have enough good pencils or keep them around. People will steal your pencil and do their homework with it or stir their coffee with it or clean their ears with it—and you won't want it then. It will make your coffee taste funny. Get enough to lose some.
- *A really big eraser:* There are lots of kinds out there, just like pencils. If you want to make your life easier, get an electric model. (But then everyone will hear it and know you made a mistake.)
- *Graph paper:* In a pinch some designers have done without everything but a straightedge, scale rule, and erasable bond graph paper—four squares to an inch. If you get it in nonphoto reproductive blue, you can have copies made and the graph lines won't show.
- *Templates:* These come in ½″ and ¼″ scale for furniture pieces. They are very handy for your initial layouts.

➤ **TIP** If you want to investigate CAD, go to http://www.sketchup.com and download their trial version of *Sketch up*. It's a user-friendly 3D design program that will produce professional-looking results in a hurry. It even has a function that sections large drawings to print out on letter-size paper so that you can tape them together. A student version is available.

Sketches and Drawings

Initial Sketches, or You Can't Lean Against the Fourth Wall

Now the real design work starts. Based on the conversation you had with your director, take a look at your "what" list. Where did she see the major acting area in each setting? Start with that area. Now go through your graphic resources and look for ideas based on those images. Label them and keep them handy as references.

At this point you should start to see the basic shape of the setting beginning to form. Sketch a rough floor plan of what this room would look like if it was in a real house. You can even measure a real room you think to be similar in size and work from there. Your templates would be useful here for actual furniture measurements (or you can

Figure 6.1: *Initial sketches of* Arms and the Man *set with four walls.*

refer to the Standard Dimensions table found on page 251 of the *Backstage Handbook*[1]). Now draw it again, but leave out one wall. We call this the *fourth wall*, and it's the audience's window into the world of the play. Move anything from the fourth wall that would obstruct the audience's view and locate it on one of the other walls (Figure 6.1).

Locate on your sketch the major acting areas you and the director spoke of. Do they work with everything else, or are they buried in the set, necessitating that you move them to where they will catch more focus? Look at your action list: What else happens in that setting? What kinds of exits do you need? Where are the characters sitting? How many acting areas can you give the director? Work for at least two areas, depending on the size of the scene.

Heightening Reality, or Spin-Doctoring the Set

If you can't draw focus for the areas you want, there are a couple of solutions you can try. Remember what we said about height? Height gives emphasis and allows areas in the back to be seen more easily. Can you logically make one of those areas higher than

[1] Carter, P. *Backstage Handbook: An Illustrated Almanac of Information*, 3rd ed., New York: Broadway Press, 1999.

Figure 6.2: *Removing the fourth wall, raising Raina's windows up on a platform eight inches, and adding a hallway behind the door to solve a couple of design problems.*

the others? Main entrances, stair landings, and window seats are just a few suggestions (Figure 6.2). If you can't move the acting areas because of the action of the play, can you tilt the set on the stage to show them more prominently (Figure 6.3)?

Floor Plans and Scale Drawings

Back to the Floor Plan and up with the Model

Now that you have the theatre's floor plan, trace it and lay your sketch inside the stage house. How does it work with the sightlines? Adjust if necessary. Now you are at the point where this plan view stuff is going to drive you up a tree. You are itching to see what you have done in three dimensions. Your cross section of the theatre is the first thing you should reach for. Check and see how high your overhead limitations are. These are set by lighting instruments, proscenium heights (if you have one), and the height your setting should logically be. Estimate the average height of your walls, and draw simple block elevations of your floor plan. (You already know the flat's width from your floor plan.) Don't worry about the finer details yet; you just want basic shapes. Label each flat on the elevations and on the floor plan so that you can assemble them in the right order.

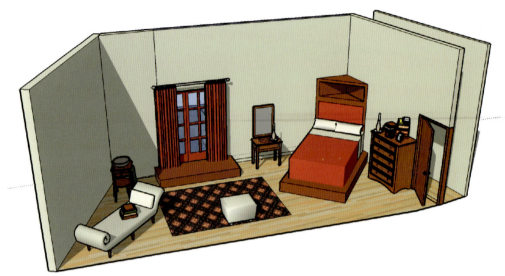

Figure 6.3: *Raising the windows even more, adding a platform under the bed to give it more height, opening the walls up, and tilting the set to add interest and push the action downstage. Note set decorations and props. Which are missing from the author's description?*

Take copies of these drawings and a tracing of your floor plan and spray-glue them to some card stock. With an Xacto knife, cut out the shapes of the elevations. Now tape these pieces down on their corresponding lines on the floor plan. You've just made a *white model*, a basic study in the shapes of the scenery and their inner relationships. Do the same thing with the theatre's floor plan and cross-sectional drawings, and create a theatre box in which to place the set model. Don't forget to include the wings and fly tower, if any, as well as any other strange architectural whoozis that can affect your backstage life.

Get some long, thin dowels or wire rods, cut them to the width of the stage, and tape some black fabric or paper the width of your proscenium opening around the rods—you've created pipe lines for masking. Refer to your cross sections and ground plans for the actual location of the line set positions, and see how you can mask your stage off.

Drop Me a Line

If you look at the shape and aren't crazy about the basic lines, attempt to change them. An abundance of vertical lines makes the set look taller. A lot of horizontal lines makes the set look squat. Taller sets look more epic; shorter sets seem more intimate. You can't just work with one type or your design will be uninteresting and actually hard to look at. By contrasting shapes, you can make a greater statement. Curves soften hard lines and blend lines together.

Long unbroken expanses of wall lines aren't that interesting to look at. If you don't need a wall to be long to accommodate furniture, break it up. Slide a wall in and create an alcove; as an added plus, the more often you change directions the better the scenery self-supports. Play around a little. You should also add basic shapes to represent your furniture and see how their basic lines affect the composition. Little cubes of card stock or wood will work, or you can have some real fun and invest in some *pop-out furniture* (http://www.rosebrand.com is one source).

If all of this seems arbitrary, well, some of it is. That's why we call it art—it's your interpretation of reality. But, as we said, don't reinvent the wheel. Look back to your graphic resources for inspiration on lines and shape. Do these basic shapes you've come up with say anything about the director's concept? Also, don't forget those special images you saved that didn't work with the period but inspired you or said something to you about the theme of the play. They're worth a look now. Another major consideration is that inventory of stock scenery you got from the theatre. Their size and shape can help you define the size and shape of the lines. Make scale cutouts of these shapes, and substitute them for pieces in your model, or label similar ones of the same size and shape stock. Monkey around a little with these. Once you are happy with the result, pull up the tape and glue them down with a hot-glue gun.

> **TIP**   If you are drawing in CAD, you can create a model in virtual space. That's one of the attractive features of CAD. But even then, most directors like to see a physical model. The process isn't that different in CAD: Draw the flats and then print them out directly onto card stock.

Perspective Sketches

Perspective drawings are a method of translating the two-dimensional elevations into three-dimensional information. By looking at the perspective sketches, you get an idea of how the entire set looks from a centrally located seat in the audience. There are two schools of thought on this. Some people love to do the perspective sketch because the process of doing it gives them new information about the set as they are doing it. Other people say the model does the exact same thing and prefer to do it that way. The problem with a sketch is that it isn't a model; you are limited to one view of the set. The problem with a model is that it isn't a sketch; you can't neatly tuck it in your notebook. Some designers do both. It's all in what works for you.

If you work in CAD, you have the best of both worlds, since you can print out any view you want, you can print your elevations to make models, and you can make changes very easily. But if you don't have the software, you can't do anything. So it doesn't hurt to know how to do a basic perspective sketch. After all, some of the best designers in the world have worked out their design problems with a felt-tip pen, a cocktail napkin, and a working knowledge of single-point perspective.

Putting It All in Perspective

There are many types of perspective used in drawings: single-point (parallel), two-point (angular), three-point (oblique), and drop-point (mechanical) perspective. But the easiest to master is *single-point perspective*. You've no doubt made a drawing like this in grade school art class if you had to draw a railroad track trailing off into the distance lined by shrinking telephone poles. The concept goes something like this. Things in the distance appear smaller, so you draw them smaller. The resulting drawing gives the illusion of depth. There are two key terms that make this effect work: the vanishing point and the horizon line. The *horizon line* is the line out in the distance that is the horizontal limit to your perception. Early sailors thought the horizon line was the drop-off of the end of the world; it's why they thought the world was flat. Although we never heard from Columbus' fifth ship, we know now this isn't true.

The second term is the button on the perspective game. Somewhere on that horizon line is what we call the *vanishing point*. This point is where all of the lines converge in the distance. By drawing guidelines to this point from everything in the drawing, we ensure that the objects in the distance get proportionally smaller as we go toward the vanishing point, where they just vanish.

There are two ways to make a perspective drawing: freehand and mechanical perspective. Drop-point perspective is an art unto itself and not easily grasped. A quick and dirty explanation involves two other terms: the observation point and the picture plane. The *observation point* is the point from which you are observing the set. In film terms it would be the camera angle. The *picture plane* is a little more difficult to grasp. It is basically what you are seeing in front of you as you look at the set if you imagine that this image is "on a glass sheet."[2] In a proscenium house the size and shape of the proscenium usually define the size of the picture plane. If you then laid this sheet on a piece of paper and slid the ground plan's centerline above the observation point, you could drop corner points down to your perspective drawing. It's a handy skill to have. If you want to pursue it, look at *Designer Drafting for the Entertainment World* by Patricia Woodbridge.[3] She devotes an entire chapter to this process as well as the gridded perspective sketch.

Freehand perspective, while not as accurate, is often all you need to get the point across or to get a design idea straight in your head. To make a freehand perspective drawing, imagine you are in an audience seat in the theatre; dead center of the theatre's house, the seat everyone fights for. Grab your white model and put it up on a few books to approximate where it would be if you were in the audience. The model in front of you approximates your picture plane; where you are sitting is the observation point.

[2] Woodbridge, P. *Designer Drafting for the Entertainment World*, Burlington, MA: Focal Press, 2000.
[3] Woodbridge, P. *Designer Drafting for the Entertainment World*, Burlington, MA: Focal Press, 2000.

Draw a ½″ border around your paper, and use the bottom border as your ground line, the line that represents the end of what you're looking at or the bottom of the picture plane. Your eye level relative to the model's base is the horizon line. Since you are sitting dead center in front of your model, this puts the vanishing point in the center of the horizon line.

Estimate the height of the horizon line and draw a horizontal line to represent it on the page. You can try using your pencil and thumb as a gauge, the way the artists in movies do, or you can just eyeball the distance. Do the same thing to judge the walls to the extreme right and left of center, and draw vertical lines to represent their height. To draw the bottom and top of the flats, trace a light line from the vanishing point to the bottom of the flat, and do the same at the top. This gives them the angle that creates the illusion of depth. Move along the rest of the model toward the center, working your way in from the sides. Get the basic outlines in first, and fill in the details later. Darken the lines around the objects and erase the guidelines.

Digital Images and CAD

Color Renderings

Once you have the shape down, you can begin to think about what color can say for you. Look again at your graphic resources. Find colors and textures that work with the period, appeal to you artistically, and speak to the concept of the production. For example, if your production has an underlying threat, perhaps you could have black encroaching around the edges or a predominance of red. Refer back to the graphic resources to which you had an emotional response. Compare them with your impressions of the play and the director's concepts.

Everyone has a color medium with which he or she enjoys working. If you don't, the easiest to start with is colored pencils. They involve a short learning curve and are very forgiving. Mistakes are easily erased. Make a few copies of your perspective sketch and try some of these color choices. If you like them, try them out on the flat elevations.

> **TIP** Watercolor pencils are a bit more expensive than the traditional colored pencils, but they give you a few more options. By adding varying amounts of water on a brush, you can smooth out a large block of color or move the color around, creating textures and shading, and even blend colors into each other. It's sort of a low-impact introduction to painting.

> **TIP** CAD (computer-aided design) allows you to render your sets in perspective simply by changing the way the object is viewed in virtual space. Color rendering techniques vary from simple paint bucket techniques to creating virtual surfaces and applying them to the objects. For every program out there, there are books and user groups to help you. Once you've rendered the set, you can select

views from several observation points and print them out. You can also print out color renderings of the elevations and create a simple color model, the same way you made the white model.

Making Designer Plates

We've already spoken of designer plates in Chapter 4. Now you are going to create some. You have already drawn a floor plan and elevations. You now need to present them in a way that someone besides yourself can understand. The next section presents a basic checklist of items you need to include. (An excellent resource for drafting techniques is Patricia Woodbridge's *Designer Drafting for the Entertainment World*.)

Plan Views, or Floor Plans

Plaster Line

In a proscenium theatre this is the back side of the proscenium portal. All horizontal lines will need to be parallel to this line. It's one of the two major lines by which we navigate the stage. Think of it as our longitude line. These are shown as alternating long and short dashed lines in a medium-to-heavy line weight (Figure 6.4).

Centerline

This is the other major line. It's down the center of the proscenium portal, not necessarily the center of your stage floor, where your wing space could vary from side to side. This way, the audience perceives it as the center of the opening (Figure 6.5).

Border and Leg Maskings

Since you are looking through the borders, we see them as medium-weighted dashed hidden lines on the drawing, the way you see invisible stuff drawn in a comic book. The legs, depending on whether they are hard or soft, full or flat, are drawn in solid lines since we see the top edge of them hanging below the line set position.

Line Sets

These aren't just for borders and legs. These lines mark the overhead locations of each line set in your theatre. These line sets can hold scenery, electrics, as well as drops and scrims. The main rag or act drop line is usually the first line set; the cyc line is usually the last. The cyc line sometimes curves in as if it were hugging the other line sets from behind. You want to represent this on the drawing; the lighting designer will need to know how wide the cyc is for his strip lights; and directors and stage managers will want to know its location for upstage crosses and side entrances. Draw only the line

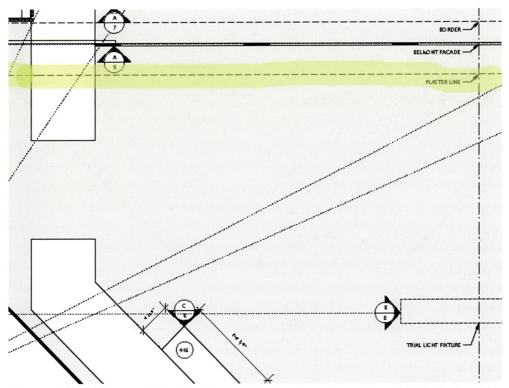

Figure 6.4: *A close-up of the* Merchant of Venice *floor plan with a highlighted plaster line. (Courtesy of Steve TenEyck.)*

sets you are using, and draw a key on the side of the stage from which these line sets are controlled (Figure 6.6).

Border and Title Block

The *title block* tells you the name of the show, the director who drafted the drawing, the plate number, the drawing's view, and the drawing scale as well as any special notes you want to give. The border doesn't tell you anything except that there is no usable information on the final ½″ of paper below this line. These are usually done in a heavy line weight.

Flats and Flat Labels

These are usually drawn in little triangles, as we said before, and they point to the flats. Also, you need to indicate which ways the doors swing and the window locations in the flat. These details will be fleshed out on each individual flat's elevation.

273

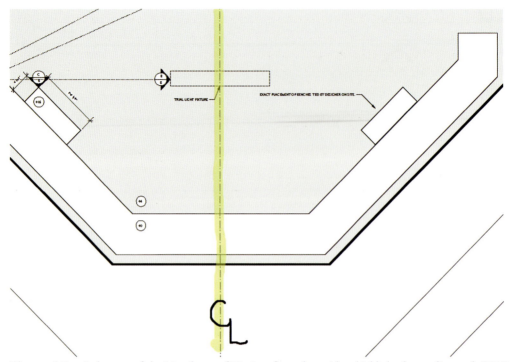

Figure 6.5: *A close-up of the* Merchant of Venice *floor plan with a highlighted centerline and "CL" centerline mark. (Courtesy of Steve TenEyck.)*

Facility Details

It's good to know the shape of the building, the locations of doors and other exits and the fire curtain, and other architectural whoozis. They give you an idea of what your offstage space is and critical sightlines. These should be on the stock plot you get from the theatre.

Scenery

That's what we're doing right? Make sure these pieces have solid outlines and are labeled in some way. Platform shapes should be outlined, and elevations should be noted. You'll also need to indicate any escape stairs wherever necessary and their elevations. If a piece moves, such as a wagon, you should indicate its path by drawing a dotted line from its offstage position to its onstage position. This will indicate the travel path so that the TD and director and stage manager can make sure the path is clear (Figure 6.7).

Section Views

These involve pretty much the same story as for the ground plan. You need the same information, but only what you can see of the set from that section view (Figure 6.8).

274

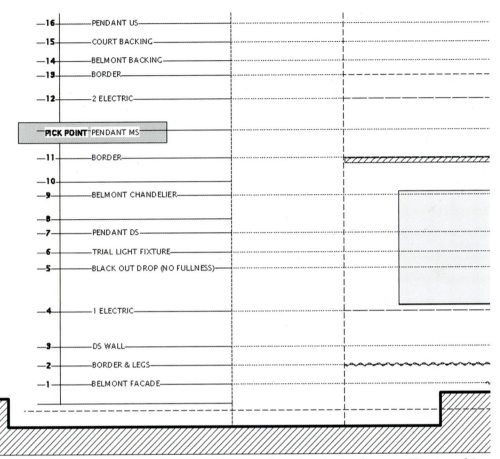

Figure 6.6: *A close-up of the* Merchant of Venice *floor plan showing line sets. (Courtesy of Steve TenEyck.)*

All the line sets are represented, and on the drawing you need to give a clear representation of the facility, including proscenium height and trap space below stage.

Elevations

Here is where you need to add details to the individual pieces, including the following.

Dimensions

If you are drawing in scale and indicate the scale on the plate, theoretically you don't have to dimension the elevation. But no one will like you. Some dimensioning is necessary as a reassurance that what you have drawn is in the scale you said it is and that what they see is what they think they see. It all comes down to how much help you

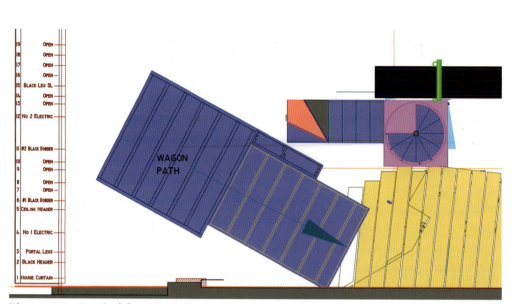

Figure 6.7: *Detail of floor plan indicating the travel path of a wagon.*

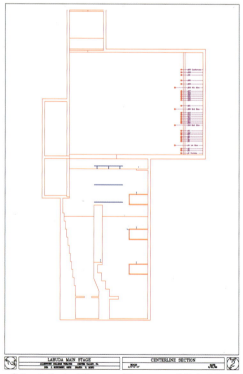

Figure 6.8: *Section view of the Labuda Theatre. (Courtesy of Bob Mond.)*

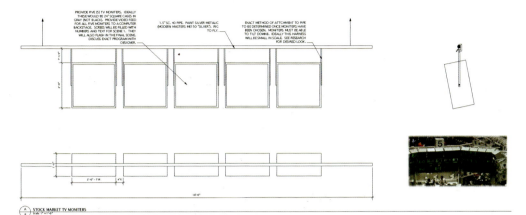

Figure 6.9: *Breakout detail elevation from* Merchant of Venice. *(Courtesy of Steve TenEyck.)*

want to be to the carpenters and TD. They like information, but not confusing information. Some designers dimension the outside details and leave the inside for the TD, to avoid the confusion of crossed dimension lines. The more you work with a particular shop, the more you'll know what they need from you. Don't hesitate to give the shop more detail if they ask for it. After all, you want the set built, don't you?

Breakout Details

These are just one more way to give the TD more detailed information. They can be in the form of images from catalogues or zoomed-in details drawn in a larger scale and indicated as such. Think of them like the traveling zoom shots from the police crime scene shows (Figure 6.9).

Views

These could include front, left and/or right side, plan, and even section and hidden views. If your piece is asymmetrical, you will need to give them as much detail as you can. Include any views that show the object changing shape from the front elevation. If the scenic unit is a basic symmetrical rectangle or any other symmetrical shape, you only need to draw one side, put a centerline down the unit, and list "R&R" (or "reverse and repeat" (Figure 6.10).

Paint Elevations

These are a combination of the elevations and the color renderings. They give your scenic artist a guide as to what paint treatment you want and where. They should include the same views as the scenic elevations. Make one for each elevation, showing the colors and paint treatment for all the details. Breakout information can include your

TOP VIEW

MEMORANDUM
½"= 1" SCALE
R&R ALL DETAILS

FRONT VIEW

Figure 6.10: *Elevation detail showing the R&R method of detail.*

graphic resource images, paint swatches, wallpaper, and even small sample textures of the scenic treatment you've done as an example. One designer we know brought a small colorful tiled mirror he found in Spain as a paint sample. Use whatever will get your point across. It is not unheard of to give the paint crew a large painted model as a paint elevation. Label and attach the details to the elevations. If you want the elevations to remain usable, it's not a bad idea to laminate them for protection.

In the long run you want to think of yourself like Michael Keaton did in the movie *Night Shift*, in which he said, "I'm an idea man, Chuck." You have the idea, but it's no good if you can't express it to the people who will work with it. Give them detail, and in the process you will see your pocket universe come to life.

Chapter 7
How Do I Get Them to Believe It?
Adding Realistic Details

Now you've done it. It's built. How do you finish it? We'll describe some simple techniques everyone should know about paint treatments and wall coverings. The key to all of scenic artistry is careful observation. What do these things I want to mimic actually look like? Your designer should be able to help you there with graphic resources and painter's elevations. If you are the designer and scenic artist, begin by studying the textures and colors of the scenery you want to paint. This chapter will by no means be all inclusive, but we'll get you started with some simple techniques that require practice (and a minimum of special equipment) and point you in the right direction with several resources.

Paint Treatments

The Paint
We all know how to use paint, but what is this stuff, anyway? Paint is a colored film that gets applied to a surface and remains once the surface has dried. Depending on its chemical composition, it can display various properties of wear, drying time, and ease of use. There are three parts to any paint: the binder, the vehicle, and the additives. Arguably, the *binder* is the most important part of the paint; it's the stuff that holds the paint together. The *vehicle* is just a substance, such as water, that you add to make the paint thicker or thinner, or to adjust its viscosity, if you want to say it in fancy talk. The *additives* are the rest of the stuff in paint, such as pigment, which gives the paint

its color, and other substances that affect the way the paint wears, such as additives that make it an *exterior* paint to withstand weather or the fillers added to make the paint cover or hide well. Since we rarely deal with anything that has to last more than a few weeks, the main additive we discuss is pigment.

Paint Finishes

Before we go further, we should clear up a few terms. *Paint finish* refers to the quality of a painted surface when it dries. Here are some common ones.

- *Flat finishes:* These are preferred for theatrical work since they don't reflect light. All theatrical scenic paints come in a flat finish. Flat black paint is such a theatrical staple it is hard to imagine theatre without it. Rosco's Velour Black is one good example of a flat black that absorbs light, creating the no-see-me black we often look for in theatre. Aside from being nonreflective, the flat finish hides surface imperfections easily. The major disadvantage of flat paint is that it scuffs easily. This isn't a disadvantage on drops, but it is on walls and floors. Your run crew will complain that they have to mop the stage floor each night; however, your lighting designer will love you for it since no light will bounce off of the scenery. Most books on scenic painting wouldn't mention the following finishes, but we'll discuss them so you can see the contrast with flat paint.
- *Eggshell:* Actually looks like the dull sheen on an eggshell. This finish is a bit harder than flat finishes and a bit more durable. It holds up to scuffs, but the down side is that slight sheen we spoke of.
- *Satin:* Whereas eggshell has a slight sheen, satin has an undeniable shine to it, resembling brushed metal. It is much harder than flat finishes and stands up to scuffs well, making it a nice floor treatment. If you use this paint for a floor surface, you will have to mop it less to maintain a good-looking floor, but you will get some bounce light from it as part of the deal.
- *Glossy:* This is the most durable of the common finishes, but it really makes lighting designers crazy. The hard surface of the paint reflects light like mad. Glossy surfaces are also hard to repaint since the hard, slick surface does not adhere to binders well. A primer coat is always needed to cover a glossy surface.

Just because we generally do not like the harder, shinier surfaces does not mean we do not use them. As an accent, the change in paint finish can be quite effective in making a statement. For example, glossy finishes look fancier, and a bit of glossy trim around a door can really add a nice pop to your set. If you intend to use glossy surfaces, warn the lighting designer as soon as possible. In addition to being reflective, hard surfaces tend to be slippery, so it would not hurt to warn the costume designer as well so he or she can treat the actors' shoes.

Types of Common Theatrical Paint

Before we were taught stagecraft, dry pigments were the thing. In fact, even recent books on scenic painting list dry pigment mixing and the stinky glue pots used for it and other messy, time-consuming, as well as hazardous methods of preparing paint that we won't even go into here. There are people out there who make a good living mixing the paint into more user-friendly products; we want to do our part for the global economy by supporting them. Besides, hardly anyone makes his own paint anymore; there are easier and more productive ways of showing off your opposable thumbs.

The paint and finishes we refer to in this chapter are water soluble. Oil-based paints have their place in the world, but the longer drying time and the flammable cleaning and thinning solutions it requires make them less desirable than their water-based cousins.

We're Casein the Joint

Casein paint is milk-based or soy protein–based binder paint and one of the most common theatrical paints because of its flat finish and vibrant colors and because it dries quickly to a flexible film that is not water resistant. We call this *rewettable* paint. If you paint over a section of dry casein, the bottom colors will bleed into the colors you just added. This may work for you or against you, depending on how you plan your work.

The major disadvantage is the shelf life of casein paint. Since it has an organic protein–based binder, it may spoil; once it goes bad it smells like rotted cheese, and any drops or scenery you paint with it will as well. Everyone who has worked in this business a while has a horror story about rotted paint; for example, one road company we know was asked to leave a theatre because their drops smelled so bad. Once a can of rotted paint is opened, bacteria in the air or more especially in water make the paint spoil.

This stuff comes in a concentrated formula that you scoop out into another container and add water as a vehicle until you get the consistency you want. By mixing only what you need, you can avoid excessive spoilage. Unused portions should be topped with an inch or two of a product such as Lysol™ or Simple Green™ liquid cleaner and sealed tightly to prevent air from reaching the paint. In spite of this disadvantage, many designers and scenic artists love casein and swear you can't get the same color formulations with any other paint. Casein may be thinned out to make glazes and other transparent finishes or simply thinned out to stretch your paint budget and still provide desirable coverage and color.

Nothin' Could Be Finer Than to Use Acrylic Vinyl After Casein: Vinyl Acrylic Paint

This paint behaves like casein but has a vinyl acrylic binder that will not go bad. Rosco's website lists the average shelf life of their unopened Idding's Deep Color casein at two years and at three to five years for their Supersaturated and Off Broadway lines, which are vinyl acrylic paints (follow this link to Rosco's website: http://www.rosco.com). These paints stick well to almost any surface and can be thinned out quite a bit for different effects and paint techniques. Supersaturated paint is intended to be thinned out to at least 1:1 water and paint, but it can be thinned to at least 20:1 for transparent finishes. It comes in quart cans and is very thick; it's essentially pigment and binder with a little water as a vehicle. The Off Broadway line is made to a viscosity like house paint, but it can be thinned as well. The advantage to the Off Broadway line is the metallic paints it offers.

The Two Dirtiest Words in Scenic Artistry: House Paint

There are very few trained scenic artists that will allow acrylic or latex house paint to be used on their sets. One reason is that flat house paint just is not as flat as a flat scenic paint. Another reason is the pigment used to tint house paint. Scenic paint is made from pure artist's pigment, while house paint is actually a blend of many pigments. This creates what they describe as "muddy colors" when different house paints are blended. House paint is formulated to go on a wall, that is, a wall in a house. It is not meant to be folded, rolled, or treated in any of the other hundreds of ways we beat and abuse a poor paint surface in the course of a show's run. As a result it may chip, crack, and flake off. Scenic paint has a more flexible binder to allow bendable adhesion to all kinds of different surfaces.

House Versus Scenic Paint

All this aside, the question remains: "Can I paint a set with house paints? I mean they are right there in the paint aisle! I don't live in New York! I can't just run around the corner and pick up some Supersat on my way to lunch! I don't want to pay all that shipping! Paint is heavy!" Just calm down—the answer is yes. There are many productions that have done an adequate job with house paint. Since the advent of home improvement TV shows and the popularization of faux painting, the big-box do-it-yourself stores have begun to stock a plethora of paint, painting DVDs, fancy brush whizbangs, and all kinds of clinics. Many of the techniques they teach are the same ones used in theatre, and they have been redesigned to work with house paint. Sometimes the availability of house paint and the variety of colors that can be mixed and formulated for you is just too easy and convenient to pass up. But as we said before, convenience has its trade-offs. If you are going to use house paint, you should design with that in mind. If a show was designed with scenic paint, the chance that you will be able match the designer's color choices in house paint are not good. And don't forget, house paint has sheen.

White house paint and black house paint are cheaper than their scenic counterparts, and we use them like mad. If you are looking for a way to stretch your paint budget, these two solutions will be the least noticeable. A highlight here and there done in house white or a house white mixed with another color is not going to be that awful. Is the flat house black really flat? No. Are you going to light something you paint black anyhow? Probably not.

Equipment: Layout Tools

With most layout work, you need a towel, a good supply of water, a flat surface, good tunes, some good sunscreen, sun, and some sort of bathing suit. With paint layout tools, what you need is a little different. (It is not uncommon, however, for summer stock companies to have an outdoor paint deck, so you may be using the aforementioned tools. Bathing suit is optional and really not recommended—you are painting, remember.) Actually, you will be using many of the same techniques we mentioned in carpentry layout. A framing square, a chalk line, a straightedge, and a tape measure are all common instruments used in paint layout. Gridding is one prime example and projecting a layout is another (see Chapter 4).

Pouncing Patterns Produces Painting Productivity

> **TIP**   Full-scale patterns are really particularly useful in scenic painting. To transfer them to the scenery or drop we can use a method called *pouncing*. Once you make your layout through a grid or a projection, you take a tracing wheel and trace all the lines in the layout. This puts little holes in the pattern paper. Then you take some scrap muslin and rip it into small squares of six inches or so. You pour charcoal dust into these squares and tie them with elastic bands or tie line. Then, with your pattern positioned securely over your drop, you pat or pounce the charcoal bags over those little holes you just traced. This transfers the pattern in charcoal onto your drop (Figure 7.1).

If you have enough room and the equipment to project, you can project your layout drawing directly and trace it in vine charcoal (Figure 7.2).

The advantage of charcoal for layouts is that the charcoal is easily removed after you paint. Floggers are made of scraps of 2 × 2 or 1 × 1 with scrap muslin wrapped around them and stapled on one end. Slits are cut into the other end, and the result looks much like a cat o' nine tail (Figure 7.3) (while it is very temping to chase freshmen down the hall with these, again, this is not encouraged). You swing these gizmos at the

Figure 7.1: *Artist working with a pounce.*

Figure 7.2: *Artist working with a projected layout.*

Figure 7.3: *Flogger.*

drop, and the resulting force lifts the charcoal off of the drop, similar to the way you beat a carpet clean (if you have not beaten a carpet, it's similar to flogging a drop).

Brushes

Brushes are the most personal of the scenic artist's tools. There are many sizes and shapes, but the parts of a paintbrush are standard among them all: the handle, the ferrule, and the bristles. The *ferrule* is the shiny metal thingy that holds the bristles together on the handle. The ends of the bristles are epoxied into it, and it in turn is epoxied and/or nailed to the handle. The better ferrules are made of a rust-resistant metal, such as brass or stainless steel. Sometimes a plug or a bar is placed inside the ferrule between rows of bristles, creating a gap, or paint well, allowing the brush to hold more paint (Figure 7.4).

Bristling over the Debate on Natural Versus Synthetic

The bristles are the heart and soul of the paintbrush. The bristles we use for water-soluble paints are most often natural bristles, made from animal hair, but, as you may discover in the paint store, there are many synthetic bristles that can do the same job. Scenic artistry is just that—an art. And like all fine arts, there is a certain amount of tradition connected with it. When a paintbrush is dipped in paint, we call it *charging* the brush. Scenic artists traditionally gravitate toward the natural bristle for its superior charging ability. If you look at animal hair (if you are grabbing an animal to do this, make sure it is one you know), you'll see that they're tapered at the end opposite the root. When you bring these ends together at the tip of a brush, they naturally slide

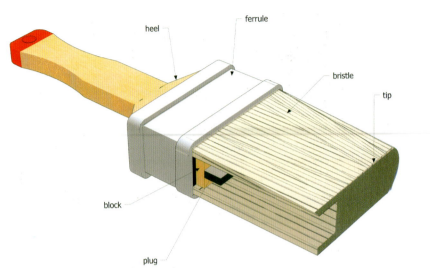

Figure 7.4: *Cutaway of a brush showing the parts.*

together to hold the paint inside the brush's paint well until you put pressure on them. Their shape also causes the paint to flow toward the end of the bristles, allowing you to direct the flow through pressure and movement of the brush.

Synthetic bristles in the past tended to be uniform in size and shape and did not charge as full as a natural brush. The upside of a synthetic brush is the reduced cost and its simpler care and maintenance. New brush technologies are evolving all the time, and synthetic brushes are catching up to natural bristles. In some respects, synthetic bristles are better than natural bristles. However, making paint go where you want it to and look the way you want it to is an almost mystical art and as much about the right feel as it is about technique. Just as the golfer and the bowler choose the right equipment for their sport and the carpenter chooses the right hammer for the job, the scenic artist needs to find the right brushes for the job.

Pack Up Your Fitches in Your Old Kit Bag

Everybody has a specialty in theatre, and most people have enough knowledge of everyone else's job to be dangerous. Scenic artists never seem to get enough respect, and their tools get the least. To everyone else a paintbrush is a paintbrush and perfectly good for applying glue, dusting a benchtop, or cleaning one's ears (it happens). That's why scenic designers tend to guard their paint kits with their life. The last thing they want is for the perfect brush with the right-feeling handle to wind up stirring someone's coffee. A *kit* is a collection of tools designated to perform a specific task. While, as we said, a painter's brushes are subject to personal taste, we can suggest some standard brush types that are commonly used.

Figure 7.5: *Dutch (primer) brush.*

Dutch (Primer) Brushes

These brushes have a flat ferrule and usually two to three rows of bristles 4–8″ wide. As you probably guessed, they hold a lot of paint. These brushes can quickly base, or prime, large areas. They have a large handle to offset their large size; however, their large size keeps them from doing detail work (Figure 7.5).

Lay-in Brushes

The lay-in brush is another type of flat ferrule brush, and it can be anywhere from 1″ to 4″ wide. These brushes have fewer rows of bristles than primer brushes and are usually finer bristled in nature. They do not hold as much paint as a primer brush but work well for laying in large areas of color. The finer bristles allow them to do more detailed work. Most common painter's brushes fall in this category.

One of the more useful of this type of brush is the *sash brush*. This brush was made to paint the details on window sashes; its chisel-pointed end allows it to pull a tight, straight line. It is really nice for cutting-in work. When you *cut in*, you are painting on the edges of walls under, above, or beside a molding, floor, ceiling, or some other structure that is of a different color than the area you are painting. These cut lines need to be particularly sharp to define the color changes. Once the cut line is made, another person may come in behind you and lay in the rest of the color. This speeds up the work considerably since the lay-in worker has your cut line as an extra safety margin. By the same token, you also cut in on a drop when you go from one block of color to another.

A good mixture of these brushes would include a handful of 1″, 1½″, several 2″ and 3″ sash brushes, flat-bristle brushes, and two or so 4″ brushes for doing larger lay-ins (Figure 7.6).

Figure 7.6: *Variety of lay-in brushes.*

Detail Brushes

These are any brush of a fine bristle that you use to add detail to your painting. This is one of the areas where the artist's tastes take over. *Fitches* are one preferred type; they have a round or oblong ferrule and resemble large versions of artists' brushes. *Scenic line brushes* are another type of round ferrule brush, but the ferrule is crimped at the end, flattening it out a bit. This helps you hold a line when the brush is held against a straightedge. These brushes are more expensive than common painters' brushes and can be found online at theatrical websites, such as www.rosebrand.com and Gerriets International (http://www.gi-info.com), sold in kits or at better paint stores. A typical kit contains ¼″, ½″, ¾″, 1″, 1¼″, 1½″, and 2″ fitches (Figure 7.7). (The size here is actually the measurement of the paint stroke, not the ferrule.)

Just as with any other tool, you need to see which types of brushes work the best for you. Borrow a friend's brush and see how that works. Do not be surprised if she stands over you while you use it. She's just making sure it stays out of your coffee cup. There are a few other items that might creep into your bag as you progress in your scene-painting skills, and these are more specialized brushes and tools for paint techniques. We will point them out as we discuss the techniques.

Shop Supplies

There are items every paint shop should have; some are common sense and some seem out of place until you learn more about how we use them. We describe them next.

Figure 7.7: *Fitches and scenic liners.*

Figure 7.8: *Working down with a bamboo paint extension.*

Bamboo Sticks

These are practically ubiquitous in every paint shop. By splitting the end of the bamboo pole to create four sections, inserting a brush handle into them (the way you would chuck a bit into a drill), and securing the end with a rubber band, you have an extension with a "sphincter-like grip."[1] These may be adjusted to hold just about any brush as well as charcoal and markers for lining. Remember, bamboo is sharp. Sand the edges well before using (Figure 7.8).

[1] *Stock Scenery Construction Handbook*, 2nd ed., New York: Broadway Press, 1999.

Straightedge or Lining Stick

This is different from the straightedge we have used for layout work. When drafting, straight lines may be drawn with a T-square or a triangle straightedge that is lying directly on the paper and tracing the edge of the drafting straightedge with a pencil. Paint, being a liquid, behaves differently from pencils. If you used a similar technique with a paintbrush, one of two things would happen and quite often both. The edge of your straightedge will get paint all over it. The next time you set the straightedge down, this paint will get on your painting, causing an unwanted line. Also, unless you make a very tight seal with the straightedge, the paint will seep under the straightedge and cause a blurry line, and the paint on the straightedge will again cause an unwanted line.

On painting straightedges or lining sticks, the edge is engineered to rise above the paint surface. You create the line by running the ferrule of the brush, instead of the brush tip, against the edge. Scenic liners have that crimped ferrule that runs nicely against these edges. These function best for floor work, and to that end they have stick handles that allow you to lift and place them without bending (Figure 7.9).

Hair Driers

You may have seen these used in paint stores. Wet paint always looks different from dry paint. Since we never have enough time for anything in theatre, we speed up this process by using a hair dryer. Also you may notice that most scenic artists are perfectly coiffed.

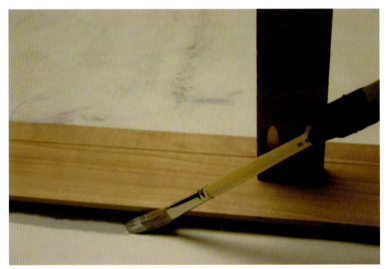

Figure 7.9: *Lining with a scenic liner and a straightedge.*

290

Garden or Deck Sprayers

These are pump-action sprayers that spit out a fine mist. They can be used with hot water to restretch a wrinkled muslin flat (make sure it isn't painted with casein first) or to spray a mist of watered-down paint to create a spatter effect. They would also be great water guns for chasing annoying people, but we do not recommend that and have never done it ourselves.

Window Screening

When you rinse off your dinner dishes (or your mother rinses the dinner dishes—and aren't you ashamed of yourself? Doesn't she do enough for you?) and the gunk collects in the sink strainer, you simply lift the strainer out of the sink and dump the gunk into the trash. Paint creates tons of gunk—goopy, chewy gunk that never wants to leave a drain and will make you the enemy of every plumber and maintenance worker around you. An aluminum window screen (nonrusting) placed at the bottom of your paint sink makes it easy to degunkify your sink.

Stirrers

In the old days when we went for that nickel loaf of bread and the 50-cent quart of paint, the baker/paint salesman would give you an armful of paint stirring sticks; and if you were nice, he would give you a couple of carpenter's pencils to boot. These days there are not many bakery/paint stores around, and, really, was it a good idea in the first place? Good thing you can get all the stirring sticks you need from the scene shop. Have them save pieces of scrap for you that are in the neighborhood of ¾″ × ¾″. While you are there, check to see if you can weasel an old heavy-duty drill from them. An old heavy-duty cordless drill and a squirrel-cage mixer may be your best friends when stirring a five-gallon bucket of paint. These stirrers look like the little exercise wheel your mice or hamsters run on—but on a stick. When chucked into the drill, they can stir your paint pretty darn quick. Just shut the drill off before you take it out of the paint.

A Bucket of Sawdust

Totally random right? Paint spills all the time, and if it is black paint on a black stage floor it is a slip hazard. Sawdust will quickly absorb the spill, and it can easily get brushed away.

Masking Tape and Drop Cloths

Did you know that masking tape was invented for painting? Blocking off an area to keep it from getting painted is called *masking*. While we have seen people use this tape to block off windows and doors, parts of scenery can be masked while we cut in around them or use messy techniques like spattering and puddling. The removed masking tape also recycles into very nice ball that can be used in conjunction with a paint stick or a bamboo pole for a quick game of tape ball.

Drop cloths such as bogus paper, craft paper, or plastic drops can be used to cover and shield walls and scenery from spatters, but they can also be taped down to mask large areas from sprays or spatters. Quite often they are used underneath drops to smooth out rough surfaces and protect the floor from wet-painting techniques.

Empty Buckets of Various Sizes

Once you mix a shade of paint, glaze, or a wash, you have to keep it somewhere. (Actually, how did you mix without a bucket in the first place?) One of the most common practices in theatre is never to throw anything away. As you empty buckets, wash and store them. This is where the window screening in your sink will come in handy. You can also buy various sizes of paint buckets, but that's cheating.

Rollers and Roller Buckets

Rollers are great for laying in vast amounts of color quickly and are available in wide widths and a variety of naps. The downside to a roller over a brush is that a roller really just lays the paint down, whereas a brush adds the character and texture of the brush stroke. Texture rollers are available at the paint store, and they work with varying degrees of success.

Roller buckets are different from the more familiar roller pans; they are actually a bucket with a grate or ridged surface to wipe the roller when charging it. The advantage is that they are not as easily kicked or stepped into.

Here's the Messy Part: Common Painting Techniques

One of the most amusing things in life is to see students arrive at a paint call in their nicest, most fashionable attire. What were they thinking? Guaranteed they will get paint on them. So here it is in print: **You will get paint on you. The paint doesn't care how stylish your clothes are (or were)**. Actually, studies are being done right now with your tax money to prove that the amount of paint on you is proportional to the cost of your clothes.

Painting Down and Painting Up

Where are you going to paint that scenery? You have two basic choices. You can paint the scenery down (on the floor), horizontally (on sawhorses), or up, which would place the scenery vertically in front of you. Each has its advantages.

Up, Up, and Away

One method of painting up is with a *paint frame*. This is a complicated system that uses a frame to which the drop is attached that lowers the drop into a paint well or raises the painter on a paint bridge. These are expensive systems that require specialized equipment, not unlike a second fly system, and they need trained personnel to run them. (For an excellent description and several really good illustrations of paint frames, consult *Scenic Art for the Theatre: Histories Tools and Techniques*, 2nd ed., Burlington, MA: Focal Press, 2005. That is one of the few places we've seen a paint frame.)

Another method for painting up is very similar to painting a house. Once the scenic walls are assembled, you can paint them just the way you paint a wall. The obvious advantage to painting up is you are painting the scenery the way you will be using it; you can step back from it and look at it the same way the audience will see it (provided you aren't on a ladder). The disadvantages are that paint frames take up space and there is that old gravity bugaboo again, making certain wet techniques more difficult.

Getting Down to It: The Lowdown on Painting Down

This is probably one of the most common ways of painting large scenery and drops. It does not require any more specialized equipment than the stage floor and brush extensions to keep from bending over all day. Also, the techniques used in this method are more like those used with watercolors: You can work wetter and blend more easily. Multiple painters can work on different parts of the scenery without the use of ladders or fall-arrest equipment, and few painters have ever fallen off the stage floor—well, a few. But chances are they were going to fall sometime that day anyhow, probably just after they stepped into the roller pan.

The disadvantages include walking through wet paint, lumpy floors, and tight scheduling of the floor space. Quite often in summer stock situations the scenics are pulling the third shift late at night into early morning after rehearsals and build calls have finished. Also, unless you look at it from the balcony, load rail, or grid, it's hard to get a good perspective on what you are working on.

Base Coating

We have mentioned priming and sizing; base coating is sometimes thought of as the same thing. However, the base coat may be the start of a texture technique.

Scumbling

We will start with this method first because it is the most fun to say. Scumbling is the process of blending several colors together to create a texture effect. This effect is achieved by blending three or more colors together with random strokes while they

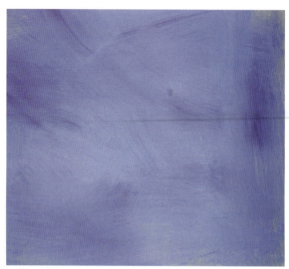

Figure 7.10: *Sample of scumbling.*

are still wet, directly on the scenery. When the colors are carefully chosen, this technique can provide the base for many other texture effects or can stand alone as a mottled texture background. Portrait photographers use a similar background to add texture and interest to a shot without distracting from the subject (Figure 7.10).

Wet Blending

Wet blending mixes three or more colors on a surface, similar to scumbling, but there is usually a direction or grain that the paint is pulled toward. The key to successful wet blending is moving quickly and blending before the paint dries. Two colors are laid down and then a third color is pulled over them in the grain direction. Wood grain is a common use for this technique; carefully observe a board and you will see it is not one color but many. Keep the board or graphic resources handy as you work with this technique (see Figure 7.11).

Ombré

A good example of this is a painted-sky effect that gradually gets lighter as it approaches the stage floor. Several colors are used, creating a gradation. Bands of color are painted under each other with separate brushes or rollers, and then a clean brush is used to blend the areas between, usually working light to dark (Figure 7.12).

Figure 7.11: *Sample of wet blending.*

Faux Texture Techniques

Spattering

If you have ever shaken a paintbrush out that still had some paint in it, you have already tried this technique. By watering the paint down to a thin texture, you can easily spray the paint into little drops. This creates a pebbled texture that is great for creating a rough surface treatment. For example, if you combine scumbling and spattering, besides sounding like you deserve disciplinary action, you may create a convincing stone effect. Spattering can be achieved by charging your brush with a thinned color and shaking the brush or holding the brush horizontally over your work and tapping the ferrule from underneath. It's a really good idea to mask areas you do not want to be spattered. Another good idea is to test your spatter pattern techniques before you try it on the scenery. This may get way out of hand partly because the mixture of paint and water can be tricky and mostly because it is really fun and you are likely to overdo it. Garden sprayers can also be used to spatter, and their nozzles can be adjusted to vary the spray cone (Figure 7.13).

Figure 7.12: *Sample of an ombré base.*

Figure 7.13: *Sample of spattering techniques.*

Figure 7.14: *Sample of a puddling technique.*

Puddling

Let's say, for instance, you really hated that kid next to you in preschool and you may have "accidentally" knocked over your brush water onto his watercolor painting. You know what you did? You ruined his painting, you horrid child. But you also utilized a scenic technique known as *puddling*. When you spray or drip water onto a wet-painted surface and allow the colors to run and blend together, you have puddling (not pudding, no matter what spell-check tells you) (Figure 7.14). This technique softens and blends areas; it's most effective when used to create marble textures. Puddling can easily be achieved with water in a garden sprayer or a stiff brush in a method similar to spattering. Another method of puddling involves charging the paintbrushes with different colors of paint and letting the paints half spatter and half drip over your work. The paint will flow and blend together. With a little work, you can achieve this effect with pudding as well, but you already tried that in preschool, didn't you? What did that kid ever do to you?

Dry Brushing

You have done this before if you ever ran out of toothpaste and just brushed your teeth anyway. The paint technique involves getting just the tip of the bristles in the paint and

Figure 7.15: *Sample of a dry-brushing technique.*

lightly dragging it over a surface. Just like spattering, this technique involves careful control of the brush. This technique is often used to create wood grain over a wet–blended base coat. It's also useful to accentuate existing textures to add contrast or to age or distress a scenic piece (Figure 7.15).

Stencils

Stenciling is a quick way of repeating a shape multiple times. This can be useful for creating regular shapes such as wallpaper patterns and bricks. A stencil can be as delicate as a lace doily or cut from a sheet of luaun. The basic effect is creating a shape that masks the paint from some areas while shaping it through cut designs in others. You can apply the paint with a special stiff brush called a *stippling brush*. This brush's bristles are not meant to bend like other brushes; the paint sticks to the end of the brush and is pounced into the stencil. After you paint one area, the stencil can be lifted and moved to the next. Multiple stencils can be used to create multicolored designs. This method can be used up or down (Figure 7.16).

Stamping

This is sort of the reverse of stenciling. Stamps are not that different from rubber stamps, except they can be a whole lot larger. Blocks of rigid upholstery foam are carved to create the negative of the design you wish to stamp. By dipping the stamp into paint the way you would dip a rubber stamp into an ink pad, you can create a repeated pattern on the scenery. Large stamps are best used down, but smaller stamps can be used when painting up (Figure 7.17).

Figure 7.16: *Close-up of the DeSales University production of* The Memorandum's *set showing a sample of a stencil technique.*

Figure 7.17: *Sample of a stamping technique from the DeSales University production of* The Foreigner.

Glazes and Washes

A *glaze* is a thin coating that is painted over a finish. Whereas these can be clear coats, satin, or a gloss, a glaze can also be tinted with a color to soften a treatment or add depth. An orange glaze is often used to "antique" props. By layering glazes over paintings, you can create a look of depth; glazes used with puddling and spattering can create convincing marble techniques. Rosco and other scenic paint manufacturers make acrylic glazes in clear, satin, and glossy finishes, and glazes have also become readily available from the big-box do-it-yourself stores as well.

A *wash* is similar to a glaze, but it uses water as a vehicle instead of a glaze compound. It's just a lot of water and some paint. Washes are very good for adding shadow; "dirty-water washes," made of black and occasionally other colors, are often used to create this effect. Washes are also used to shade scenery to direct focus. For example, by darkening the perimeter of a set with varying degrees of wash, you actually punch up the areas you want the audience to focus on.

Sponging

Sponging is not that different from stamping. Either a natural sea sponge or a synthetic or man-made sponge is dipped in paint, often a glaze, and stamped in either regular or random patterns. Man-made sponges have a close cell texture; whereas natural sea sponges have a random texture. You can search through many natural sponges until you find one that you can become friends with, or choose several with different textures for your kit. Man-made sponges do not vary in texture that much (Figure 7.18).

Rag-Rolling: Ragging On and Ragging Off

These techniques are used with a glaze. In *ragging off*, the glaze is applied to the base coat and a rag is twisted or gathered into a long roll. Then the roll is rolled across the glaze, creating a random pattern by lifting the glaze off. *Ragging on* is just that: The glaze is applied to the rag and the rag is rolled across the surface. What is the difference? Ragging off needs to be done faster than ragging on, and it is best done down. Ragging on can be done down or up, but it tends to be bolder and less subtle in inexperienced hands. The resulting texture looks a bit like crumpled fabric. There are as many ways of ragging as there are things you can crumple and dip in glaze; each material adds its own texture. Cotton shop rags, terry cloth, newspaper, and even plastic shopping bags can be used. Experiment and find what works best for your design (Figure 7.19).

Painting Actual Textures

With the realism expected from TV, many demands are placed on a designer and scenic artist to create very real-looking sets. The style of scenic painting called *trompe l'oeil* is intended to mimic reality with tricks of perspective, highlights, and shadow. While it is

Figure 7.18: *Sample of a sponged glaze technique.*

Figure 7.19: *Sample of a rag-roll technique from the DeSales University production of* The Memorandum.

very beautiful, it is also an art unto itself and not quickly mastered. (*Scenic Art for the Theatre*, noted on page 293, is a wonderful resource on this technique, its history, and the other techniques we have mentioned.)

"So thanks a lot, I have to plan this design and I don't have time to find an Italian master to train me intensively in an ancient art of scenic painting." (Before you go further into scenic artistry, perhaps you should look into anger management and stress reduction.) There is a faster solution than that, and it involves creating textures and painting over them. Since the advent of hard-cover flats, a world of options has opened to us that were not possible with soft flats. Shadows do not have to be mimicked; they can be created and enhanced.

Appliqués

Anything you tack onto a flat can be considered an appliqué. Moldings are one prime example, so are cut Homasote® bricks, foam stone block, and vacuuform panels. These materials are chosen because their own inherent textures mimic the texture you want to create. They can then be spattered, sponged, glazed, or washed to create the finished color and textures you want (Figure 7.20).

Wall Coverings

Wallpaper

You can wallpaper a hard flat and call it a day. There are also textured wallpapers that mimic stone, wood, or even brick. This is a quick and dirty method. But if it is texture-painted carefully, it can read quite well, as long as your seams are nice and tight and

Figure 7.20: *Fireplace with appliquéd bricks from DeSales University's production of* The Diary of Anne Frank.

Figure 7.21: *Textured floor from the DeSales University Production of* The Butterfingers Angel.

your patterns match. Cloth can also be used as a wallpaper and adhered in a similar way. Textured cloth with a nap, such as terry cloth, can be applied in strips with a glue-and-water solution, like papier-mâché, and create a convincing stone texture.

Textured Paint

Adding the texture right into the paint is another option. Sand or sawdust mixed into the paint will create a texture that can mimic stucco or stone. Joint compound mixed 50–50 with glue and tinted with paint can be shaped and formed on sheets of luaun to create tiles or flagstone or even pulled and grained to form weathered planks. As you might imagine, these take some time to dry, and you should experiment with the mix based on the hardness you need to meet the floor's traffic needs (Figure 7.21).

So whether you use house paint or scenic paint, remember that it's your world; it can look the way you want it to. None of the techniques described in this chapter represents the ultimate way to achieve an effect. Sometimes the best work is done using a variety of effects and improvised equipment. The main thing is that it should create an environment to serve the play.

Chapter 8

What Should It Look Like?

Choosing Props, Dressings, and Floor Treatments

You've painted the set, but you are not done yet. You need to dress it and prop it. What is *dressing a set*? This is the part where you add draperies, rugs, chairs, knickknacks, and other items that will flesh out the world of the characters.

Set Dressings and Props

How do you choose these items? You need to go back to the script. Remember the lists we filled out in Chapter 5? These are the guides you can use to step into the characters' minds. What would they like? Where would they put it?

Illuminating Practical Prop Questions

There are a couple of questions you have to answer with any prop: What does it look like? What does it do? Let's go back to the first scene in *Arms and the Man*. We will use the candle props as an example. We know from the description on the script page shown in Figure 5.1 that there are two candles, one "on the chest of drawers and another on the dressing table with a box of matches beside it." We should start by consulting the Actions Sheet (Table 5.5), the Who Sheet (Table 5.6), and the Where Sheet (Table 5.8). What do these tell us? From the Actions Sheet we know these candles are lit and blown out. From the Who Sheet we know that the room belongs to Raina and that her mother, Catherine, as head of the house, has some influence on the room and its furnishings. From the Where Sheet we know that the play takes place in 1885.

Figure 8.1: *Small electric fan that blows an electrically lit silk used to simulate open flame on stage.*

The Candle and the Man: Open Flame and Safety Concerns

First let's look at the action. Whatever the candle sticks ultimately look like, we know that they need to be easily lit and easily blown out. The thing about theatre is that we really do not like open flames, and local fire codes often prohibit them. While a candle does not seem like that big of a deal, every surface that the candle is near or in contact with needs to be fireproofed, and any costumes and fabrics near it need to be flame tested and fireproofed as well. Quite often it is simpler and less expensive to use electric candles (Figure 8.1).

Back to the Text

When we look at the Who Sheet, we see that the candles are in Raina's room and that she is a romantic young girl. We would like the objects in the room to reflect that quality. Her mother, Catherine, is obsessed with Viennese fashion. That gives us another option, since, as the lady of the house, she would have some influence on the choices of objects in the room.

From the Where Sheet we know that the play takes place in 1885. There is no mention of gaslight, so we assume that candles are the principal source of night illumination in the house. Therefore one candle would have to be more or less movable to allow her to move around the house at night should she need to. Notice that Shaw has indicated that the candle on the dressing table has a box of matches beside it. This suggests that this particular candle is the first one she might go for to move about the house. The other candle can be more ornate, but they should still seem easy to light and extinguish.

Light My Fire

So where are we? We need a practical candle that can be lit and blown out, that does not violate fire codes, and that is romantic looking. Before you get any further, realize that prop making is often a compromise. We already decided that the candle needs to be electric and that it needs to go on and off. When you are dealing with practical props, the first concern should be the *action* of the prop. Will it work when it needs to? Will it be safe? Will it take abuse? Will the effect be realistic? So you need to locate a reliable electric candle flame and work from there.

Electric props have two options. They could be wired into house electrics and controlled from the light board, or they could be battery operated and actor controlled. Directors may want a say in this decision. Some like to leave technical elements under the technician's control, and some want the actors to run the cue. Most often in the case of a practical lamp, the actor puts her hand over the switch and holds it there for the brief half second it takes for the light board operator to run that light cue.

Candles are different. Candles need to be lit by matches. Match flames are more acceptable than candle flames since the match is under the actor's control when lit. Still, the ashtrays need to have a tiny bit of water or petroleum jelly in them to extinguish the match completely. Since there is no easy way to fake the lighting of a match and you can't light an electric candle, you have a cueing nightmare. Each production will have to solve this on its own, but a likely choice would be to have the actor turn upstage to light the candle, masking the match and flame from the audience and allowing the operator to run the cue from the board.

Problem solved, right? Well, let's take a closer look. Since this is only the first scene of the play and the candles and the set have to shift, the electric cable could become a problem. There is an act break between shifts, and you could easily unplug the candle then, but is there an electric nearby? Does the set design allow the cable to be masked? Another solution for those with big budgets involves radio-controlled candles that can be operated from the control booth. An even simpler solution involves battery-operated candles that the actor controls. Discuss these options with the design team and see what action the director will be most comfortable with. Then you can work out where the switch will most easily be reached by the actor, where a cue could happen, or how the candle will shift. Then you can begin to shape the look of the prop based on its electrification and action needs.

Figure 8.2: *Dressings in the Barrymore Apartment in a DeSales University production of* I Hate Hamlet.

Dressings and the Character and Everybody Else

One would assume that when a prop does not need to be touched by an actor, it is relatively easy to fake. However, actors are unpredictable. They might try to pick up and flip through the fake book that has no pages or some other equally embarrassing action and subject your set dressing to abuse and ridicule. A rule of thumb is that if you do not want an actor to move it, fasten it down. This goes double for all of the dressings on wagons: If it can move, it will fall off during a scene shift. Nail, screw, hot-glue, or tape the object down (Figure 8.2).

A Revolving Wagon Dressed for Interior and Exterior Sets

In the long run, people like props. They are fun. It is like playing house, and that is really the spirit with which you should approach set dressing. "If I were the character, what kind of drapes would I buy? What type of chair would I like to sit in. And what chair will I keep other people from sitting in by covering it in plastic?" All the little collected objects that one person or family accumulates through life speak volumes about character, and you get to pick them out. Realize, however, that the more inter-esting the dressings are, the more likely the actors are going to touch them. And to a certain extent you should let them. These things are their characters things, and they are improving their performance.

While you may have done tons of research and found exactly the right shade of purple for a tapestry, understand that the director may come in and say, "I hate it. Can it be green? Can you spray it down? Can you wash it out? Can you just get rid of it?" You

Figure 8.3: *Stanley's house in DeSales University's* A Streetcar Named Desire.

do have to understand that the dressings are not all yours. You may be right that this is the way it should look historically. But as we said before, there is a lot of compromise in props and the director may actually be right. Although we are creating a reality, it is not *the* reality; it's a reality that serves the production of the play (Figure 8.3).

There Is Never Enough Money for Props and Set Dressings

That said, what can you do? Hopefully, the production team is onboard and realizes that the scale of the production needs to stay within the budget. Still, no matter what, you will be expected to work miracles with what you are given. You need to prioritize your budget. First, ask early and often about consumable props, and set aside 10% more than you think you will need. These are the expenses that will creep up and bite you if you do not watch out. Second, anything the actor touches needs to be safe and well constructed so a good chunk of money can go here, depending on the production needs. Quite often the set dressings get what is left over. So how can you make your budget stretch?

Borrowing

You may borrow set dressings and props for the run of your production. The golden rule of prop borrowing is to return the prop in as good a condition as or better than you received it. Make no changes to any borrowed props or dressings without the owner's permission. It is a great idea to take photos of the items before you take possession and when you return them. That much said; Jimmy Durante's most famous quote was: "Everybody wants to get into the act." Put the word out to the cast, the production team, and family members. Visiting local antiques shops or retailers and offering them show credit or advertising in your program is another option if your producing organization is onboard with the idea. They may bite. After all, it's show biz. The worst that could happen is that they say no. Or you might have to listen to their story of their third-grade play. If you get a prop for free, it's worth it.

Altering Stock Items

Stock props can be altered for a current production. For example, chairs are easily reupholstered, painted, or distressed with paint washes. The amount of alteration should be in proportion to the productions needs and the universality of the individual prop. The idea of keeping a stock of anything is to save you money. There is always a trade-off: The more you alter and destroy props for productions, the less stock you will have to pull from. Still it is a viable solution.

Faking

If you cannot afford or cannot borrow the right prop or dressing, find something that looks like it. Start with the object's basic shape. Is there anything that mimics that shape? For example, a production of *Pajama Game* required 20 sewing machines, and with a $200 budget that was not going to happen. Recycled tomato juice cans, rat traps, scrap lumber, some convincing scenic paint, and the manner in which the actors used the props sold them to the audience. Some great ideas can be inspired just by looking at the shapes of objects in the plumbing aisle of a hardware store. Vacuuform is another option. Companies often have molds of the strangest things, from radiators to '57 Chevy grills, and sometimes they aren't in their catalogues. It never hurts to ask.

Casting

You can always make a mold of the original object and cast it from urethane resin, plaster, or other plastics (Figure 8.4). Accordingly, www.smoothon.com is a great resource for casting supplies and information.

Thrift Shopping

If you have to buy a prop, thrift and secondhand stores as well as flea markets and yard sales are good places to start. You may not find the exact period, but you might find something that mimics the line and alter it from there. Also, when you do find the perfect piece, you will feel as if you bagged big game.

Renting

Prop rental houses are also an option. Most often budgets do not allow for rentals for the entire rehearsal period. Rehearsal props are then used in the finished prop's place.

Figure 8.4: *Silicon casting of a bourbon bottle to make a breakaway prop bottle from "smash plastic" urethane resin.*

Make sure that you rent the prop for the tech rehearsal period through the strike of the show. This gives the actors time to learn how the prop works and to get used to it. As with borrowed props, photographs are a good idea. Discuss at the time of rental what alterations, if any, you may make to the prop, and get it in writing on your contract. Plan the return date in advance, and make sure you get the prop back in time.

Dangerous Props and Environments

The Care and Feeding of Actors

First, keep your hands clear of actors when they eat, especially if it's free food. Seriously, food is a great concern for the production, and careful consideration needs to be made in its choice. First, while you are checking on the amount of consumables, you need to find out if any of the actors have food allergies. The wrong food in the wrong mouth could be serious and even life threatening.

Figure 8.5: *Blanche and her drinking problem. After Blanche drank from this glass, she snuck it back on the shelf. That glass was struck, washed every night, and returned to the set.*

Drinking Problems

Liquid onstage is also a big concern. Any time an actor has a glass with liquid, it could spill, or it could spill and break. Be ready with replacements, mops, and brooms in the wings. Also, anything the actors place in their mouths, such as a glass, a cup, a fork, a spoon, or a knife, needs to be washed every night (Figure 8.5). Even if it is just water in the cup, germs could spread through a cast like wildfire and kill a show. There is no need to bring Typhoid Mary back to life.

Can They Smoke 'Em If They Got 'Em?

Cigarettes are also big concerns if there is smoking in a play. Can the actor smoke? Can he or she smoke the brand you chose? Lighter cigarettes may be substituted for other brands, and unfiltered look-alike cigarettes can be made from light filtered ones by cutting them to the unfiltered length. Check your Where Sheet and look for brands that were popular in the play's era. If you cannot find a particular brand, scan an image of the cigarette pack and print a label to fake another brand.

Ashtrays need to be treated with water or petroleum jelly to extinguish ashes. Not only is it safer to do this, but a smoldering butt that just will not go out will be terribly distracting during a scene—and so will the one in the ashtray (Figure 8.6).

Food Prep and Security

Do you have any refrigeration? If you have nowhere to keep food from spoiling, do not use food that will spoil. The area that the food will be stored and prepared in needs to be clean and free of any kind of contaminants, such as dust, dirt, or chemicals, and

Figure 8.6: *The cigar smoking scene from* The Memorandum.

the food needs to be secured every night—seriously. Actors have been known to raid prop food, unsuspecting people pass by and eat it, and stupid people like to play high school pranks such as spiking the food or water to make the actors gag on stage. Not only is your consumable budget on the line, your reputation is as well. Limit access to the food. What might seem like a harmless prank could trigger a food allergy, and you will have the ultimate responsibility for it.

Weapons
Anything used in combat of any kind needs to be approved by your fight director before it gets placed in the actors' hands. Combat weapons are serious business and should never be improvised out of decorative pieces or shop-made by anyone who is not a qualified weapons maker. It's just a bad idea. If there is combat in a show, you need to talk to the fight director right away. Weapons are expensive and can eat up a budget quickly. And they may be dangerous; they are designed to hurt people, aren't they? The fight director will be your greatest resource for these props. He will know what you need to get and how the actors will use it. He will often have resources for procuring the props and perhaps will rent or loan you some of his own weapons. He will also have suggestions for rehearsal props until you get the real weapons. Also, it does not have to be a traditional weapon; anything with an edge or that is swung is considered a weapon, needs to be safe, and needs a fight director's approval (Figure 8.7).

Maintenance and Security
Often a fight captain is appointed from the cast who is trained in the fights and how to care for the weapons. If not, you need to learn from the fight director how to do it. For example, edged weapons for combat are not sharpened—that is no surprise. But

313

Figure 8.7: *Fight scene in* Streetcar *with a broken breakaway bottleneck. This was cast from the mold in Figure 8.4 and was a mimic of the bottle she used in the opening scene we mentioned in Figure 8.5. Labels were scanned and copied for each bottle.*

when you take two metal surfaces and bang them together, they will nick each other; these nicks might cut and scratch an actor, causing serious harm. Each night, the weapons need to be inspected and maintained to prevent injuries such as this. Guns need special care as well; aside from maintenance they need to be watched and treated with care. You should always treat a gun, loaded or not, as a loaded weapon, even the toy ones. Never point a gun directly at a person; even when it is fired onstage, the actor points it slightly upstage of the person. Guns, even prop guns, can expel burning powder and sparks that can burn and injure anyone nearby—it has happened and we have the scars to prove it.

The weapons should be locked up each night and always given limited access. Only the fight captain, the actors using them, and the prop person in charge of the weapons should be allowed to touch them. Weapons are even cooler to play with than set dressings, and inexperienced actors will want to play with them. Experienced actors have had their heads chewed off for doing this, so they know better. Sharpen your teeth. If they drop the weapon, they could cause damage that might not be visible immediately. At best, with a rented weapon you could lose your deposit; at worst, the weapon might malfunction and cause an injury.

Floors

Floors are only a concern when the actors dance, crawl, fight, drink, eat, or walk across them. Moving across a floor causes a lot of stress and scuffing on the treatment you choose. Each type has its uses and concerns.

Painted Floors

Probably the most common type of floor treatment is to paint it. The level of detail the painted treatment gets depends on the sightlines in the theatre; if the audience cannot see it, you do not need to do that much. One problem with painting a floor is that you need the floor in order to do it. That is why floor painting often gets scheduled late in the production but early enough that the actors can use it and get used to walking on the finish.

If scheduling is tight, a floor deck can be laid out and painted somewhere else and installed when dry; the fasteners will get touched up to match the design. The finish of the paint should meet the design needs; it should be durable as well as decorative. If traction is a concern, as on raked stages, there are commercial additives that will add a bit of texture to the paint. Consult with the costumer; that is the person who is in charge of the shoes.

And, of course, if you have a flat finish you will need to damp mop it with clean water and mop each night to give the stage a fresh look when the audience first takes their seats. At the very least you need to sweep before each performance. Theatres seem to create their own special brand of dust, and it creeps up onto your floors at night (Figure 8.8).

Snap-Lock Laminates

A quick and dirty (but easily cleaned) way of executing a floor treatment is by using snap-lock laminates. Armstrong™ and Pergo™ are two name brands that are available

Figure 8.8: *Crew member from* A Streetcar Named Desire *clears the stage of all props and sweeps the painted floor of breakaway bottle fragments.*

in home improvement stores. They are easy to lay down, and with care they can be reused. They are durable, hold up to spills, and are easily cleaned. But they can be a big investment. Still, if you are looking to do a lot of nice floors over a season, you might consider these as part of your stock.

Carpets and Area Rugs

These give a room a cozy, finished look, but they need to be well secured. Carefully placed fabric staples will do the job if it's a stock carpet. If you rented or borrowed the carpet or if the carpet shifts, they might frown on that solution. Nonskid carpet pads can be placed under the offending treatment to arrest its forward progression. Consult with the director, choreographer, and fight director about what action needs to take place around it. And, of course, if you have a carpet, you will need to vacuum it. (Area rugs that have not been fastened down may be beaten; it's just like flogging a drop.)

Marleys

These are primarily used as a dance floor, but any production that requires a lot of movement will like them (Figure 8.9). They are large sheets similar to linoleum that get rolled out and taped down to the stage floor. (Dance studios have these permanently installed by fusing the plastic sheets together.) Once the first end is laid down and the seams are taped, the fun part begins. You get a bunch of people to stomp around on the marley to stretch it out. This is lovingly referred to *chugging,* since the stomping action makes the group look like a train starting down the track. It's also great fun

Figure 8.9: *Dancers on a full-stage marley.*

and releases lots of aggression. Marleys are durable and just need a damp mop between shows (except Jacob Marley, who had other issues). Each type and manufacturer will have its own care instructions.

In short, if you are going to create a world full of props and dressings for actors, they are eventually going to be in it. They will stand in front of your dressings, walk on your carefully mopped floor, and eat your beautifully prepared food. The best you can do is organize a safe environment for them with safe props, dressings, and floors, carefully labeled prop tables, and prop cabinets that secure their props for them each night and set them free in the world of the play to find their own way—and enjoy this time; they grow up so fast.

Section 3

Lighting the Set

Chapter 9
The Basics of Lighting

Once the sets have been designed and built and are onstage, the next step is the lighting. Often this is one area where little time is spent to create the final mood. Months may have been devoted to building the set, but the lighting is often an afterthought and the process rushed through. Lighting is like the paint that is applied to a new car off the assembly line. No one wants a vehicle that isn't finished (without paint), and that "paint" is the signature that completes the vehicle. You are essentially doing the same thing when lighting your set. You are adding the last coat of paint to the scene and creating the final product.

Lighting not only illuminates the set but also allows you to create a mood, time, setting, and look for your environment. Carefully placed lighting units will highlight certain aspects of your set, and no lighting in other places will hide defects. Once again, your goal is not just to turn on a light so that the audience may see the action, but to carefully place each unit to establish the time of day, whether it's an interior or exterior location, and the mood of the piece.

Now that you know what lighting is and can do, how do you go about making that happen? The first step is to understand the concept of lighting and how it can work for you. The ground floor of lighting is *three-point lighting*, the subject of the opening section of the chapter. The chapter then goes on to discuss the types of lighting instruments and their intended uses, how to use diffusion, gels, and cookies, and what to light and what not to light.

Three-Point Lighting

As the name implies, three-point lighting is made up of three lights: a key light, fill light, and backlight. This is how people have been lighting for ages. With three-point lighting, the person or object has depth within a space. When looking at a photograph, a two-dimensional object, it is sometimes difficult to separate the subject from the background. The same concept applies on a set. By using lighting and creating depth in your three-dimensional space, objects stand out from the background and look three-dimensional. This is accomplished by modeling the object with your light and "placing shadows" so that your characters or sets do not look flat.

Anyone can just point a light at something and blast it. Yes, you have illuminated it, but you have not *lit* it. Flooding the area with light makes things easier to see, but they are flat, lifeless, and dull. But with three-point lighting, you as the creator are chiseling the object out of darkness, much like a sculptor creates a statue from a block of marble. Think of yourself as that sculptor and your set the block of marble—now sculpt.

The *key light* gets its name because it is the main light providing illumination on your subject or set. The key light is used in theatre, film, and still photography. It is the main (key) light that is the starting point in your lighting setup. The key light is usually not pointing directly in front of the object—let's say your set. Why? If you point a light at a set wall rising four feet from the stage floor, the wall is now lit, but it is flatly lit—it has no dimension or depth (see Figure 9.1). When you point a flashlight at a wall, you have a bright spot where the beam hits, but that's all. We talk about spotlights in the next section, and they do precisely what you have just done with your key light—allow the spotlight to blast light on something—but we have better purposes for the key light.

The reason for this lifeless look is the lack of a shadow. Whenever you turn on a light and point it at something, it creates a shadow. Something is blocking the beam of light and a shadow is created. Where that shadow falls is very important. Some think that it doesn't matter where the shadow falls or that you have no control over where it falls. Nothing is further from the truth. We are the ones with the brains, and the shadow from the light will fall where we want it to.

Novice news photographers attach a bright light to the top of their camera, and a strong beam of light falls on their subject, washing out any detail and burning a strong shadow behind their victim. The photo looks lifeless and flat. They have just illuminated the object, not lit it.

But if you move that same light (the one on the photographer's camera or the one pointed at your four-foot wall) slightly to the left or right, you are creating a shadow and giving the wall texture. With the addition of this one light, you can tell if the wall is brick, stone, freshly painted, rough, smooth, etc. This may seem like common sense to some, but it is what separates the novice from the rest of the pack.

Figure 9.1: *A flat wall.*

That's all it takes for the key light—move it slightly to the left or right (it does not matter which) so that the light is striking your wall at a slight angle. Of course you can use the key light to light a person, but for this exercise we just use the wall as an example. Notice what moving that light does. The wall is beginning to have some depth because we now see a shadow falling on the ground. Move the light around until you are happy with its placement with regard to the shadow. Figure 9.2 shows what moving the key light can do.

The sun is the biggest and brightest key light around. On a summer day, notice what the sun does when its beams hit a tree. The shadow of the tree falls either to the left or the right (depending on the direction of the sun). This is basically "one-point lighting." But there are several other factors at play that we will get into shortly (see Figure 9.3).

Sometimes this is all the illumination you need on a particular set piece if you want to suggest a specific time of day: early in the morning or late in the day when the sun is lowest in the sky, creating long, strong shadows. If this is the mood or time of day, that might be all the light you need. But this is generally not so. Do you see how just by moving your one light to the left or right you have established a time of day? By

Figure 9.2: *Effect of moving the key light slightly.*

raising or lowering that same key light you are lessening or strengthening that same effect. The shadows change drastically as you move the light up or down, suggesting a different time of day. From the safety of your lighting grid, move the key light around and see how the shadows are changed. Once you have the desired result, lock the light into position.

The *fill light,* the companion to the key light, is placed opposite the key light. Also, as the name implies, the fill light "fills" in some of the shadows created by the key light—basically it is a fine-tuning, balancing effect. You can never really get rid of shadows; you just move them somewhere else. The more lights you add to your set, the more shadows you create. The intensity of each shadow may be different, but every light will cast a shadow (dying, paying taxes, and creating shadows with lights are three things you may count on in life).

With your fill light to the left of your key, that same strong shadow on your wall is softened slightly. If the time period in your scene is early afternoon, the addition of the fill light will soften the harsh look of the key and change the time period so the lighting is slightly flatter. Each of these light placements may be subtle, and moving the light to the left or right a small amount as well as raising or lowering it will add

Figure 9.3: *A tree lit by the sun.*

tiny nuances to your lighting scheme. Figure 9.4 shows what happens when you add a fill light to the equation.

One other thing should be explained about the fill. Not only do you have control of where you place the light (to the left or right, up or down), but you also can change the intensity of the light by dimming it. The fill light is usually not as strong as the key light because you want a little less light to fill in the shadows. If the fill light were as strong as the key, you might just have two key lights. As in a movie, each light in a scene should have some purpose (where the light is coming from and which light source on the set is creating it) besides illuminating the scene.

When someone looks at your set and asks, "Which light is the key?" your answer should be "the brightest light," whether it is on the left or the right. If both lights are of exactly the same intensity and placed at the same distance, height, and angle, you have two key lights.

Lowering the intensity of the fill by dimming it or moving it farther away enhances the key rather than competing with it. The shadows are softened and are more pleasing. In Figure 9.3 (the tree on a sunny day), since the sun is the key, what is the fill?

Figure 9.4: *Wall with fill light added.*

There is only one light source, so this is not a trick question; there are many other things in that "scene" that could act as fill.

The fill can be anything else in that outdoor setting that reflects or bounces light. A *reflector* is something that takes the rays of light and returns almost 100% of that light. A mirror is a great example of a reflector, because you when look in it, you see all of your reflection (unless you are a vampire). An object that *bounces* light collects the light and absorbs most of it and sends the rest of it on its way. The amount of absorption varies with the bounce object (a white card will bounce more light than a gray or blue card). With a bounce card, you might have 60% absorbed and 40% reflected light.

We also have these reflectors and bounce cards in nature. Some of the sunlight is bounced off the grass, a nearby white building, and the sky. Clouds also bounce light in nature. A white card may be parked just outside of the frame that is throwing light onto the tree. Look at Figure 9.3 again. Notice how strong the shadow is. This is a great indication that there is very little fill light available—the sun as the key is doing most of the work. That is why people like to lounge in the shade of a tree because in a cloudless sky, it might be the only place to find shade. If an outdoor fill source is very strong, you won't find too much shade under that tree. Figure 9.5 illustrates a

Figure 9.5: *Tree with a strong fill light.*

different tree with a lot of fill light. Notice how faint the shadow is. It is almost non-existent because the fill light level is almost that of the sun (key light).

Therefore every object has some reflective or bounce qualities. Even a black card has some (very, very little but still some). Next time you're outdoors, observe God's lighting and see if you can determine what the fill source is (you already know what the key is).

Even with two-point lighting, your wall looks better than it did before. But we are still not finished because the wall does not have the depth a three-dimensional piece should have. With the addition of a *backlight*, we will now have our depth. The great thing about three-point lighting is that the name of each light explains its purpose. The backlight is placed behind the object to separate it from the background, giving it depth.

If the backlight is placed behind the wall and its beam strikes the top edge, the wall now stands out from the background. This essentially gives your key light more prominence. You are not changing the time of day by adding the backlight (because the key and fill lights are still striking the front of the wall); you are giving depth, separation, and three-dimensionality to the wall. If the top of the wall were jagged or broken, the

327

Figure 9.6: *Wall with backlight.*

easiest way for those in the back rows to see this would be with the backlight. In film-making, the backlight is sometimes called the *kicker*, because it seems to "kick" the object away from the background. Figure 9.6 shows the effect of adding the backlight.

Look at Figure 9.4 again. Notice how the wall blends into the background even though they are of different colors. Figure 9.7 shows a young man with a key and fill light standing against a background. The back of his head and the wall seem to blend together. With the addition of a backlight (Figure 9.8), a young woman's illuminated hair is now a strong contrast from the background, giving her distinction. The strength, or *intensity*, of the backlight depends on the subject's hair color (if a human) or the darkness of the object (if it is a set piece). Lighter hair (blond) has more reflective qualities, so you might want to have less illumination (unless you want it to glow). Darker colors absorb more light, so black hair needs more intensity.

Notice how appealing the subject looks with a strong backlight (Figure 9.8). The image is even more attractive because of the almost dreamlike quality of light. You can achieve the same result on your set with strong backlighting.

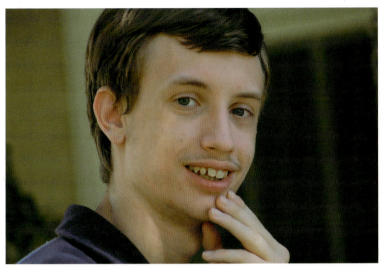

Figure 9.7: *No backlight present—the person and the background are one.*

Figure 9.8: *Girl with a strong backlight.*

While we are still on the subject of people, you should give every person a backlight (for separation), but it does not have to be a *hair* light (a light pointed at someone's hair). By pointing the backlight at their shoulders, you get the desired effect. Most people use the backlight as a hair light also, because it highlights the hair (like good shampoo). You've seen the results in every shampoo commercial. Before applying the product, her hair is lifeless and dull (no hair light). Once the shampoo has been applied (the hair light is illuminated), the hair has bounce and it shines. Some people realize this ploy, but it works to sell the shampoo. If your subject is bald, don't use the backlight as a hair light—it's not flattering and looks bad. Instead, point the back-/hair light on his shoulders and you will still have your separation.

This same three-point lighting applies in nature with the tree. Even though the sun is the key light, we still have other objects reflecting and bouncing light to add as the fill and backlight.

Do you really need three lights for every object or person in your scene? No. Just as in nature, different things on the set will bounce light to add some fill. This now introduces two new concepts to lighting: hard and soft light. *Hard* light, as the name implies, creates a strong shadow that is well defined. The sun is an example of hard light. It is bright and casts a strong shadow.

Soft light, or *diffused* light, can still be provided by the sun, but it is filtered by the clouds. Soft light has less defined shadows and is typically a more flattering type of light. Bad guys and scary people are usually lit with hard light, and women, children, and pleasant people are lit with softer light. Later we discuss ways to soften or diffuse the light, but for now just know you have that option. Figure 9.9 shows a woman lit with hard light, and Figure 9.10 shows a softer approach. In these examples the roles we previously mentioned were reversed (soft light—female, hard light—male). It just proves that with lighting you can do almost anything you want to achieve a desired result.

The best way to learn three-point lighting is to practice it. If two people are standing close together, the same key or fill can be used for both. The same concept applies to your set. Know the time of day for your scene and practice lighting the same objects

Figure 9.9: *Hard lighting: heavy shadows, but still attractive.*

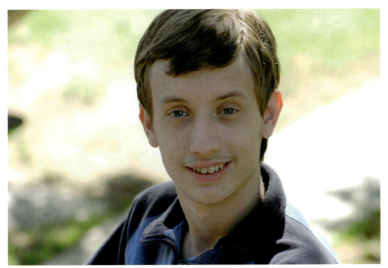

Figure 9.10: *Soft lighting: pleasant person.*

for early morning, noon, mid-afternoon, and late evening. Do this as an exercise. With the same lights, create a different time of day through their placement. Leave the late-night effect until after you have read Chapter 10.

In Figure 9.11 we have two people on the set, each with his own three-point light. As mentioned earlier, this does not always have to be the practice. But in this instance the director wanted it that way. Each person was also far enough away from the other that using the same lighting instruments for both would not have been practical.

Types of Lighting Instruments and Their Intended Purposes

Now that you understand three-point lighting and what it can do, you need to become familiar with the specific lighting instruments themselves. In this section we discuss several lighting instruments, though this is by no means an exhaustive list. The day this book goes into print, new innovations in lighting will already be appearing on stages. The units mentioned in this chapter are some of the models currently available and the ones we use during our productions. This section is just to be used as a guide.

We do not discuss how a bulb operates in this chapter. There are great books on lighting that delve deeply into the process of lighting, but that subject is beyond the scope of this text. If you really must know how a filament works, read *Placing Shadows: Lighting Techniques for Video Production*, 3rd ed., by Chuck Gloman and Tom Letourneau (Burlington, MA: Focal Press, 2005). Now that that's out of our system, let's continue with the instruments themselves.

Figure 9.11: *Three-point lighting for each character.*

Send in the Broads

We'll begin with broads because alphabetically they come first in the lighting food chain. A *broad* is a basic light utilizing a lamp and a reflector, not much else. The *lamp*, or bulb, may be clear or frosted. A frosted lamp has a softer light quality, much like when you purchase a soft white light bulb for use at home. The angled reflector (you already know what that does) is shallow (very close to the lamp), and the light emits a very wide, harsh light. Mounted behind the lamp, the reflector sends the light's beam from the unit. Used when you want to fill a large area with light, a broad does the job easily, but it creates the side effect of strong shadows.

Broads usually have *barn doors*, which are pieces of black metal that can be positioned to control the directionality of the light. In layman's terms, a barn door allows you to keep light from falling where it should not. These barn doors are limited, in that they usually are very basic and will not rotate from their fixed position. The barn doors on other instruments are more flexible. Also know as a *flood light*, a broad will flood the area with light reflected from the open bulb. The *throw*, or how far the light beam travels, is mediocre and works best as a fill or background light where a large area must be blanketed with illumination.

If a broad is pointed at an actor (it sounds like something Frank Sinatra would sing about), it should be diffused because of the harshness. The most common application of a broad is sunlight (or moonlight) streaming through a window or door on the set. Sometimes placed along the floor, broads will cover the stage with light.

Fresnels

Next in the alphabetical list is the *Fresnel*, named after its inventor, Augustin Fresnel (we could be calling the light an Augustin). Having been around for over 200 years, the Fresnel is familiar to most people from its use in lighthouse illumination. Lighthouses would use this same type of light, the Fresnel, to send its lifesaving beam out to sea. Their size was determined by order (first-order Fresnel being the largest and fifth-order being the smallest). The one thing that makes a Fresnel unique (and a great test question) is that its lens is made up of a series of concentric rings (circular rings that get progressively smaller) on the front surface of the lens.

Because this glass lens has two surfaces (the glass and the rings), light passing through it is angled, much as with a prism, and the result is a unique light pattern that only a Fresnel can create. The other special feature of the Fresnel is that it is focusable (you can focus other lights, too, but more on that later). A reflector (just as in a broad) is positioned a fixed distance from the bulb. By moving the focusing knob, you slide the bulb and reflector closer to or farther from the lens. The reflector itself never gets closer to the lamp, but the lamp/reflector unit moves in tandem. The movement can change the light beam from flood (a wide area of light—"flooding" the area with light) to a spot (a narrow area, or "spot," of light).

The closer the reflector/lamp moves toward the lens, the wider the beam of light (flood). If you prefer the unit to be in "spot" mode, the lamp travels farther away from the lens toward the back of the Fresnel. All the operator of the light needs to know is to move the level closer to "flood" or "spot" and the unit does the rest of the work. Drawing 9.1 illustrates how moving the reflector/lamp changes the light output of a Fresnel.

Fresnels have several other features that make them a versatile light: barn doors; gel, diffusion, and scrim holders; and snoots that allow total control of the light. A *snoot* is a metal tube placed in front of the light to create a small spot of illumination. Measured either by size (an "inch" classification signifies the diameter of the lens, such as a 6″ Fresnel) or by wattage (starting at 100 watts up to—really big), a variety of sizes of Fresnel are commonly used in virtually all stage productions. Figure 9.12 shows some of our Fresnels.

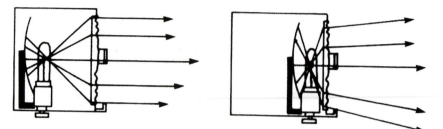

Drawing 9.1: *Fresnel moving from flood to spot.*

Figure 9.12: *A few 750-watt Fresnels.*

We cannot list all of the various manufacturers of lighting instruments, but several of the more popular will be mentioned—like Strand–Century (www.strandlight.com). The unit pictured in Figure 9.12 is one of our 20 1 K units (1 K = 1000 watts). A 750-watt lamp may also be used in this size unit or something as strong as a 2 K (2000 watts). Normally, a 1 K is most efficient because the wattage is just bright enough (in either spot or flood) and the throw distance is great. The Fresnel is the oldest unit, but the Leko is by far the most popular.

Anyone Have a Leko?

The Lekolite, developed by Century Lighting, is unique in appearance. It has a long, cylindrical shape called *ellipsoidal*, and no other lighting unit has a sharper focus of light output. There is virtually no spill of light with an ellipsoidal. The reflector has an ellipse shape (it's all in the name), and various lens types are available to meet specific throw-distance and coverage requirements. The reflector of a Fresnel is spherical or concave in shape. The ellipse shape of the reflector in an ellipsoidal surrounds the lamp (see Drawing 9.2). The light pattern may be further shaped by means of the four built-in shutters. Moving them to different positions gives each light a specific output.

If that weren't enough, specific scenic templates can be added to project a pattern on the set. Called *gobos*, these may be bought commercially (Gobos to Go: www.gobostogo.com) or homemade. These gobos are inserted into the light (on holders), behind the lens but in front of the lamp. Figure 9.13 shows an example of a manufactured gobo.

If you want to throw a circular pool of light or a pattern on the floor or background of the stage (such as a window or a tree), moving the lens barrel will sharpen or diffuse the image. The design of the Leko (with one or more Fresnel lenses) is unique. The redesigned axial Lekos (Drawing 9.2) has the lamp in the center of the reflector, and the instrument can be used in any position (pointed up or down).

Although we touch on maintenance later in the chapter and discuss what should be done to an instrument, just know now that Lekos can develop problems with age (just like people). Abused and older Lekos can become problematic when the alignment of the filament in the elliptical reflector causes their light output to decrease. This mis-alignment can create dead spots, hot spots, and strange colors on the set.

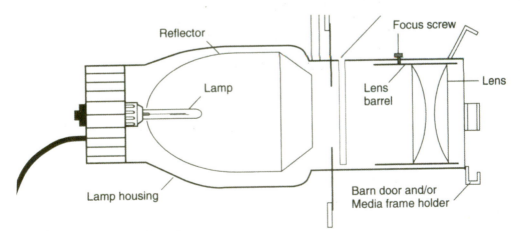

Drawing 9.2: *Makeup of a Leko.*

Figure 9.13: *What a nice gobo you have there.*

This alignment is adjusted by means of the joystick in the base of the housing. If a Leko is misaligned and you must correct it:

Make an alignment gauge and cut a rectangle of 16- to 22-gauge sheet metal to the exact size of the color frame holder of the Leko to be aligned. Use a #50 drill to make a small hole in the exact center of the metal rectangle. You now have your alignment gauge. Place the instrument about 3 feet from a white wall with its beam perpendicular to the surface of the wall. Insert the alignment gauge in the color frame holder and darken the room so you can see the image of the filament and the reflector projected on the wall through the small hole of the gauge. With a poorly aligned instrument there will be light and dark areas of the reflector caused by the incorrect filament location. By adjusting the four or five screws in the cap of the lamp housing you will be able to realign the filament within the reflector. The object is to move the filament to the center of the reflector. When it is properly aligned you will see the bright glowing areas of the reflector increase in number and in area. When you have maximized the bright areas of the reflector and created an even pattern of light on the wall, remove the hot gauge with a pair of pliers and aim the instrument at a wall 25 feet away. You should see a much brighter, even field of light. If not, some minor adjustments of the alignment screws may be necessary.[1]

The versions we own are Strand-Century 750-watt axial Lekolites. Figure 9.14 shows two of our Lekos in operation. The "750" on the back signifies the wattage.

---

[1] Gloman, C., and LeTourneau, T. *Placing Shadows: Lighting Techniques for Video Production*, 2nd ed., Burlington, MA: Focal Press, 2000.

Figure 9.14: *Two Lekos are better than one.*

Figure 9.15: *A Leko bank.*

With over 50 units per stage production, the idea is to use these in "banks" of light where each Leko has a specific purpose. Mounted on either horizontal or vertical pipes, these lights are aimed at specific areas on the stage. See Figures 9.15 and 9.16.

Any light must be mounted and positioned properly to be effective. In our stages, each Leko, once in position, is clamped tightly to a steel bar. As an added safety feature, a wire cable should be looped around the light's mounting hardware and the bar. Obviously this should be in place before you turn your attention to tightening the clamp's mounting screw. With this safety cable in place, if you lose your grip when maneuver-

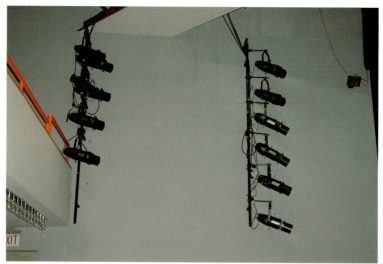

Figure 9.16: *Another Leko bank.*

Figure 9.17: *Lekos safely attached with cable.*

ing the light, nothing will be damaged and no one will get hurt. It takes only a few seconds to attach this cable, and problems only arise when you do not take the time to place safety first. I've seen more than my share of broken lights because someone "thought" they had or "forgot" to attach the safety cable. Figures 9.17 and 9.18 show more Lekos in place, each with a safety cable.

Your lights can also be mounted to a catwalk with clamps, as long as the safety cables are in place. Any sturdy overhead grid is fair game for clamping lights (see Figure 9.19).

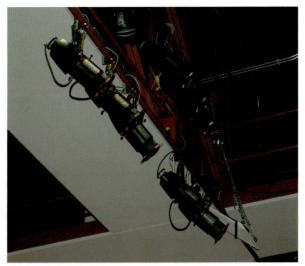

Figure 9.18: *Brand-name products with safety cable.*

Figure 9.19: *Lekos clamped to a catwalk.*

Electronic Theatre Controls, Inc. (ETC), produces the Source Four ellipsoidal spotlight. Made of lighter aluminum, with shock mounts on the reflector and lens and 20-gauge stainless steel shutters (to prevent corrosion), these units are workhorses (see Figure 9.20).

Putting Spotlights in the Spot

Spotlights are essentially either Fresnels or ellipsoidal lights that pound the light onto a set. This is the only instance where pointing a beam of light at something is

Figure 9.20: *Electronic Theatre Controls Source Four spotlight. (Courtesy of Electronic Theatre Controls.)*

acceptable. Several manufacturers make spotlights, and they are usually much larger and beefier than the grid-mounted Lekos.

Spotlights are mounted on a stand and usually operated by someone. The Strong Corporation (www.strongint.com) makes the Trouperette IV (we are still using the Model III), which in their own words is "the standard by which all other spotlights are measured." Using a 1000-watt bulb (like our Model III), the Trouperette provides a strong white beam of light that can be masked by means of the shutter blades. With a weight of 90 pounds, this unit needs its own stand and stays were it is placed. Because of the high temperature in the lamp bulbs and the precise color rendition, its life is short (approximately 250 hours). Table 9.1 lists the specifications of the Trouperette IV.

Another member of the spotlight family is the *Intellabeam*. This automated, moving light takes the muscle out of hand operation and can be programmed for movement as well as output. With features like an 11-color dichroic wheel, strobe, 12 gobo patterns, and a 700-watt lamp, this unit is a lighting designer's dream.

Other Types of Lighting Instruments

A few of the other lighting types you might run into include the scoop and the floor light (footlight). The *scoop* is an open-faced light housed in a metal reflector, much like a broad. However, the scoop reflector (essentially the back of the scoop itself) has a matte finish. Basically uncontrollable, scoops are only used when you need large areas filled with light without controllability (no barn doors).

Table 9.1: *Strong Trouperette IV Lighting Specifications (Courtesy of Strong Entertainment Lighting)*

Throw Distance		Largest (Flood) with Iris Open				Small (Spot) with Iris Open				Minimum Diameter with Iris Closed			
		Diameter		Intensity		Diameter		Intensity		Diameter		Intensity	
Feet	Meters	Feet	Meters	FC	Lux	Feet	Meters	FC	Lux	Inches	Meters	FC	Lux
20	6.6	7.6	2.5	207	2,228	2.5	0.8	990	10,657	6	0.15	990	10,657
30	9.8	11.4	3.7	92	990	3.75	1.2	440	4,736	9	0.23	440	4,736
40	13.1	15.2	5	52	557	5	1.6	248	2,664	12	0.3	248	2,664
50	16.4	1.9	6.2	33	357	6.25	2.1	158	1,705	15	0.38	158	1,705
60	19.7	22.8	7.5	23	248	7.5	2.5	110	1,184	18	0.46	110	1,184
70	23	26.6	8.7	17	182	8.75	2.9	81	870	21	0.53	81	870
80	26.2	30.4	10	13	139	10	303	62	666	24	0.61	62	666
90	29.5	34.2	11.2	10	110	11.3	3.7	49	526	27	0.69	49	526
100	32.8	38	12.5	8	89	12.5	4.1	40	426	30	0.76	40	426

Figure 9.21: *Floor light (footlight).*

As seen in Figure 9.21, the *floor light,* or *footlight,* is placed on the floor of the stage and pointed at the set and actors. Used as a source for a wash of light, floor lights raise the ambient level of light on stage so that the audience has a better chance of seeing what is going on. In conjunction with any other light, the floor light's purpose is just to get the level of lighting higher and possibly illuminate the actor's feet.

Taking Care of What You Own

Luckily, maintenance is not a big problem with theatrical lights, but it is still something that must be done on a regular basis. Remember where lights usually live (in high places), and any light source attracts varmints, in the form of bugs. Just like we are supposed to walk toward the light, insects are drawn to the light and heat. Even indoors after a short period of time, the bodies of these units collect bits and pieces of fried bugs.

Sometimes cleaning these instruments is as simple as opening the lens and removing the offending debris. The lens and internal workings should be gently cleaned, but under no circumstances should the lamp bulb itself be touched with your fingers. Moisture and grease from your fingers will adhere to the lamp's surface and cause it to fail prematurely, sometimes after only a few hours. Each lamp is extremely expensive and can be replaced or cleaned by holding it in a cloth so that your fingers do not come in contact with the lamp.

If the lamp is hot, you would never touch it with your fingers anyway. But if by accident you do inadvertently touch the lamp, don't panic. Immediately wipe it clean with a soft cloth, and you are again loved by the world. You can always tell when someone

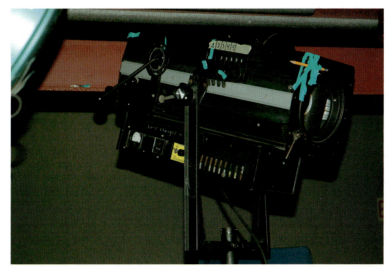

Figure 9.22: *Well-maintained light.*

has touched a lamp's surface and not cleaned up afterward. The bulb will blacken and swell in the area where it was touched, showing the offense for everyone to see. Always keep an example of one of these "touched" bulbs in plain view so that others will avoid the same mistake.

Figure 9.22 shows an example of a well-maintained spotlight. Although it looks messy with blue tape all over it, the cleaning or lamp-changing schedule is clearly marked on the unit, and a pencil is always available. Feel free to write anything necessary on the tape (not on the lens) so that whoever uses the light knows the shape it's in. Develop a cleaning routine with each instrument and you will have a better chance of its working when you need it.

Diffusion, Gels, and Cookies

Now that you know how to light and understand what each type of lighting unit does, it is time to finesse the light to get the desired effect. There are three things that affect a light's output (besides turning it off): diffusion, gels, and cookies.

I'm Slightly Diffused

Diffusion is the transmission of light through a translucent material, usually for the purpose of softening that light and reducing glare. Diffusion is also the name of a semi-transparent material, made up of different thicknesses of material and/or metal, that is placed in front of the light to decrease or soften its output. You can do just about anything you want with diffusion. First, let's look at the metal types of diffusion, called *scrims*.

A *scrim* is a piece of screen (such as found on a screen door) that is housed in a frame placed in front of the light. Available in varying thickness, this "screen" decreases the output of the light when its beam shines through it. The mesh of the screen breaks down the light's rays, lessening the output. The denser the mesh, the more light is broken up.

You may be asking yourself, "Why don't you just dim the light to decrease its output?" That is one possible solution, but not all lights can be on dimmers. If not, a scrim is a great way to knock down the light. A variation on this theme is *half-scrims*. As the name implies, the bottom half of the scrim is screen and the top half is clear, with nothing there. If you have a half-scrim that has the screen on the top, then it is just upside down. Half-scrims are used when you want part of the light blocked and only part of it. This is something that cannot be done with a dimmer—the dimmer reduces the wattage of the entire light, whereas a half-scrim works on only part of it.

When might you use a half-scrim? Suppose one Leko is pointed at a blue background wall, illuminating it. One of your characters walks in front of the wall, wearing white, and suddenly appears blown out, almost effervescing. This is where a half-scrim comes in handy. Because your character in white is closer to the light than the wall, scrimming the lower part of the unit (the part of the light that hits the person because she is closer) will lessen the light falling on her and still allow the full intensity of the top of the light to strike the wall. This is almost like using one light instead of two. The blue wall is absorbing most of the light and needs more wattage on it; the woman is reflecting light and needs less. The old adage comes into play again: Dark colors absorb light and light colors reflect light. To prove this point, put your hand on a dark-colored car in the middle of summer; dark colors absorb light (and heat).

No one in the audience can tell that the Leko is scrimmed, but if you had not half-scrimmed, then the light on the actor would have been too intense. Because all actors hit their marks on the stage, they will always walk to the correct spot and be half-scrimmed. If they miss their mark, they should be able to feel the intensity of the light and find it again (see Figure 9.23).

An example of where you might not want to use a half-scrim is when you want the character to glow and appear too white. Figure 9.24 is an excellent illustration of this. In Charles Dickens's *Scrooge*, the Ghost of Christmas Past was meant to radiate light—or to glow. By having that character wear white and putting an undiffused light on her, she exudes light where Scrooge appears normal.

Scrims also come in meshlike fabric. These are put a little farther away from the light but have the same effect. Used more in filmmaking than on the stage, the stockinglike fabric does not hold up as well as the metal screen. But if you ever run across one, you'll know what it is.

Figure 9.23: *Half-scrimmed light in use.*

Figure 9.24: *Glowing ghost.*

The other type of diffusion is a paperlike, semitransparent material that is also placed in front of the light. If you hold a piece of writing paper in front of a light, it diffuses the light, allowing some of the illumination to pass through it. Of course a plain piece of paper might burn when in front of a light, so a strong material must be used. We discussed this look earlier in the chapter—soft lighting. The diffusion material softens the light falling on the object, making the shadows less intense. Available in almost 100 different types, diffusion material can be as thin as wax paper or as thick as Plexiglas.

How do you know which type to use and when? The easy answer is that it all depends on the look you want. Extremely thin paper (such as wax paper) allows most of the light to pass through it and creates an effect called *light diffusion*. This level of diffusion is almost transparent and is used when you want subtle softening and stronger shadows.

Rosco (www.rosco.com) and Lee (www.lee.com) are the largest manufacturers of diffusion material, and they make swatch booklets that contain samples. For a more textured look, try Tough Spun, which looks like a Bounce dryer sheet. Whether used on people or sets, the fabric of the Tough Spun allows light to pass through only in certain places, resulting in a very textured look.

Tough White Diffusion (sounds like a heavy metal band) is a moderate diffuser and uses three and a half stops of light. F-stops are not really important on the stage, but this at least gives you an idea of how much light is blocked or diffused. Table 9.2 lists various types of diffusion and how much light they block. This is only a partial list containing some of the more popular diffusion materials.

Note in number 6 that the effect is "painting-like." When using this type of diffusion in front of a light, the tiny holes in the netting make the actor appear as if he or she were textured as if in a Renaissance painting. This same effect is often achieved when a "net" curtain is used on the set. Looking through the millions of holes makes the characters behind the net appear as if they are in a painting.

As a last bit of information on diffusion, Rosco supplied a partial listing of their diffusion material and what it offers (see Table 9.3).

What's Swell About Gels?

A *gel* is a colored piece of gelatinous material that is also placed in front of a light to cast its particular color. There probably has not been a set constructed that did not use gels of some sort. The easiest way to tell what kind of light effect you will get from a gel is to look through it. A red gel will cast a red light, a blue a blue, a green a green, and so on.

Figure 9.25 illustrates the use of red and blue gels on Lekos. In Figure 9.26, notice that each of the colored gels has a grease pencil marking on it (R42 means red gel 42).

Table 9.2: *List of Diffusion Materials*

Number	Diffuser Name	Diffusion Level	Number of Stops of Light	Effect
1	Tough Spun	Slight	2½	Textured
2	Tough White	Moderate	3½	Silky
3	Opal Tough Frost	Slight	1	Color enhancing
4	Soft Frost	Moderate	2	Even diffusion
5	Light Grid Cloth	Heavy	3½	Strong
6	Net	Heavy	2½s	Even/painting-like

Table 9.3: *Tough and Soft Diffusion Types (Courtesy of Rosco Corporation)*

Name	Purpose	Name	Purpose
Tough Sun Light Tough Spun Quarter Tough Spun	Feathers the beam edge and softens the overall field. Beam shape is maintained.	Tough Frost Light Tough Frost Opal Tough Frost Powder Frost Light Opal Tough	Moderate beam spread, yet maintains a discernable beam center.
Tough White Diffusion Tough Half White Tough Quarter White	Wide beam spread creates an even field of soft, shadowless pleasing light.	Tough Rolex Light Tough Rolex	Wide beam spread creates a dense, even, soft field of shadowless light.
Grid Cloth Light Grid Cloth Quarter Grid Cloth	Reinforced woven material, soft, shadowless quality and large area diffusion.	Tough Silk Light Tough Silk	Spreads light beam in one direction, usually for a "slash of light" effect.
Soft Frost Wide Soft Frost Half-Density Soft Frost Hilite Silent Frost	Stronger shadows and only moderately heat resistant. Used only on low-wattage lights.		

Labeling the gels this way is easier than trying to determine the exact shade of a gel by holding it up to a light. When the lights are turned on, you won't be able to see the writing on the set when the beam shines through it, as seen in Figure 9.27.

Each of these gels has different levels of color intensity and nifty names. One of my favorite is the Chocolate gel. When lighting dark wood or chocolate, the gel makes it come alive. Other colors, like Bastard Amber and Rose, create exactly the hue that the name implies.

Unlike in the world of movies, less is not necessarily more on the stage. If you are portraying a red light district, use a red gel and not a straw or amber color. Lee and Rosco make a line of theatrical gels that are quite different than their film gels. The tolerances

Figure 9.25: *Red and blue gels on Lekos.*

Figure 9.26: *Gels are labeled with grease pencil.*

Figure 9.27: *Invisible writing once it's illuminated.*

Figure 9.28: *Blue gel used to create moonlight (or nighttime).*

for color temperature do not exist on the stage, and the discriminating camera lens needs those nuances visible.

Let's look at a few examples of what colored gels can do to a set. A blue gel (Figure 9.28) often signifies night, even though moonlight is not really blue. But a blue gel on a Leko signifies moonlight on the set. The effect should not be too strong, just enough to convey the mood desired. But onstage, even though the moon does not produce blue light or a strong shadow, the audience will understand that "blue" means night. A

349

Figure 9.29: *Straw gel adds warmth.*

strong, directional blue light means the moon is out and one should be on the lookout for creatures of the night.

A straw gel adds warmth of color to a summer scene (Figure 9.29). The look is subtle, and an orange gel might be too much in this instance. When looking at a photograph, an orange tone, or *color temperature,* gives a warm, appealing look. On the other hand, a blue-tinted image looks cold and less appealing. You do not always want to call attention to your colored gels. You never want someone to say, "Look at all that green light!" Instead, a slight amount of green gives the desired result without giving away the secret.

If you want a strong result, use both red and blue light on the set to give the illusion of a dream scene, as seen in Figure 9.30.

A combination of gels (a red and a blue) exudes a purple color, a shade of royalty. Perfect for a Shakespearean production, the purple hue shows richness. Basically, if you shine a light with a specific-color gel on front, any objects with that color of light will be enhanced.

Pools of light can also create specific moods on the set. In Figure 9.31 we have three different types, or pools, of lighting. The group dancing is bathed in a warm straw light to show happiness, Scrooge is in a white light (he is a spectator and is not part of the group's warmth, so his light color is different), and the Ghost of Christmas Past is covered in blue light because she is a specter and removed from the warmth of the group and Scrooge's white light.

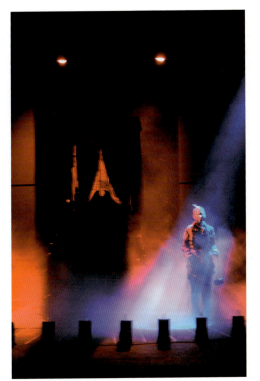

Figure 9.30: *Red and blue gels in a dream sequence.*

Figure 9.31: *Three moods, three colors of light.*

Figure 9.32: *Separation by colored light.*

In Figure 9.32, Scrooge and the Ghost of Christmas Present look on as another group talks. Once again, the group of outsiders being observed are clothed in warm, orange light, and the observers are off in the cold blue light—at a distance. The magic of lighting creates this not-very-subliminal effect of separation.

At times, even Scrooge has to appear normally lit and others in the cast might have a touch of color to signify their moods. In Figure 9.33, the boy in the background is slightly blue. Why?

With lighting, you can also make the audience look where you want. And with these same pools of light, the viewer will not look at a darkened area of the set if action in bright light is happening elsewhere. Since this does not really work in the movies, on the stage it is acceptable to say with light, "Hey, look over here!" (see Figure 9.34). That is the reason all of the set lights are turned off when changing scenes—you don't want the audience to see anything.

Even an empty set says something when lit with colored gels. What do the colors of light on the vacant set in Figure 9.35 say?

Another way to make a character appear invisible is to light him or her differently from the rest. Although Scrooge in Figure 9.36 is dressed in his bedclothes (and the other characters are not), the lighting is what makes him seem out of place. In this instance he had a slightly blue cast and everyone else was warmly lit. In a movie you can have someone disappear; that's more difficult on the stage.

Figure 9.33: *The main character is normal and the other has the blues.*

Figure 9.34: *Calling attention to the action with light.*

As a variation on the theme, trying using a salmon or pink gel on your set. In Figure 9.37, the pink gel is used to signify early morning on a bright new day because Scrooge is a changed man.

Cookies, Anyone?

If you do any kind of lighting, you've probably used your share of cookies. A *cookie* is an object with a cut pattern placed in front of the light. The important point to remember here is "in front of" the light. A gobo is placed in front of the lamp or bulb but

Figure 9.35: *The director creates a mood with lighting.*

Figure 9.36: *Invisibility with lighting.*

behind the lens (the front of the light). Cookies come in all shapes, sizes, and materials. I've recently come across a few plastic cookies that are inexpensive in the short term, but they seem to like to melt. Let's deal with those of you using the more inexpensive plastic or cardboard cookies.

If you are using Lekos on your stage, their cookies (called *gobos*) slide in front of the lamp and behind the lens. This instrument is great for projecting the effect on the stage with extreme clarity. In Figure 9.38, we see two gobos in use: one on the wall behind

Figure 9.37: *Pink is in, and be happy about it.*

Figure 9.38: *Two cookies at one time.*

Scrooge and the ghost and another (a window frame cookie) falling on the floor. You can still use your colored gels for the result they create.

If your lighting design calls for a venetian blind effect, I know all of you with budget restraints have purchased a piece of cardboard and cut slats in it. Foam core works better, but it costs more than cardboard. After you have carefully cut the horizontal slats, hold it in front of the light source to see what pattern it throws. However, it's hard to judge just how long and how wide these slats have to be.

It's best to start by making the slats small and then enlarging them as the need arises. The old adage in woodworking still applies: Measure twice, cut once. It's very difficult to cut less when you've already cut more. Once you're happy with the size and shape of the cut slats, you must determine if your slat material is going to burst into flames when placed in front of the light for extended periods. If you place the makeshift cookie in front of anything stronger than a 600-watt unit, the cookie won't be long for this world. One way to keep the cookie from burning or warping is to put some diffusion between the light and the cookie. Even if the diffusion is attached to the cookie itself, this will decrease the heat and light intensity enough to get a little more life out of the homemade contraption. The only drawback is that it will lessen the intensity of your shadow effect.

Gobos don't have this problem because they are usually metal, which is difficult to burn. They are much closer to the light source, but they are constructed to be durable. Try moving your cookie closer to and farther away from your light. This "pattern" will never change with any cookie you use.

We are amazed at the many uses these cookies have. They can be used right side up or upside down. Cocking the cookie at a slight angle to the light and set allows the shadow to appear elongated. A light shining directly behind one of these cookies will produce a shadow that looks exactly like the cutout in the cookie (the same with a gobo). These shapes are usually too weird or defined for subtle images on the wall. You don't want to call attention to these shadows; you just want the audience to notice them but not realize they are there.

In films, Alfred Hitchcock was a master of the cookie (no, that's not why he was so large). In films such as *Spellbound*, *Notorious*, and *Psycho*, you see massive shadows of cages, spiderwebs, and other things on the set pieces to signify entrapment. Use these elements on your staged sets. Even if the effect is subliminal, it will still register.

The whole idea of a cookie is to create an effect, but it does not have to be a subliminal one. Maybe the play calls for little splotch shapes on the wall: Tilt the cookie or move it farther from the light or, better yet, diffuse or gel it so it is less defined. Or if the actor's character is nuts, go wild and let the strange shapes appear defined on the wall.

Even though these new, store-bought cookies won't melt, we always use diffusion behind them to soften the shape, and we add a piece of single screen in front to further define the image.

You can further redefine or create new shapes with a worn-out cookie. Simply attach pieces of "stuff" between the cookie and the light. I've used rolled-up pieces of diffusion, clothespins, pieces of wood, metal sticks, fingers, or anything else that might establish a new pattern or shape. Let your conscience and imagination be your guide.

356

Sometimes I've even been bold enough to use a piece of a cookie on a set. A little piece of broken wooden cookie can be positioned in front of a light to create its own distinct shadow. I've often used smaller pieces with smaller lighting instruments. A five-inch piece works well when placed in front of 200-watt unit. Try putting a full cookie next to that same light, and notice the huge singular shape that appears. A broad light beam needs a broad cookie, and a narrow-patterned light needs a piece. There's nothing wasted in this business if you try hard enough.

Learning What to Light and What Not to Light

With all of these lighting implements at your control, it is often hard to determine what the best approach to take is and when. In this section, we discuss some more nuances of lighting to make the audience look exactly where you want them to, make them feel a specific mood at a certain time, and, like in a movie, make them identify with the character.

Any light onstage that the audience sees is called a *practical*. It may be a desk lamp, a table tamp, a chandelier, a Christmas tree, or even a candle. Anything on the set that normally gives off some type of illumination is a practical light. To make each of these appear more realistic, one of the cast or crew should turn them on during the scene. Of course, under the bright lights of the set, a single candle is not going to illuminate much of anything, but with your lighting skills, you can make the audience believe it does.

The first example we will work with is a candle. We have used *A Christmas Carol* throughout this chapter, so let's not change midstream. This Dickens play is a great example to use for lighting because it is a period piece, there are many moods and lighting types, there are characters that are invisible, and the play takes place in everything from moonlit bedrooms to cemeteries.

Lighting My World

The candle, as mentioned earlier, gives off little or no light onstage. The amount of light that one candle gives off at a distance of one foot is called a *foot-candle*. If that practical were the only existing illumination, people in the back rows would see nothing. If the character carried around an unlit candle, the effect would be lost. The key here is to have the actor have a lit candle and to light the set to make it appear as if that is the only source of light.

You've all seen bad movies where the character lights a candle and the room is filled with light. You must still light the set, but make the light very warm (orange gel) and very directional (coming hopefully from the direction of the candle). In Figure 9.39, we have a candle scene. This is another instance where you can use three-point

Figure 9.39: *Candlelight on the set.*

Figure 9.40: *Building the set with practicals.*

lighting, but the key light (the candle) has to be very bright and the fill light almost nonexistent. The character sitting by the candle is key lit from the candle side of his face, and the rest is somewhat dark. Onstage you can take some liberties by bringing up the fill level. But with warm, orange lighting and the lit candle on stage, the audience will get the picture. The characters standing closest to the candle are lit the most, and set pieces farther away are in darkness.

Another practical is the chandelier. This will cast more light, but help is still needed from above (the set lights). In Figure 9.40, the stage crew actually used the practicals

Figure 9.41: *A stage full of practicals.*

as illumination, but during the production these lights remained illuminated with additional help.

The practicals on the set are there mainly for the effect or the illusion. Everyone knows they are not generating all the light, but the audience expects the light from a candle to be warm (orange) and not cold (blue). A room lit by a chandelier is going to be brighter than one lit by a single desk lamp. Once you establish the light source (the chandelier), the audience will want to see the type of illumination that unit exudes.

Just because you now have practicals in the scene does not mean the rest of your lighting is out the window. When Scrooge visits with a ghost, they are still bathed in blue, because they are not really there with the rest of the cast. In Figure 9.41 the set is lit with light seemingly from the practicals (with the exception of the observers). Remember, if we see a practical lit, we expect to see the light from it. In Figure 9.41, the practicals above the fireplace are not lit, so no light should be emanating from them. Hopefully this all seems like common sense.

Sometimes a practical is the biggest thing in the scene. In the closing scene of *A Christmas Carol*, everyone is gathered around a huge Christmas tree. With all of the many lights, the tree will give off quite a bit of light. But in this case we also have gas street lamps (an orange light), Christmas tree light (white light), and the time of the season (winter, cold and blue light). Figure 9.42 illustrates how all this comes together.

In the finale, the cold winter light is transformed from blue to warm orange because Scrooge is now right with the world. Everything else is the same, but the director

Figure 9.42: *A Dickens Christmas.*

Figure 9.43: *Winter has been replaced with warmth.*

wanted the audience to leave with a warm glow, so he changed the last scene to orange lighting that overpowers the coldness of winter (see Figure 9.43).

Building the colored light set piece, as seen above the characters and Christmas tree in Figure 9.43, may be seen in Figure 9.44. In order for the Christmas lights to appear

Figure 9.44: Behind the scenes on writing in the sky.

invisible and look as if the sky was written with light, a piece of plywood covered in black mesh was used. With the lights pointed toward and seen through the holes in the wood, the mesh adds invisibility to the piece. Once hung, the lights appear in nothingness, which makes the final scene memorable.

Chapter 10

Special Effects Lighting

Now that you have embraced the art of lighting for the "normal" scene, it's time to look at special effects lighting, which is basically 75% of the lighting you will do. Besides, what is normal lighting anyway? Your job is now to pull off the illusion you (or the director) want by using lighting. Creativity is your biggest asset, so you must employ it in abundance. In this chapter we discuss how to use light to achieve the special effects you desire, how to get the best result with the least amount of lighting effort, and what is new out there and what it can do to make your life easier.

How to Create the Intended Effects with Light

The first step in lighting your space is to carve out your set from the void or nothingness. Again, you have been asked to chisel your intended sculpture from a hunk of rock.

Using *A Christmas Carol*, the same play we discussed in Chapter 9, we are going to let light set up our boundaries. The empty stage is our workplace. With just four items on our interior living room set (a fireplace, a Christmas tree, a chandelier, and a padded stool) we have to make the audience believe we are in Bob Cratchit's living room (even though the exterior street set is directly behind).

The first step is to turn off all of the illumination on the other background set. It will still exist in the space, but because it is dark the audience will focus their attention on what is illuminated.

Figure 10.1: *Living room set.*

Move your four pieces onto the set and begin lighting (see Figure 10.1). The fireplace with two practical lamps is the main focus. This is brightly lit with a mixture of white light and orange. Why do we use a little orange gel on the fireplace? Because the candle practicals are the source of illumination and we expect them to exude an orange light.

The only other source of light in the room is from the chandelier (because the tree's lights are not on). The scene is happy, so a brighter light is called for. But notice in Figure 10.1 that one of the ghosts is present. Why isn't he bathed in blue light like he was earlier? In this case, since he is no longer observing but part of the action, he is sharing the same light as the rest of the cast. Scrooge, however, has not fully joined the party so he is still in his "observer" blue light, far to the left.

Notice that you are only seeing what the director wants you to see. Everything else is in darkness. The footlights are on, providing ambient light to the scene. Throughout the play, these lights remain on, dimmed when necessary. This is the one constant light source (so the audience can see the action).

Lekos with orange gel are pointed at the fireplace and the group of actors onstage. Because the tree in the room is dark, a Leko with a blue gel is pointed at the tree— it's dark, so the light should be cold. Three-point lighting is in place for the actors, and their living space is lit out of a black void. As mentioned earlier, you still can faintly see the sets behind the living room, but if left in darkness, they don't exist.

Figure 10.2: *Spandex and blue and green light.*

Coming-Out Party

The next lighting special effect is Jacob Marley's entrance, as seen in Figure 10.2. This special effect was a little more complicated than just lighting. It also involved creating a "special door." Because Marley is a ghost who visits Scrooge, we needed him to make an entrance like a ghost should (through the wall or door), instead of just walking in. A spandex door was built that looked just like a real door, except the actor could spread it apart and walk through it. Spandex is a fabric that stretches and still remains form-fitting (that's why we never wear it).

Even looking closely at the door, you could not tell that it was unique. The door on the set would open and close normally until the ghost made his entrance. Dressed in chains, the actor walked through the closed door by spreading the middle apart. Lit using a blue gel on one Leko and a green gel on another, he made his grand entrance. The colors signify coldness and death. White makeup also plays a part in this illusion, but our focus is on what we can do with lighting. Using the spandex door by itself might have been enough, but the blue and green light enhanced the trick.

Dickens's novel said that Scrooge felt a cold chill just before his deceased partner arrived on the scene. How can you convey this "cold chill" onstage? Having the actor shiver is the first part, but the lighting has to carry the rest of the weight. Notice that the footlights have been turned off. We do not need warm ambient light in this scene; in fact we need just the opposite. If the footlights were gelled blue for the scene, that would be helpful.

Fog on the set would be too much for this scene. Just before Marley's entrance, we hear the wind howling, his moaning, chains rattling, etc. We are setting the stage for what is about to happen. The audience knows the story and what is coming next, but they do not know how the director is going to achieve that. In our case, the spandex door was not expected.

It would be difficult to suddenly drop the temperature of the theatre, and a wind machine would be too noisy. How else could you create this illusion with lighting? Keeping Marley in blue/green light the entire time is important, but Scrooge should still be normally lit (with maybe a slight blue cast). So how do you keep Marley in blue wherever he moves on stage?

The best way is to have a spotlight follow him. Gelled with the same colors, the spotlight will keep him bathed in coldness as he walks around. You can use programmable spots for this, but it is easier to have an operator just keep the beam focused on him.

Puffs or clouds of dust should be wafting off Marley as he moves (with the effect strengthened by his makeup; he's been dead for a while, so he should not be too neat). Flour, talcum powder, and other substances could be used. A backlight on Marley is necessary to see this "dust" vaporizing because a front light would not make it visible. The backlight separating him from the background will also separate the dust from his body so that the audience notices it.

This is why it is so important for everyone in the crew to communicate with each other. Without the backlight, the "dust" effect would not be seen by anyone. If the makeup people make this clear, the lighting designer will make it visible.

Then Came Another

The next effect involved another ghost (*A Christmas Carol* is full of them—ghosts). This ghost is a little friendlier than Marley, so we lit her in a soft blue light and gave her more wattage so that she would glow. Once you establish a character with lighting, do not change the lighting until the situation requires it. Just like characters in movies have themes (e.g., Lara's Theme), they also can have lighting themes.

This ghost's entrance had to be special, and it was up to the set people to make it a reality. Scrooge is in bed when he hears a noise. We had to get him out of the bed for the effect to work.

Remember that we had Marley walk through the spandex door? Because this ghost was also "dead," we wanted her to rise up through the bed. That would have been difficult if Scrooge were still occupying the space. An opening was made in the bed through which the ghost would be hydraulically lifted.

The hydraulic bed was built as seen in Figure 10.3. An opening was cut in the plywood top, and tattered sheets were hung in place, as seen in Figure 10.4. Hydraulics aren't difficult, but the cables must be safely out of the way of any moving parts, shown in Figure 10.5.

To add an otherworldly effect to her appearance onstage, fog was added. Fog is not always the friend of the set designer, for several reasons. Once released, it is very difficult to control where the fog goes. It takes knowledge and a steady hand to have just

Figure 10.3: *Building the hydraulic bed.*

Figure 10.4: *Opening through which the ghost emerges.*

Figure 10.5: *Cables and hydraulics in place.*

enough fog rather than too much or too little (and an awful lot of luck). And fog does not like to hang around too long. Getting it in the right spot is a challenge, and keeping it from leaving is another. Hopefully fog will remain on the ground long enough without obscuring the actors. Wafters can also be used. A *wafter* is someone with a piece of cardboard or board who corrals the fog by trying to move it in the intended direction by making wind. Too much or too little wafting is not effective.

Still another difficulty with the wispy stuff is lighting it. If lit from above, it is almost opaque, so light does not go through it, but bounces off. If you have ever driven in the fog with your high beams on, you know what we mean. Most of the light (bounce lighting) is sent back to blind you. That's why fog lights on cars are always pointed down to the ground. You never want to "light" the fog; rather, you want to see "through" it. You can see the effect in Figure 9.24 (note that part of the hydraulics are visible under the bed).

You are basically lighting a cloud that will not allow the beam's particles to pass through. Ideally, fog should be lit from below so that the light appears to be shining through it rather than just on top of it. Figure 10.6 shows a little bit of fog on the set. Since the fog is already beginning to rise, the effect was dissipating rapidly.

In Figure 10.6, also notice the presence of a gobo. This heart–shaped gobo made the ghost appear friendlier even though she was shrouded in fog. The gobo looks like trees, so this was an alternative to building a forest set behind the character. The gobo does not look like a real forest, but the scene involves a ghost, so a little imagination is necessary.

Figure 10.6: *Fog and ghosts.*

Scrooge is away from the ghost, so this separation pulls the audience's eyes to the character who deserves the attention in this scene—the ghost. By having her illumination stronger (and with her wearing white), she becomes the focus of the scene.

The makeup, the costume, the set (the bed), and the lighting all work together to create this illusion. As mentioned in Chapter 9, the glowing appearance of the ghost is part costume, part lighting. If she were wearing black, her clothing would absorb light. Since white reflects light, she radiates with an inner glow. Having two Lekos on her and a follow spot, we could control her illumination. In this case, too much light was better.

In the original *Superman* movie, Marlon Brando (Jorell), was to glow when he spoke on the planet Krypton. Before the days of elaborate CGI effects, the designer made his costume out of "movie screen" material. This fabric, laced with glass beads, is normally used to project movies on because of its highly reflective qualities. By pointing a Fresnel at Brando, they made his costume glow with an inner light.

The white, tattered costume with too much light worked well with our ghost. What other ways could we have achieved this same ghostly appearance?

Dead Tired

Since we are on the subject of ghosts, our next example uses fog and blue-gelled light exclusively. With no other lighting on the set, the fog will waft up as the Ghost of Christmas Future and Scrooge stand alone in the cemetery (see Figure 10.7). We've been in a lot of cemeteries at night (don't ask why) and have never seen fog or blue

Figure 10.7: *Fog, blue light, and the cemetery.*

light. Yet both of these are totally acceptable in a stage production because people are used to seeing it that way even though reality is different. Notice the absence of any other ambient light in this scene. The stage is empty (a vacant cemetery) except for our characters and the tombstone behind them. The looming figure of the Ghost of Christmas Future is backlit with a blue light from above. Since everything else is black (and he is wearing black), separation is mandatory.

Because this ghost is evil and silent, he should not be wearing white. His dark costume will absorb most of the light, so high quantities must be pounded on him. This ghost (in the book) is said to float instead of walk.

Creating a nine-foot actor is easy with stilts, but how do you get him to float rather than "clump" along? One way is with wheels. Having the costume long enough so that it drags on the ground helps with the floating factor, so whichever method is used, that fact is hidden.

Figure 10.8 shows another of "Future's" scenes. Here we want the Ghost of Christmas Future to be in the shadows as Scrooge realizes his fate. Scrooge is lit well with three-point lighting but still has a slight blue cast. If looking at a dead body covered with a sheet does not call for blue light, little else does.

The body draped in white should also have a slight blue cast to it. White suggests purity, and nothing in this scene really suggests that. As before, the lights are coming down from directly above the actors rather than from out in the audience area. The placement of these lights is as important as when you should use them. Normally, much of

Figure 10.8: *The future being foretold.*

the play is lit from lights mounted on the balcony or the catwalk. When you want an actor to appear isolated or inferior, pointing a light directly down on the actor suggests that. From a bird's-eye view we are looking down on the actor. The "looking down" is the effect this light suggests. How else might you make the actor look inferior and less demanding? One of our students suggested that having an actor playing with puppies makes him look less domineering—that is true, but it was not the answer we were looking for.

The opposite results if you have lights from below pointing up at the actors. That suggests power, dominance, and authority. Some of the lighting on the Ghost of Christmas Future was from below because the audience is supposed to fear that character and pity Scrooge, with his light from above. How else could you achieve the same results using different lighting?

Getting Flashed

The last special effect in this section is lightning, used often in stage productions. The easiest way to create lighting is with a strobe light. You do not want the strobe to continue pulsating because that is a different issue, but one quick flash of light is all that is necessary.

Movie studios have created lightning effects with daylight-balanced lighting. Any Fresnel with a color temperature of 5600° Kelvin will cast a blue light to the eye. The key is to have this light illuminated for only a moment to create the flash. If on too long, you have extended moonlight but not lightning. By applying power to the light for a millisecond and adding the sound effect of cracking thunder, you achieve the desired result.

There are many other special effects that can be created solely by means of lighting. Just break each effect down into smaller pieces and play around with the lighting. You would be surprised just how easy they are to do once you have separated them into simpler elements.

Achieving the Most with Very Little

As with almost anything, it is always best to get the most out of very little. It seems there are never enough lights, gels, etc. for us to do our job properly, so we must try to make do with less. That means we have to get the most out of what we have and sometimes learn to live with that.

The easiest way to accomplish this in the lighting department is to have one lighting unit do the job of two. This also may mean moving your actors closer together so that the light beam from one unit illuminates several people. With Lekos, you still have some control over the flood pattern of the lamp. If an instrument is placed farther in the back of the auditorium, its throw will be greater, but you will need more wattage. A 1000-watt unit 15 feet farther back will illuminate a larger area than a 750-watt unit placed closer. You still want the same amount of illumination, but more punch is needed if the instrument is farther away (thus the need for more wattage). Figure 10.9 shows four 1000-watt Lekos doing the same job as eight 750-watt units.

Being More Intense with Your Lights

Look at Figure 10.10 for the following example. If we have someone standing on stage, let's position a light 4 feet away from his head and pointing down. If we square that distance, we get a value of 16. Remember that number as a given amount of light. The distance from that unit to the actor's feet is approximately 8 feet. If we also square that distance, the new value is 64. If you make a fraction of that value, place the first squared value (16) and place it over the feet value (64), your fraction is $^{16}\!/_{64}$. Sixteen goes into 64 four times, so 25% of the light falling on the actor's head will reach his feet. That is a 4 : 1 lighting ratio—very shadowy and uneven.

Using the information you just learned, you can calculate that if you move that same instrument 12 feet from the actor's head, 66% of that light will illuminate his feet. We now have 41% more light ($66 - 25 = 41$). This is the same wattage unit we used in the first case, but we seemingly get more light from the same lamp.

To take the scenario even farther, if we move the light to a distance of 16 feet, 75% of the same light is reaching his feet. Our improvement is up from 25% to 41% to now

Figure 10.9: *Brighter Lekos, fewer instruments.*

Figure 10.10: *Example of lighting intensity falloff.*

50%. The actual results may vary slightly. Things like the age of the instrument, the type of lens, and the gel may change the results slightly. But the point is that you should place the units as far from the actors as possible to get rid of the sharp falloff ratio and to light the talent more evenly.

Also keep in mind that the farther you move a light source from a subject, the more the actual light level (the wattage falling on the actor) will drop. If you shine a flashlight on someone 50 feet away, that person will be darker than if she were 25 feet away. In theory, the overall lighting level is decreased by a factor that is inversely proportional to the square of the distance.

I Did Not Know That

The other misconception in lighting is that every light must be used at full power. Most instruments are hooked up to a lighting board that allows control of the intensity of each lamp. Obviously full power is the brightest, but using that same light at 75% will often give acceptable results.

During your tech rehearsal, try adjusting the intensity of each light to see if any difference is noticeable. Two lights side by side at 50% is like having one at 100% but with more control. This does not work with the less-is-more rule, but hopefully you see where we are going.

Lighting boards should not be a mystery to anyone. Basically they are just a number of dimmers together in one place. Our board at DeSales University has 48 inputs, so 48 lights can be "dimmed" at one time. The number on the board (e.g., #17) corresponds with that input light (#17). The farther up the scale you move the slider, the more power (intensity) will be sent to the unit. Usually there are percentages in relation to this slider (10%, 20%, 30%, and so on). On some boards this is digital, and on others you must read the printed number next to the slider.

As you move the slider down, the light dims. Really, that is all there is to a lighting board. Some have the added feature of programmability: You preset a particular intensity and at a given point the light to achieve that. Practice using the board and become familiar with its operation.

Other factors will also change the output of lights. Using a gel or scrim will change the intensity and "look" of the light. If, with a blue gel, you decide you need more illumination and the instrument is already at 100%, try a slightly lighter shade of blue. Remember, the darker the gel, the more light it absorbs. A half-blue uses half of the light (absorbs half of it). The "blue" color on stage might not be as deep a blue, but the audience will still see it as "blue."

Figure 10.11: *Three blind lights.*

Togetherness

Stacking lights together in a column or row will give you that bank of lights we talked about in Chapter 9. In Figure 10.11, we see three lights that (once gelled) will function as one unit, coating the actor in illumination. Each of these units might be on a separate dimmer or all three may function as one.

As mentioned in the last chapter, make sure every mounted light is secure. When tightening the clamp down to the bar with a wrench, do not force it with a torque of 10,000 pounds. This will not impress anyone except the clamp manufacturers, because that means they will be selling more clamps. Just make sure the connections are snug (all the while the safety cable is attached), and forget about overtightening.

Practice Makes Perfect

Look at Figure 10.12. Your job is to light this scene using as few lights as necessary. As you may notice in the photo, you have a set with two groups to illuminate. This is a simpler exercise because the rest of the set area is in darkness, so just the main characters need illumination.

Figure 10.12: *How would you light this scene?*

Let's start with Bob Cratchit seated at his desk, writing. Notice that his practical, or source of light, is a candle. What does that tell you? His light should be warm (orange). Now you know what is lighting his world and you know the color. Because he is not involved in the discussion with the other characters onstage, his light should be dimmed slightly. He is in the background. He still exists in the scene but is not to be noticed; he should blend in. Three-point light would not be the best choice here. Why? Because a candle could never give illumination enough even to fill in the shadows. Scrooge is cheap, and one candle is all Cratchit gets.

Notice that he does have a backlight to give him separation from the background. The two lights needed for him are a key (coming from the candle) and a backlight to pull him into the third dimension. With this one character, you have saved one light (and that amount of heat). A Leko (with an amber gel) pointed at his back brings out his hair and light-colored coat. We dim it to 60% because we do not want too much light on his shoulders, since that light is not coming from any source—it is just separation light.

The key light is another Leko, from the left side of his face (we cannot see his right). If he turns his head to face the audience, the key will illuminate his whole face. Because of the candle as the source, we dim the key to 40% and use another amber or straw gel. The paper on Cratchit's desk is supplying bounce light to his face, raising the ambient light. This paper is our "fill" light in the scene.

Scrooge and the other two actors need illumination. What is their source of light? Although you can't see it in Figure 10.12, above their heads is a chandelier. The light is coming from above because Scrooge's bald head is too bright (he's not, but his head is under the practical). The other gentlemen are wearing stovepipe hats (one light colored and the other black). Most of the illumination should come from above the stage because the chandelier is providing all the light. The candle on Cratchit's desk is too far away to add any light.

The overhead key light should be flooded enough to be the key source for all three men. You may use three separate keys, but, since they are close together, one 1000-watt Fresnel in the flood position would do the trick. This is really a trick question. If we use a Fresnel from above, the two actors with hats would have dark faces. Look at any western on TV and you normally see nothing on their faces, because the hats are blocking the light (sun). That is the reason they are wearing hats. Hollywood cheats this by reflecting light onto their faces to help lighten the shadow from their hats.

In this case, a light from the balcony or catwalk would supply illumination on their faces. You should still use a 1000-watt Fresnel in the flood position and have the dimmed Fresnel above their heads onstage be the backlight. We again have only two lights on these actors, because three would be unnecessary, and the actors can be positioned to face the audience so that they are not in profile. For four actors onstage, we used four lights instead of a possible 12.

There are other lights in the scene to brighten up the set slightly, but most of this illumination is not coming from the footlights, because they are off. Two other Lekos mounted above the set are adding ambient light, but they too are dimmed.

Exercise Two

In Figure 10.13 we have our second example. There is a greater number of people to light, but this might be easier. This photograph shows six groups of people onstage. It is nice when the actors' blocking works in your favor this way. Five of the groups will be center stage, and the last group will be in the background and not in our lighted area. Like the last time, the first question to ask is where the light source is coming from. Since we don't see any practicals on the set in this photo, the chandelier once again is our main practical source. The lights in this chandelier are supposed to be gaslight, so the color again will be on the orange side.

Look first at the actor playing the violin. He is creating the music, the ambience for this scene, and therefore should be well lit and visible to the audience. Two lights also work for him because there still will be shadows if the source of light is from above: a backlight to give him separation and a gelled Leko to provide his key light. If the instrument is out from the stage, as he turns the one light will supply all his lighting.

If you tried to light each of the other four groups of actors, too many units would come into play. This is an instance when a bank, or row, of lights will fill the stage with

Figure 10.13: *Dancing group.*

illumination without having the actors move in and out of darkness. This "bank" is still acceptable as emanating from the overhead chandelier, and anyone moving under it will be lit.

The bank of Lekos supplies pools of light as the actors dance. At times they will be more lit than others, but their "keys" are all positioned from above and are actually their backlights. Out in the audience area we have the bank of fill lighting. Their backlighting is from above (where the practical is and is called the key), and that illumination is stronger and brighter than the normal backlight, but it is really the key.

Don't get bogged down with the terminology. Actors need three lights, and what they are called is not as important as their function. Always look where the practical light source is coming from, and that will always be your key, whether from above or to the sides.

Hopefully you now have a better understanding of what you can do with fewer lighting instruments on the set. In the last part of this chapter we talk about the new innovations in lighting and how they will make your lives easier.

The Latest Techniques and Equipment

As with anything, as soon as you read this it will probably be obsolete. But great strides have been taken in the industry with new equipment. In this section we break down what we believe the future holds into three categories: fiber-optics, LED lighting, and wireless motion-tracking lighting. More innovations may be on the horizon, but we believe these three will make quite a splash in the lighting community.

Optically Speaking

Fiber optics as a light source is not new—it has been used in stage productions for several years. What makes it exciting is that the price and availability have changed so drastically.

A fiber-optic light is a single, hairlike strand of plastic (0.75 mm in diameter) that ends with a dot of light. This strand is bendable and flexible, so "light" essentially can travel around corners. These plastic optical cables are often bunched together. As early as the late 1970s, Paramount used fiber-optic lighting in the model of the *Enterprise* for the TV series *Star Trek*. These flexible instruments would illuminate the portholes of the starship without generating all of the heat that conventional lighting does.

Onstage, a single fiber-optic light would be almost impossible to see from the audience's perspective—the light is too small and the distance too great. Used often in TV commercials to make a product stand out, they also have a place onstage. The LTM Corporation (www.ltm.com) created the Micro-Set Lighting (MSL) system in the 1980s. Consisting of 100 2½′ optical strands, a single strand or a bunch could be used.

By placing a few fiber-optic strands in a glass of liquid onstage, the "light from within" appears. These cables are waterproof and are often placed inside objects to illuminate them. Since heat is not an issue, the sky's the limit.

It's Curtains!

Fiber-optic curtains have also found their place onstage. Del Lighting (www.del-lighting.com) has the K1530 (one-circuit curtain) and the K1532 (two-circuit curtain). Where a backdrop or ceiling is needed that is dotted with light, a curtain with fiber-optic lighting built in does the trick. The fibers of the two layers of flame-retardant cloth are grouped in bundles at random over the length of the curtain. Different colors of light and twinkling effects can also be implemented. See Figure 10.14.

The LEDs Have It

Light-emitting diodes, or LEDs, have also been around since the early 1970s (remember your Casio LED wristwatch?). Over 1 million different colors and various levels of dimming are produced by LED lights. If that were not enough, these lights will stay illuminated without generating any heat at all. You could put your hand on an LED light that has been on for days without feeling any heat. But probably the greatest feature of an LED is its longevity. It is estimated that an LED will last up to 300,000 hours without dimming, fading, losing its color, or burning out. That is why LEDs are used as brake lights on vehicles (they are bright and do not burn out). Think of how often your theatrical bulbs burn out and for how may thousands of shows an LED will last.

Figure 10.14: *Fiber-optic curtains. (Courtesy of Del Lighting.)*

Figure 10.15: *LED light onstage. (Courtesy of SCILux Artistic Lighting.)*

But it gets even better. Because their power consumption is extremely low, over 1000 LED units can be run off a single 20-amp (Edison) circuit. At the most you would get two 1000-watt tungsten lights to run off that same 20-amp circuit. So what is the problem? The lights generate no heat, use virtually no power, and would last for over 34 years if used continuously without being turned off. The answer is the cost.

These lights are not expensive, but they are more costly than other standard units. But when you take into account the benefits (the coolness, minimal power consumption, and long life), their operational cost is minuscule. Several companies specialize in setting up LED lighting, such as SCILux Artistic Lighting (www.scilux.com). Figure 10.15 illustrates an example of an LED strip.

Color My World

Lighting and Electronic Design, Inc. (www.ledinc.com), has created the Power Lite, which is what they call "the ultimate linear LED system." In lengths of up to 600 feet,

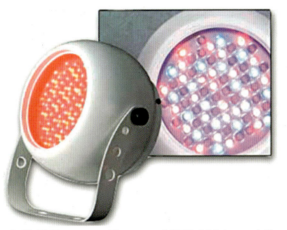

Figure 10.16: *Octopod 80 LED system. (Courtesy of SLD Lighting and Sound.)*

these 5-mm LEDs are encapsulated in strands that are water resistant, can be used indoors or outdoors, are cuttable, and can change color from red to blue or green. Although only rated at 100,000 hours of life expectancy, you would have to replace them after 11½ years of continuous use.

Does Not Sound Fishy

The Octopod 80 (*octo* means "eight") from SLD Lighting and Sound (www.sldlighting.com) has eight LED fixtures in a podlike unit. Each of the eight fixtures has 90 LEDs (30 red, 30 green, and 30 blue), or a total of 720 LEDs. Without using colored gels you can mix and match the LEDs to create a stunning display of colors. The LEDs can cross-fade from one to another, stay one particular color, or even strobe. These lights can be activated by sound and also display a "chase" function. See Figure 10.16.

Also from SLD Lighting and Sound is the Trackpod 80 Borderlight LED System. With no external controller needed, this instrument can be placed onstage or on the catwalk. With eight self-contained Octopod 80s, you have a plethora of colored illumination. With all of the benefits of the Octopod 80, you now have 5760 LEDs in a 21-pound unit that uses 95 watts of power. That works out to less than a 100-watt light bulb.

Another of the unique features with LED lights is that you can change their color just by activating that particular LED in the "pod." You no longer have to hunt for a colored gel and hang it on the light. These self-contained instruments are rotatable and are more flexible than standard units. The light throw might not be quite as far as a with a Fresnel or spotlight (these instruments are not necessarily meant to replace the older units, just complement them), but the output is still substantial, without the adverse effects created by the other units.

Great for mobile stage events, where power and space might be an issue, the LED instrument really shines brighter with less effort. The chief expense in creating an LED light is the lamp unit attached to the circuit card. At one time each LED cost around $2, but that price has fallen. Once in place, the unit lasts basically a lifetime.

These units can even be placed inches from an actor without his squinting or being affected by the heat. In filmmaking, LEDs are ideal because dimming them does not change the color temperature of the light—it stays consistent from 1% to 100%.

Stop Following Me!

The next option in lighting is a device that allows the light to follow the actor onstage without the need of an operator. If the actor wears a wireless transmitter, a receiver on the lighting unit will instruct the instrument to follow that actor wherever she moves onstage.

Wybron, Inc. (www.wybron.com), has devised the Autopilot II Model 5050; if you have moving lights, it will automate them. Whether your lights just move or focus, you can follow the action in real time, the Autopilot II may be an option. Simply connect the control box between the stage and the console and the pan and tilt of the light is automated. With this PC-controlled unit, the receivers are above the stage area and the actors wear a small belt pack with an ultrasonic element.

On the computer's screen, the setup, adjustment, operation, and diagnostics are displayed in 2D or 3D. With up to 60 controllable lights at your fingertips, more of the designer's time can be spent with the talent and sets rather than the lighting. Even if an actor misses his or her cue, the Autopilot II will still follow the individual with the light, something an operator-controlled light could not do. This way, no one in the audience knows a mistake has been made—the spotlight still follows the performer. See Figure 10.17.

Also from Wybron, Inc., is the Goboram II. With a stationary light, the Goboram will change and rotate up to three gobos in a single unit—automatically. Whether you want to change colors or gobos, these functions are programmed into the Goboram II. If several units need to be linked or daisy-chained together, that is not a problem.

Can You Cee It?

Another new development in the field of lighting is the CeeLite (www.ceelite.com). This revolutionary, paper-thin "sheet" uses light-emitting capacitor (LEC) technology to create what is considered a "flat light bulb."

Feeling like heavily laminated paper stock, the CeeLite can be conformed to most shapes and still retain no memory. The system consists of a 4 × 8 panel and a jumper.

Figure 10.17: *Autopilot II. (Courtesy of Wybron, Inc.)*

Although bright, the CeeLite is not something you would use to illuminate a room or stage. Instead, it can be applied to a surface and used as a backlight display or to suggest illumination from another area onstage. The surface is uniformly lit, without hot or cold spots of light.

As of this writing, white is the only color available, with the CeeLite giving off a slightly greenish hue. With a color temperature of around 7000° Kelvin and a life of up to 10,000 hours, this may be the new trend for the future. Where else can you use a light that allows you to bend and twist it without destroying it and still have it illuminate and adhere to a surface without adding much depth? Figure 10.18 illustrates this amazing light. It is a good thing people do not use subliminal messages anymore.

What Else Does the Future Hold?

There is no way to determine exactly what new developments will occur in the area of lighting your set. Just know for sure that the units themselves will be lighter, stronger, and more durable, will function on less power and be brighter and cooler, and will last for years instead of hours. And best of all, the prices will fall. We are seeing hints of this new technology now, but expect refinements in the near future that will make the lighting designer's job easier and more controllable.

Just look how the technology of building the set has changed drastically to a computer-controlled operation. Look for lighting to move in that direction also, with the computer controlling the design, planning, layout, and operation of the instruments. Best of all, these changes are making our lives easier and allowing us to spend more time in the more creative areas of technology rather than the mechanical.

Figure 10.18: *The CeeLite. (Courtesy of CeeLite.)*

Concluding Remarks—Finally!

So if you made it this far, you know the basics of lighting and scenery. Do not stop here. Technical theatre is an intoxicating business, and the community that surrounds it comprises some of the most fascinating people you will ever meet. They live to solve problems and create wonders. Take the basics you have learned here and work with these people. Ask questions, share ideas, and have fun. Oh, and if you can think of some really bad puns, you'll fit in (and they will probably be better than most of ours).

Index

Page numbers followed by "f" denote figures; those followed by "t" denote tables.